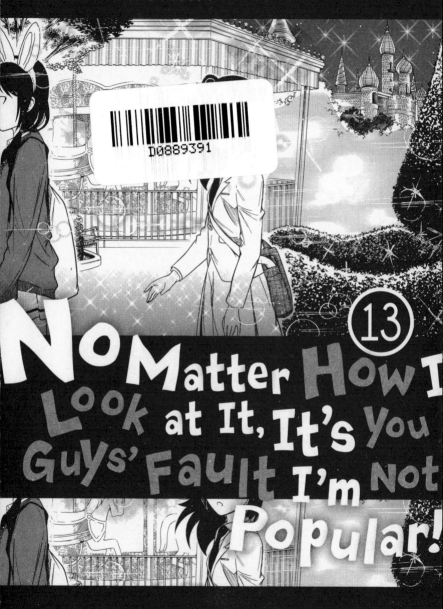

Presented by
NICO TANIGAWA

No Matter How I
Look at It, It's You
Guys' Fault I'm Not
Popular!

13

...AWW, IF I'D BEEN A WORM, I WOULD'VE HAD A MAN FROM THE GET-GO AND DEFINITELY HAVE HAD S●X, NOT TO MENTION KIDS...

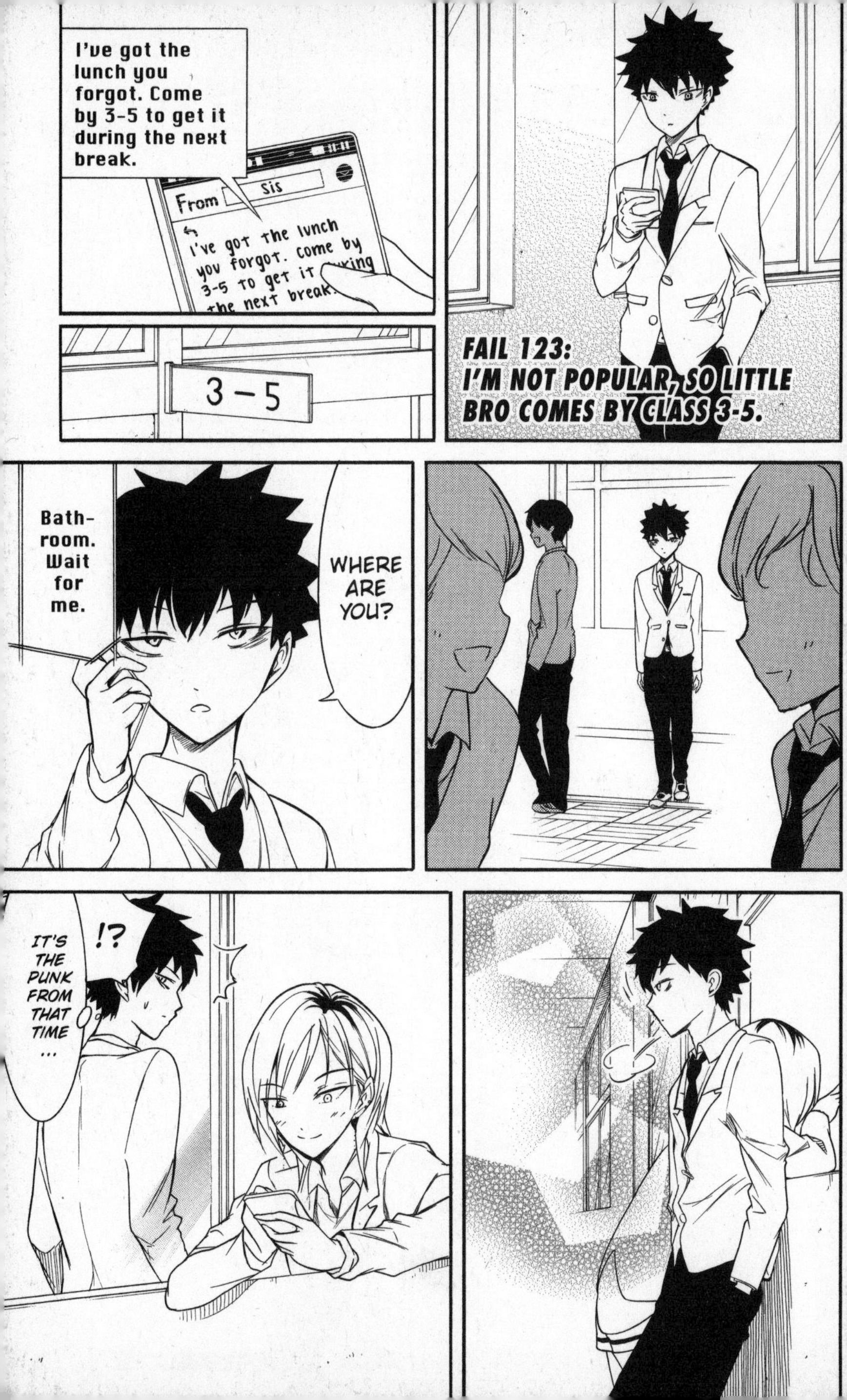
FAIL 123:
I'M NOT POPULAR, SO LITTLE BRO COMES BY CLASS 3-5.
I've got the lunch you forgot. Come by 3-5 to get it during the next break.
From Sis
3-5
WHERE ARE YOU?
Bath-room. Wait for me.
!?
IT'S THE PUNK FROM THAT TIME...

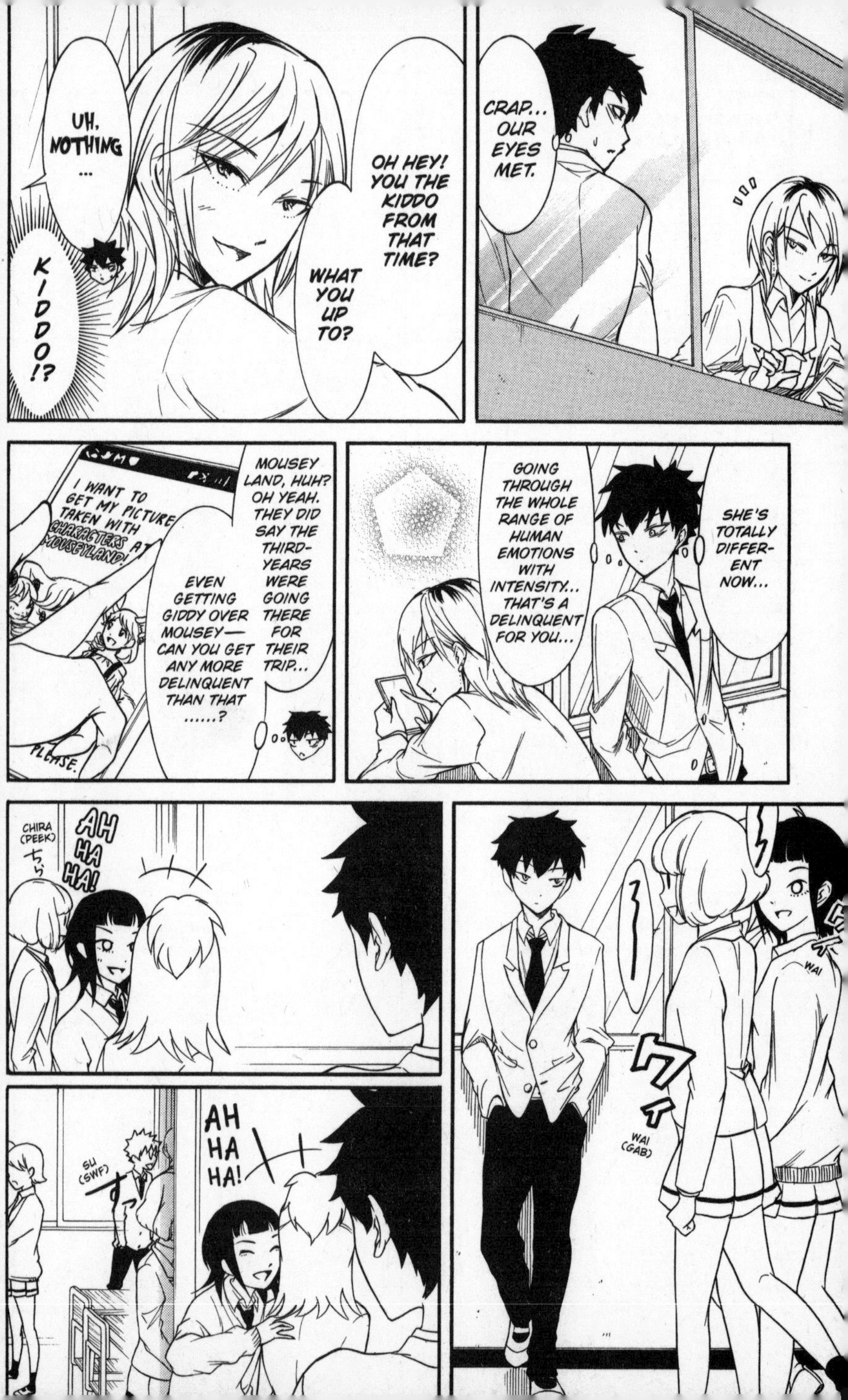
CRAP... OUR EYES MET.
OH HEY! YOU THE KIDDO FROM THAT TIME?
WHAT YOU UP TO?
UH, NOTHING ...
KIDDO!?
SHE'S TOTALLY DIFFERENT NOW...
GOING THROUGH THE WHOLE RANGE OF HUMAN EMOTIONS WITH INTENSITY... THAT'S A DELINQUENT FOR YOU...
MOUSEY LAND, HUH? OH YEAH. THEY DID SAY THE THIRD-YEARS WERE GOING THERE FOR THEIR TRIP...
EVEN GETTING GIDDY OVER MOUSEY—CAN YOU GET ANY MORE DELINQUENT THAN THAT ......?
I WANT TO GET MY PICTURE TAKEN WITH CHARACTERS AT MOUSEYLAND!
PLEASE.
WAI
WAI (GAB)
AH HA HA!
CHIRA (PEEK)
AH HA HA!
SU (SWF)

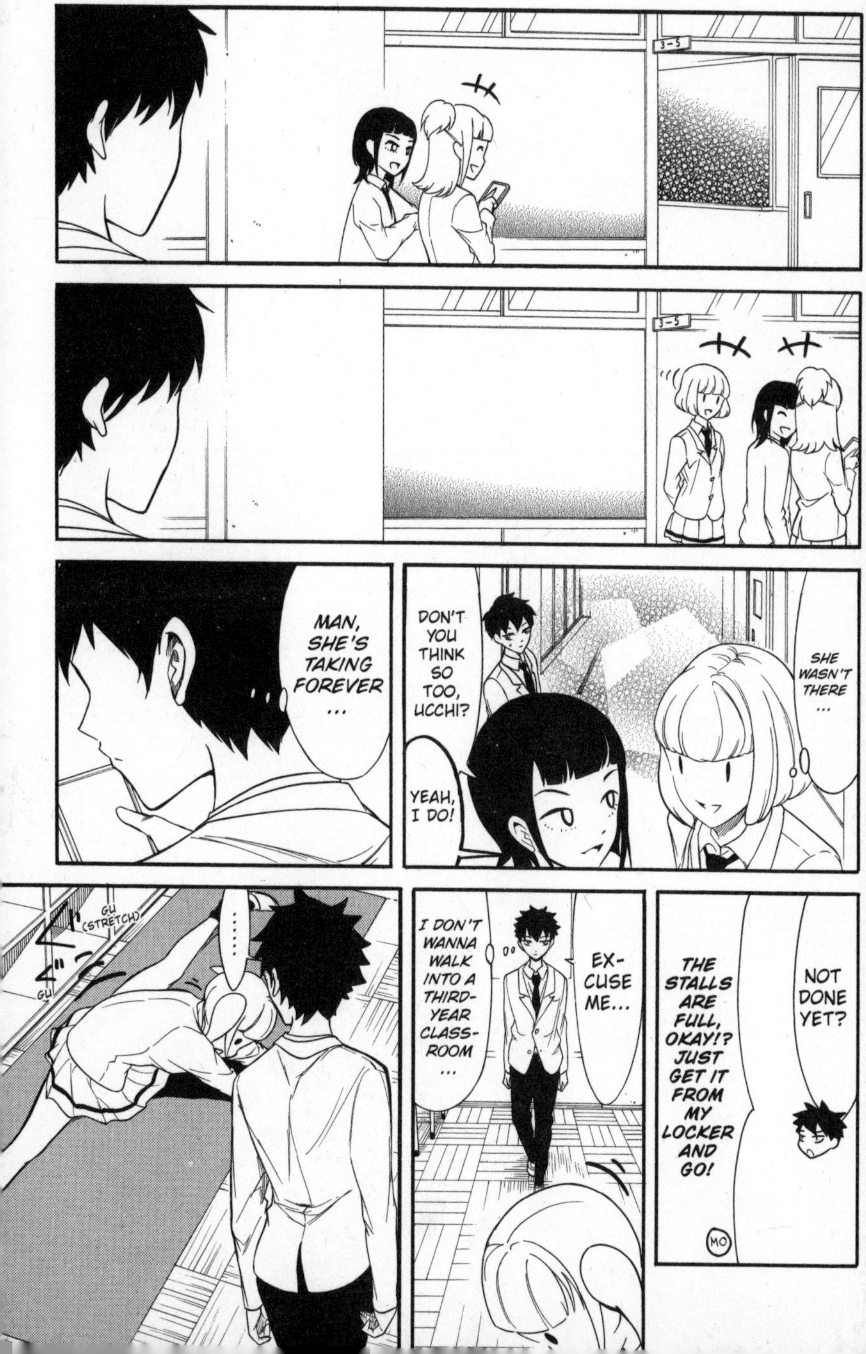
SHE WASN'T THERE ...
DON'T YOU THINK SO TOO, UCCHI?
YEAH, I DO!
MAN, SHE'S TAKING FOREVER ...
NOT DONE YET?
THE STALLS ARE FULL, OKAY!? JUST GET IT FROM MY LOCKER AND GO!
MO
EX-CUSE ME...
I DON'T WANNA WALK INTO A THIRD-YEAR CLASS-ROOM ...
......
GU (STRETCH)
GU

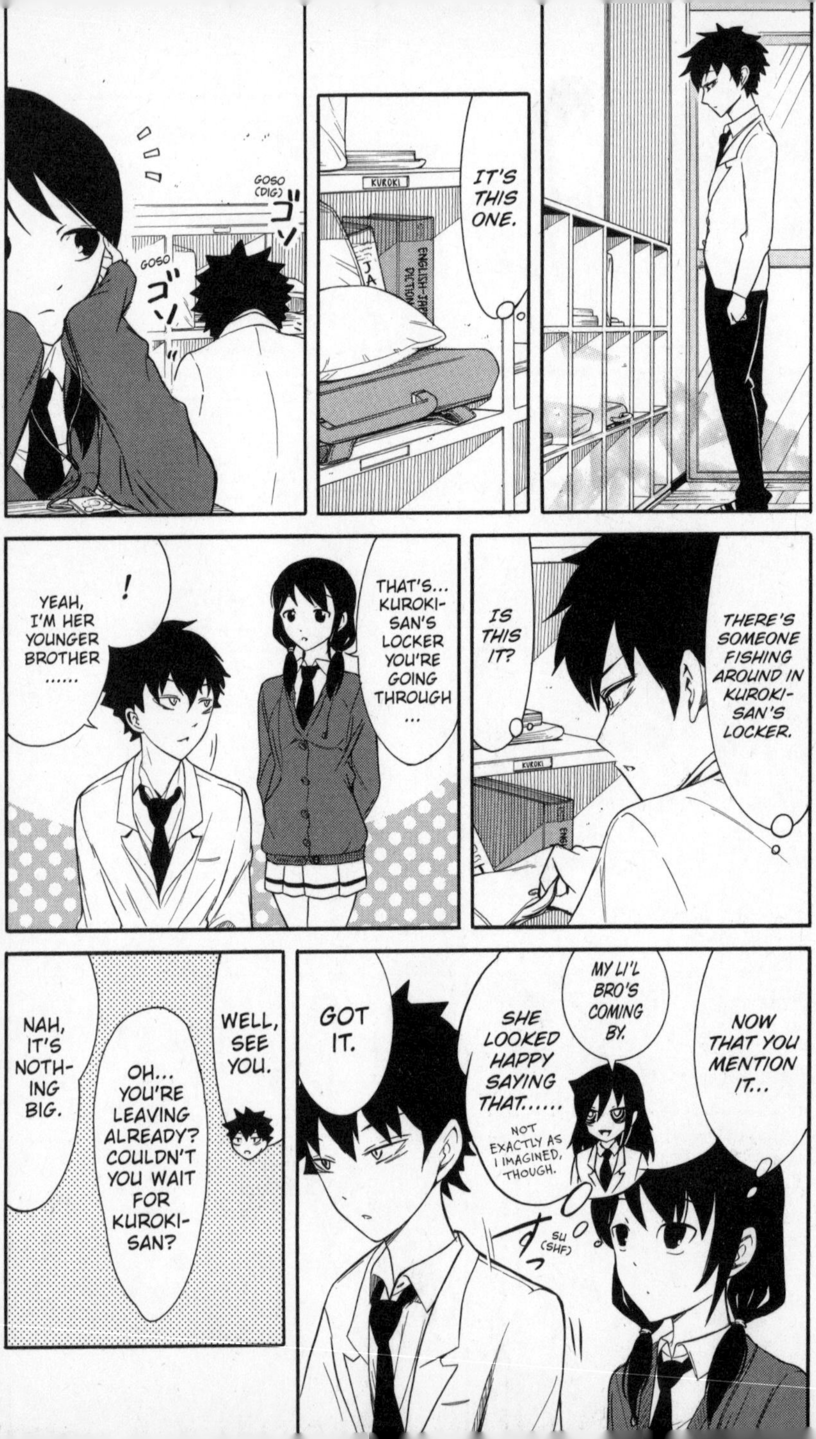
IT'S THIS ONE.
KUROKI
ENGLISH-JAP DICTION
GOSO (DIG)
ゴソ
GOSO
ゴソ
THERE'S SOMEONE FISHING AROUND IN KUROKI-SAN'S LOCKER.
IS THIS IT?
KUROKI
THAT'S... KUROKI-SAN'S LOCKER YOU'RE GOING THROUGH...
!
YEAH, I'M HER YOUNGER BROTHER......
NOW THAT YOU MENTION IT...
MY LI'L BRO'S COMING BY.
SHE LOOKED HAPPY SAYING THAT......
NOT EXACTLY AS I IMAGINED, THOUGH.
GOT IT.
す
SU (SHF)
WELL, SEE YOU.
OH... YOU'RE LEAVING ALREADY? COULDN'T YOU WAIT FOR KUROKI-SAN?
NAH, IT'S NOTHING BIG.

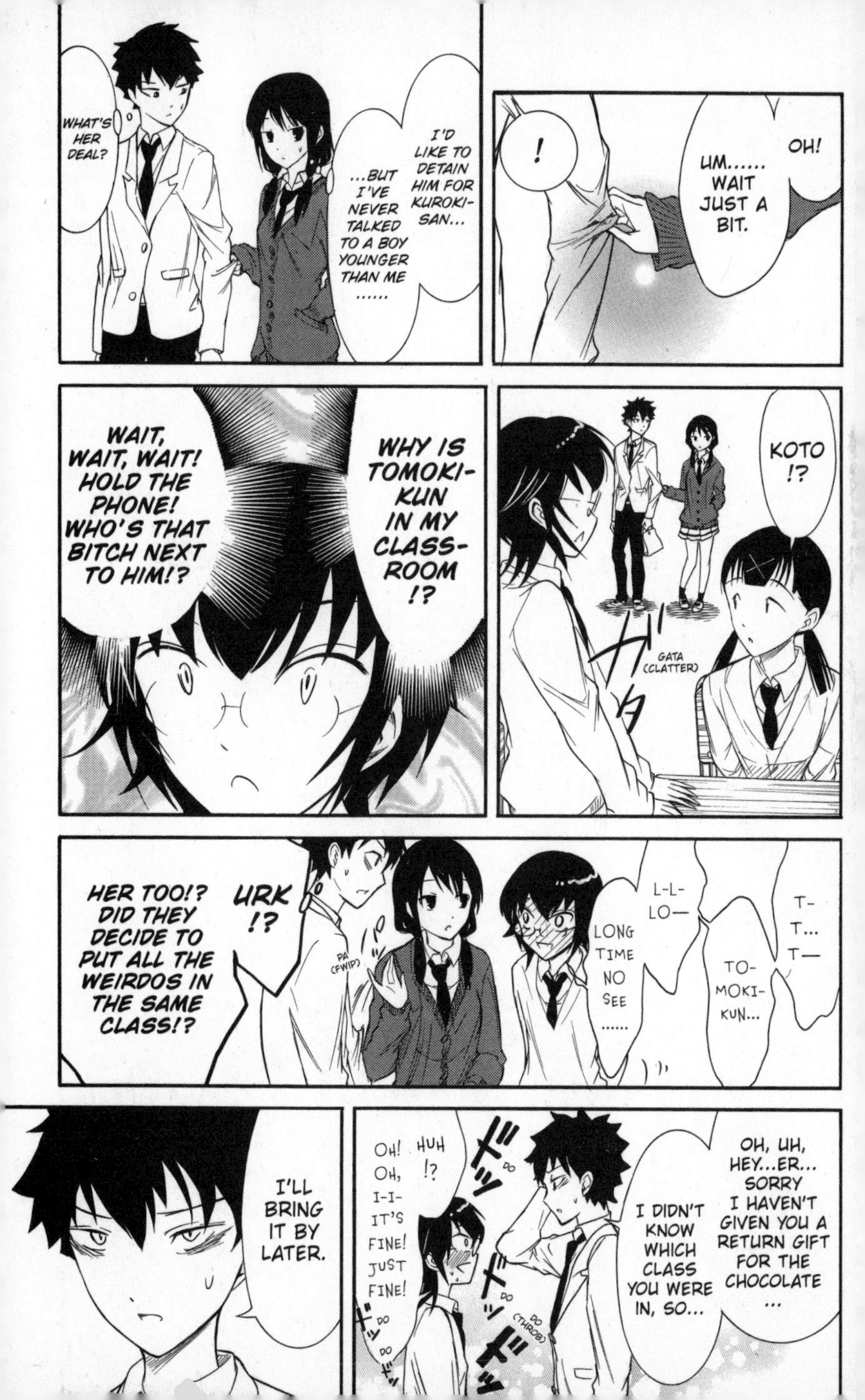
OH!
UM...... WAIT JUST A BIT.
!
I'D LIKE TO DETAIN HIM FOR KUROKI-SAN...
...BUT I'VE NEVER TALKED TO A BOY YOUNGER THAN ME ......
WHAT'S HER DEAL?
KOTO !?
GATA (CLATTER)
WHY IS TOMOKI-KUN IN MY CLASSROOM !?
WAIT, WAIT, WAIT! HOLD THE PHONE! WHO'S THAT BITCH NEXT TO HIM!?
T- T... T—
TO-MOKI-KUN...
L-L-LO—
LONG TIME NO SEE ......
PA (FWIP)
URK !?
HER TOO!? DID THEY DECIDE TO PUT ALL THE WEIRDOS IN THE SAME CLASS!?
OH, UH, HEY...ER... SORRY I HAVEN'T GIVEN YOU A RETURN GIFT FOR THE CHOCOLATE ...
I DIDN'T KNOW WHICH CLASS YOU WERE IN, SO...
DO (THROB)
DO
HUH !?
OH! OH, I-I-IT'S FINE! JUST FINE!
DO
DO
I'LL BRING IT BY LATER.

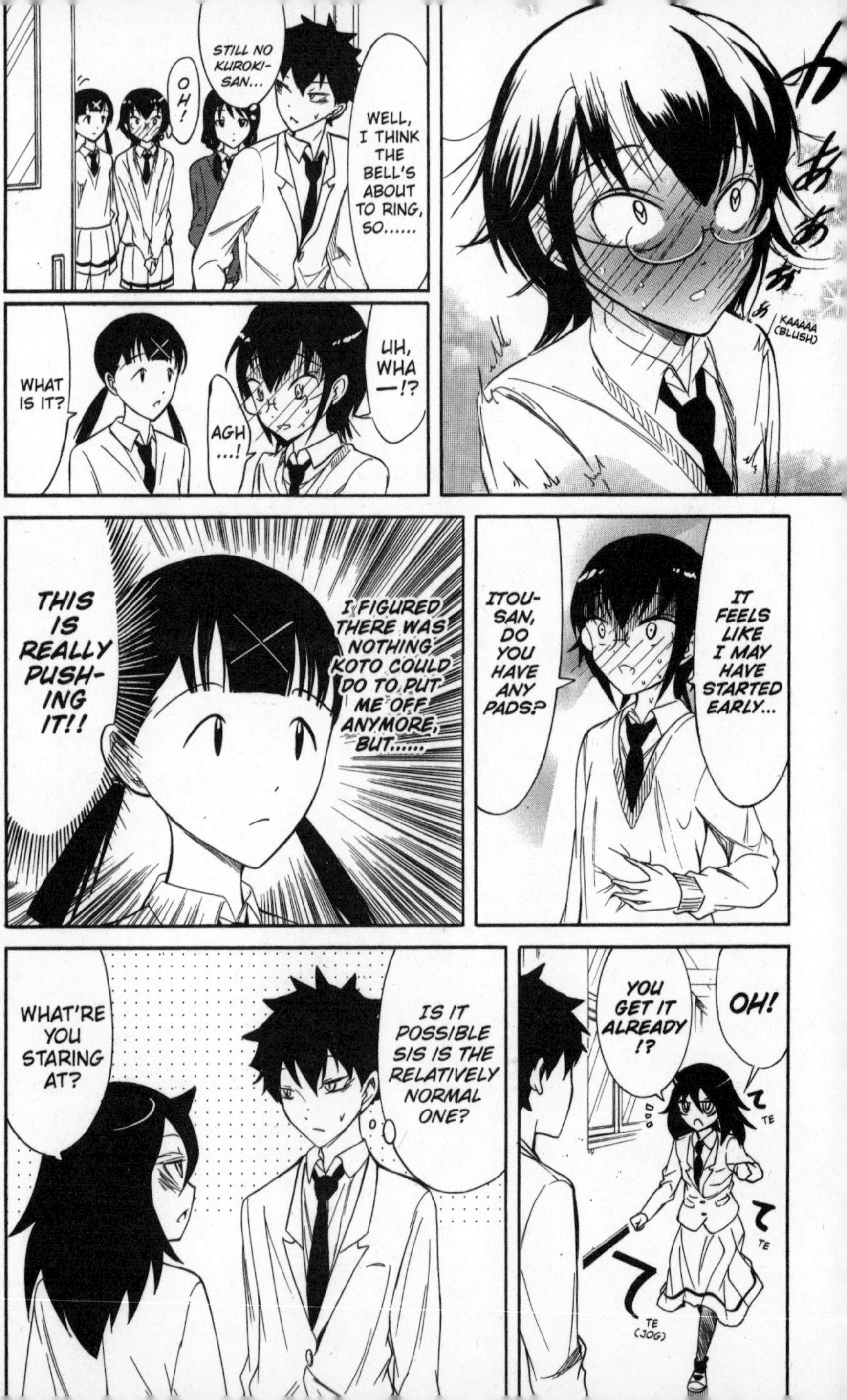
KAAAAA (BLUSH)
STILL NO KUROKI-SAN...
WELL, I THINK THE BELL'S ABOUT TO RING, SO......
OH!
UH, WHA—!?
AGH ...!
WHAT IS IT?
IT FEELS LIKE I MAY HAVE STARTED EARLY...
ITOU-SAN, DO YOU HAVE ANY PADS?
I FIGURED THERE WAS NOTHING KOTO COULD DO TO PUT ME OFF ANYMORE, BUT......
THIS IS REALLY PUSH-ING IT!!
OH!
YOU GET IT ALREADY !?
TE
TE
TE (JOG)
IS IT POSSIBLE SIS IS THE RELATIVELY NORMAL ONE?
WHAT'RE YOU STARING AT?

No Matter How I Look at It, It's You Guys' Fault I'm Not Popular!

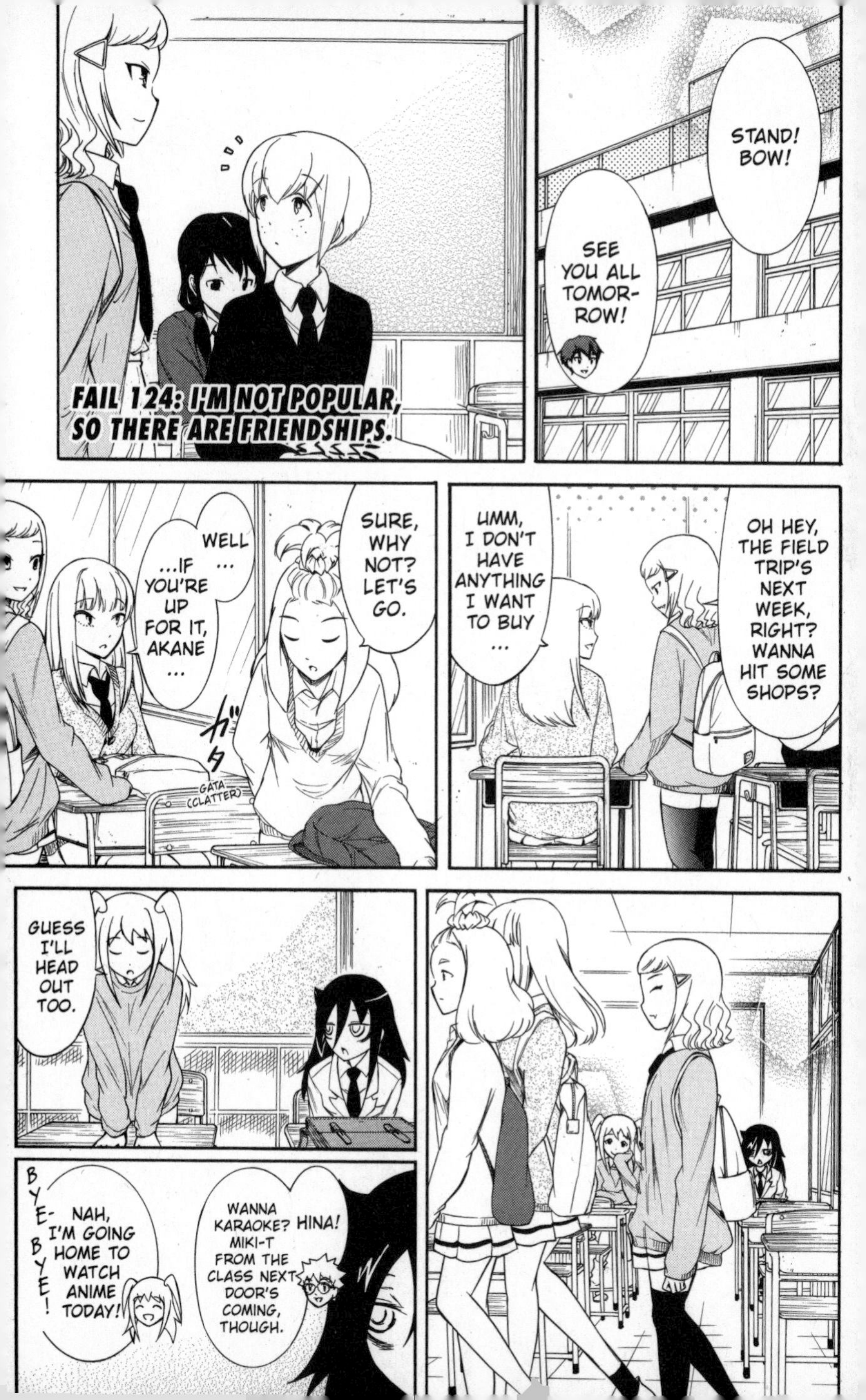
STAND! BOW!
SEE YOU ALL TOMOR-ROW!
FAIL 124: I'M NOT POPULAR, SO THERE ARE FRIENDSHIPS.
OH HEY, THE FIELD TRIP'S NEXT WEEK, RIGHT? WANNA HIT SOME SHOPS?
UMM, I DON'T HAVE ANYTHING I WANT TO BUY ...
SURE, WHY NOT? LET'S GO.
WELL ... ...IF YOU'RE UP FOR IT, AKANE ...
ガタ
GATA (CLATTER)
GUESS I'LL HEAD OUT TOO.
WANNA KARAOKE? HINA! MIKI-T FROM THE CLASS NEXT DOOR'S COMING, THOUGH.
NAH, I'M GOING HOME TO WATCH ANIME TODAY!
BYE-BYE!

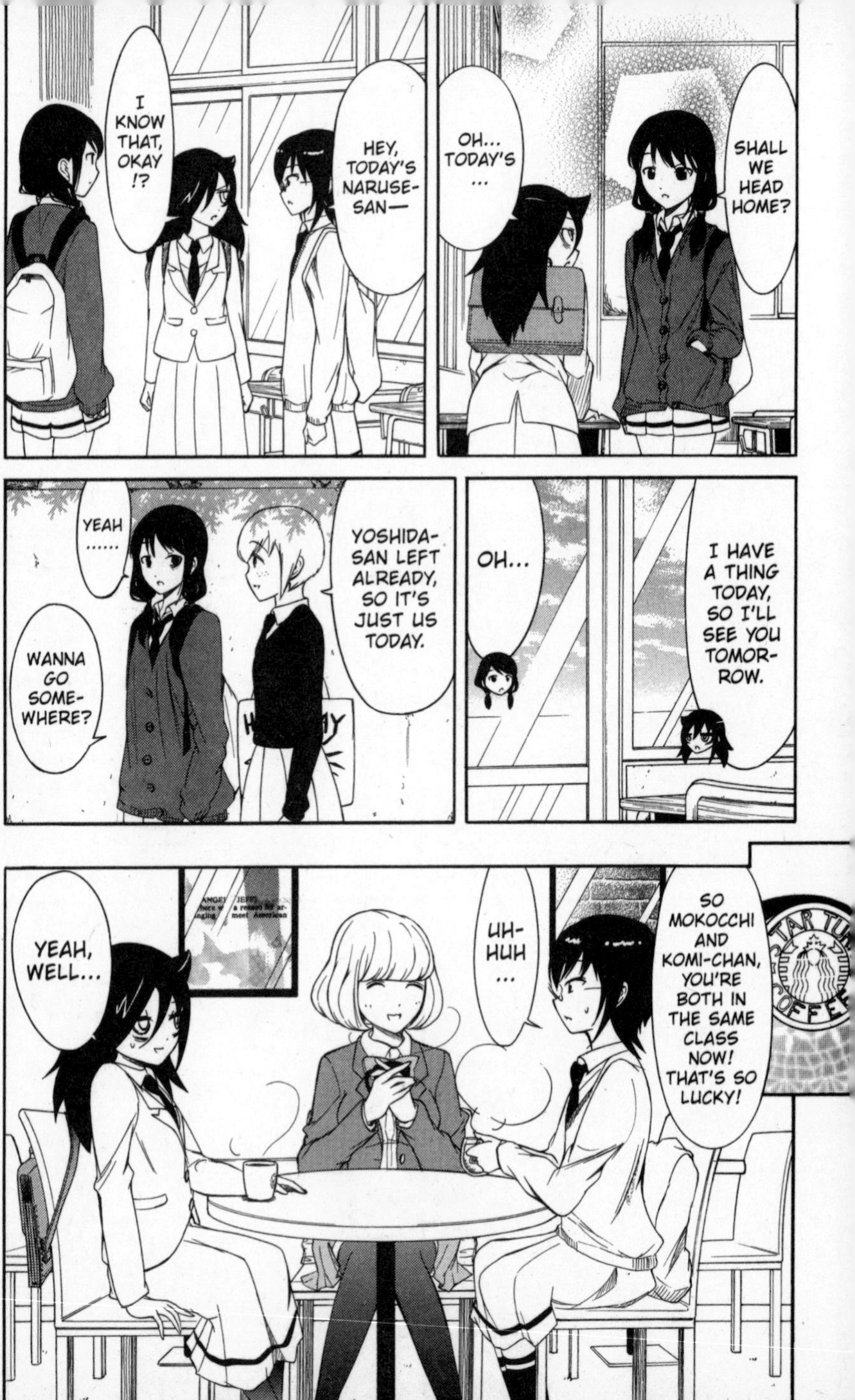
SHALL WE HEAD HOME?
OH... TODAY'S ...
HEY, TODAY'S NARUSE-SAN—
I KNOW THAT, OKAY!?
I HAVE A THING TODAY, SO I'LL SEE YOU TOMORROW.
OH...
YOSHIDA-SAN LEFT ALREADY, SO IT'S JUST US TODAY.
YEAH ......
WANNA GO SOMEWHERE?
SO MOKOCCHI AND KOMI-CHAN, YOU'RE BOTH IN THE SAME CLASS NOW! THAT'S SO LUCKY!
UH-HUH ...
YEAH, WELL...

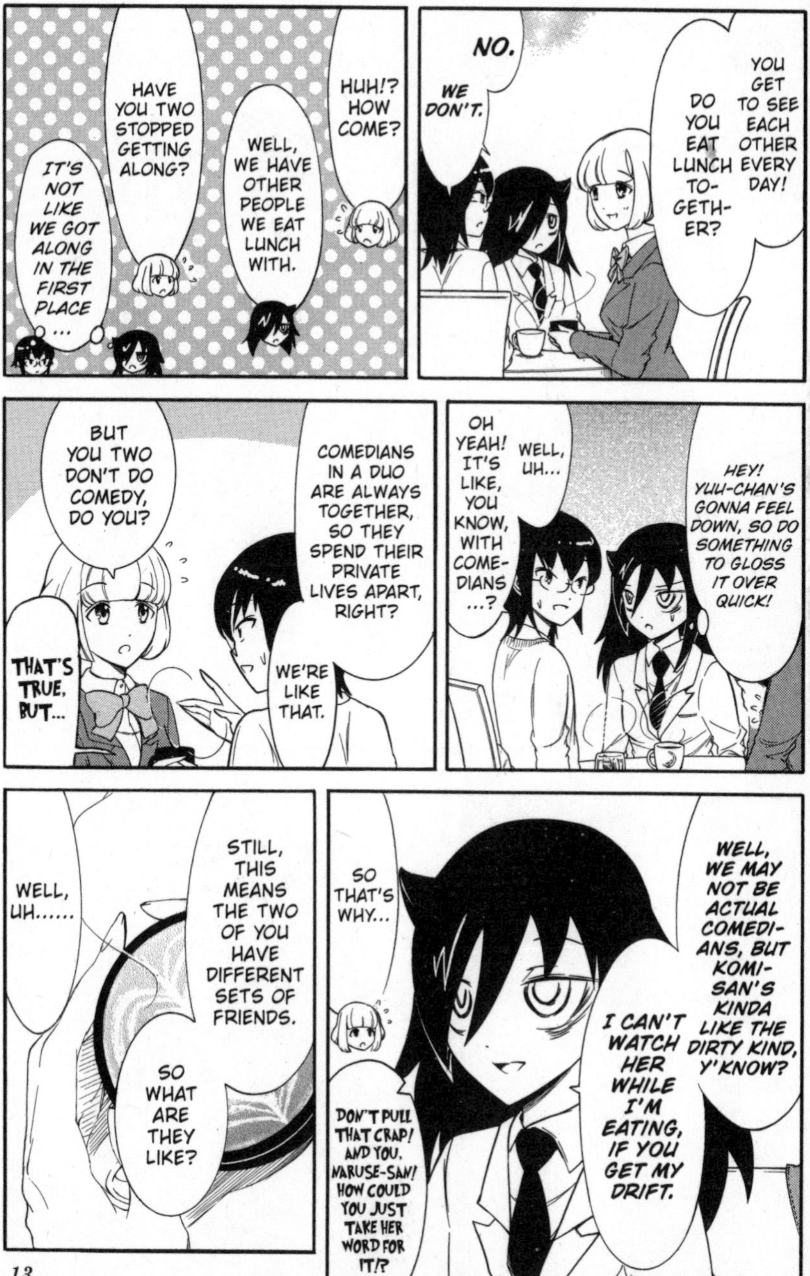

YOU GET TO SEE EACH OTHER EVERY DAY!
DO YOU EAT LUNCH TO-GETH-ER?
NO.
WE DON'T.
HUH!? HOW COME?
WELL, WE HAVE OTHER PEOPLE WE EAT LUNCH WITH.
HAVE YOU TWO STOPPED GETTING ALONG?
IT'S NOT LIKE WE GOT ALONG IN THE FIRST PLACE...
HEY! YUU-CHAN'S GONNA FEEL DOWN, SO DO SOMETHING TO GLOSS IT OVER QUICK!
WELL, UH...
OH YEAH! IT'S LIKE, YOU KNOW, WITH COME-DIANS...?
COMEDIANS IN A DUO ARE ALWAYS TOGETHER, SO THEY SPEND THEIR PRIVATE LIVES APART, RIGHT?
WE'RE LIKE THAT.
BUT YOU TWO DON'T DO COMEDY, DO YOU?
THAT'S TRUE, BUT...
WELL, WE MAY NOT BE ACTUAL COMEDI-ANS, BUT KOMI-SAN'S KINDA LIKE THE DIRTY KIND, Y'KNOW?
I CAN'T WATCH HER WHILE I'M EATING, IF YOU GET MY DRIFT.
SO THAT'S WHY...
DON'T PULL THAT CRAP! AND YOU, NARUSE-SAN! HOW COULD YOU JUST TAKE HER WORD FOR IT!?
STILL, THIS MEANS THE TWO OF YOU HAVE DIFFERENT SETS OF FRIENDS.
SO WHAT ARE THEY LIKE?
WELL, UH......

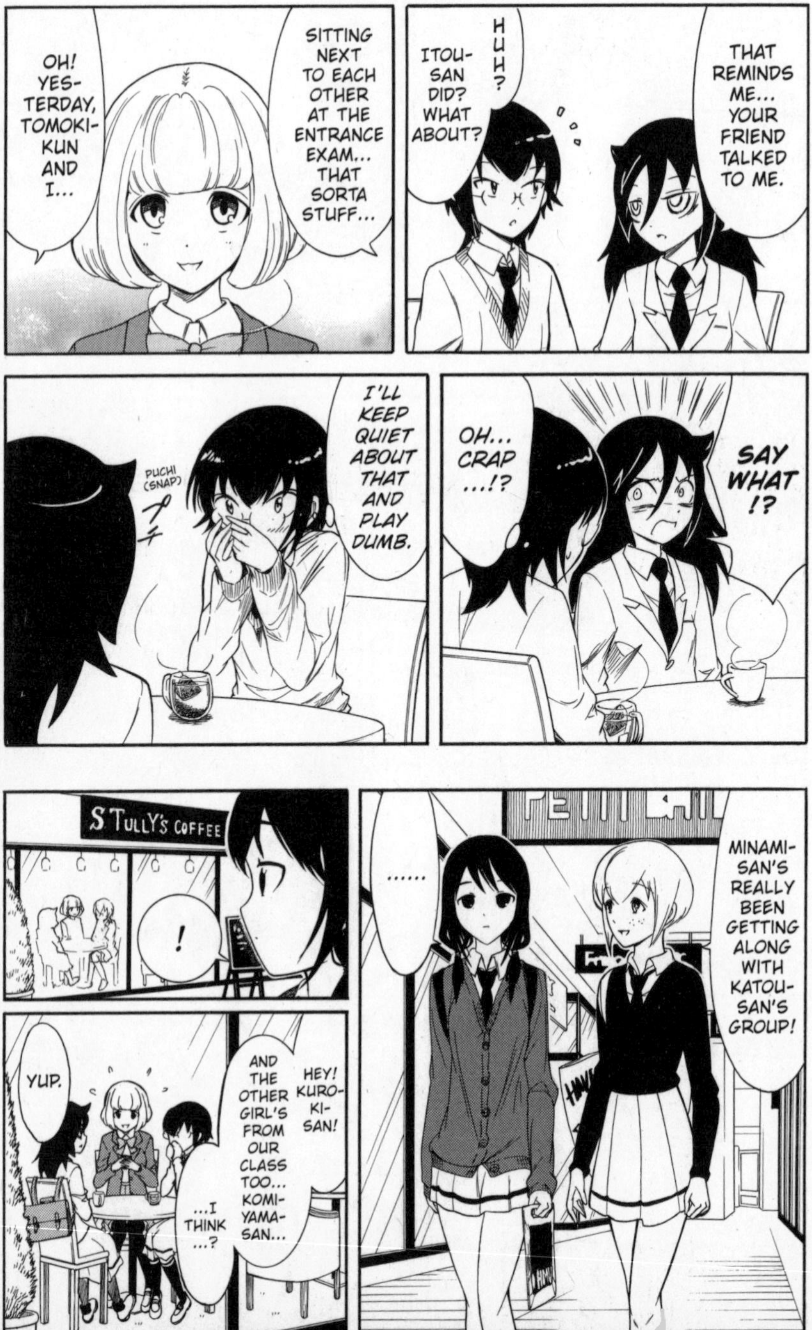
THAT REMINDS ME... YOUR FRIEND TALKED TO ME.
HUH?
ITOU-SAN DID? WHAT ABOUT?
OH! YESTERDAY, TOMOKI-KUN AND I...
SITTING NEXT TO EACH OTHER AT THE ENTRANCE EXAM... THAT SORTA STUFF...
SAY WHAT!?
OH... CRAP...!?
I'LL KEEP QUIET ABOUT THAT AND PLAY DUMB.
PUCHI (SNAP)
MINAMI-SAN'S REALLY BEEN GETTING ALONG WITH KATOU-SAN'S GROUP!
......
S TULLY'S COFFEE
!
HEY! KURO-KI-SAN!
AND THE OTHER GIRL'S FROM OUR CLASS TOO... KOMI-YAMA-SAN...
YUP.
...I THINK...?

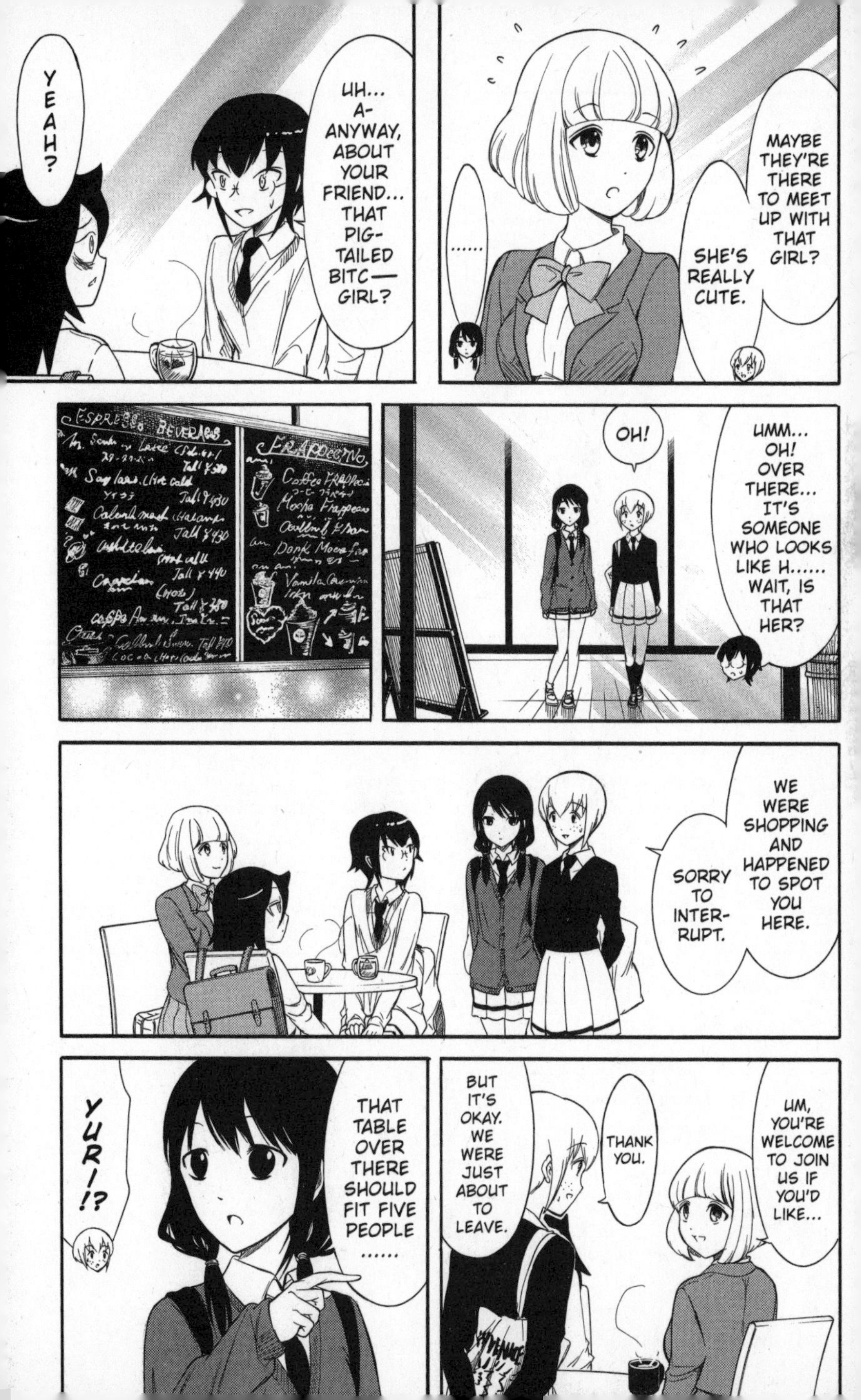
MAYBE THEY'RE THERE TO MEET UP WITH THAT GIRL?
SHE'S REALLY CUTE.
......
UH... A-ANYWAY, ABOUT YOUR FRIEND... THAT PIG-TAILED BITC—GIRL?
YEAH?
UMM... OH! OVER THERE... IT'S SOMEONE WHO LOOKS LIKE H...... WAIT, IS THAT HER?
OH!
WE WERE SHOPPING AND HAPPENED TO SPOT YOU HERE.
SORRY TO INTERRUPT.
UM, YOU'RE WELCOME TO JOIN US IF YOU'D LIKE...
THANK YOU.
BUT IT'S OKAY. WE WERE JUST ABOUT TO LEAVE.
THAT TABLE OVER THERE SHOULD FIT FIVE PEOPLE ......
YURI!?

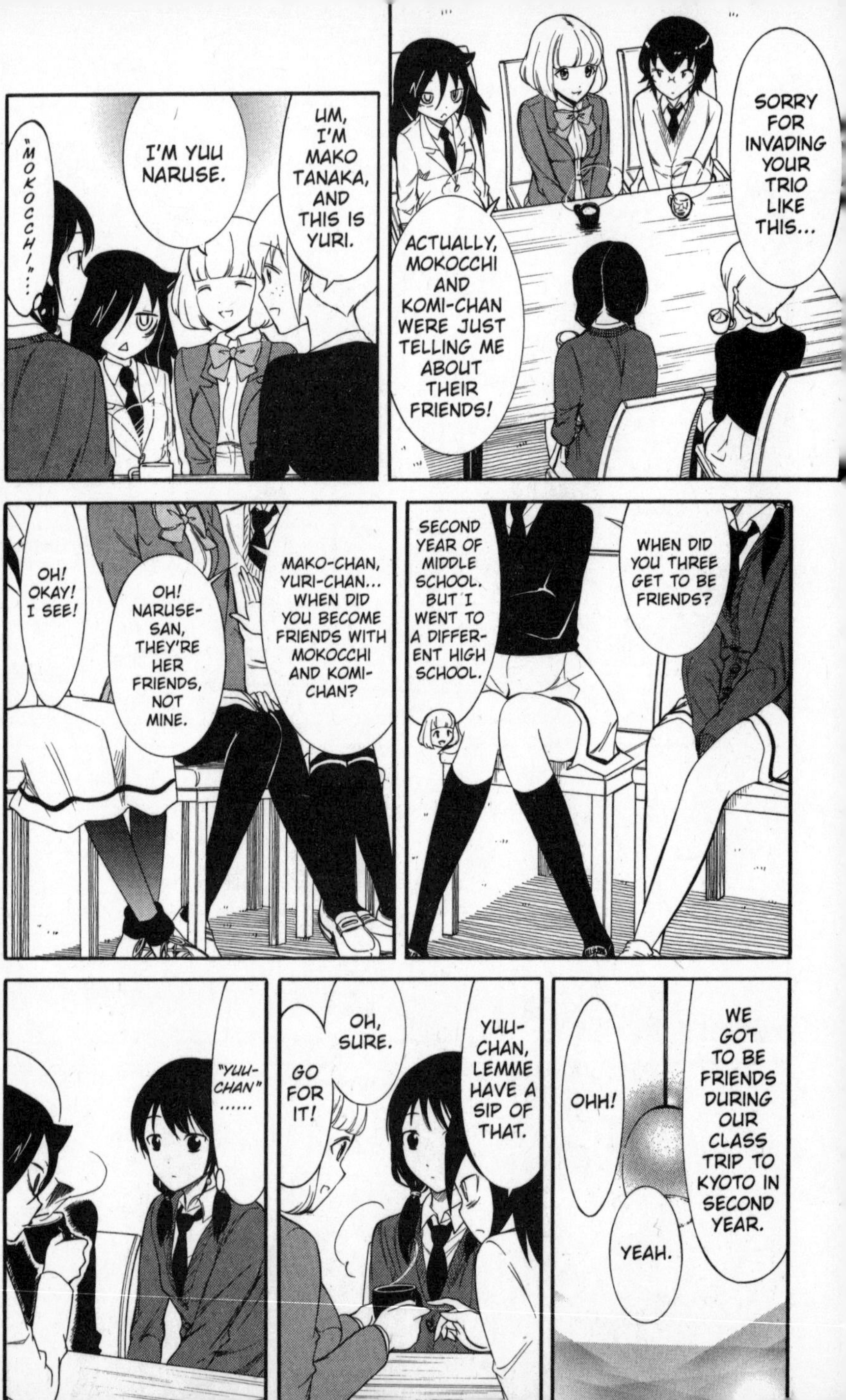
SORRY FOR INVADING YOUR TRIO LIKE THIS...
ACTUALLY, MOKOCCHI AND KOMI-CHAN WERE JUST TELLING ME ABOUT THEIR FRIENDS!
UM, I'M MAKO TANAKA, AND THIS IS YURI.
I'M YUU NARUSE.
"MOKOCCHI"...
WHEN DID YOU THREE GET TO BE FRIENDS?
SECOND YEAR OF MIDDLE SCHOOL. BUT I WENT TO A DIFFERENT HIGH SCHOOL.
MAKO-CHAN, YURI-CHAN... WHEN DID YOU BECOME FRIENDS WITH MOKOCCHI AND KOMI-CHAN?
OH! NARUSE-SAN, THEY'RE HER FRIENDS, NOT MINE.
OH! OKAY! I SEE!
WE GOT TO BE FRIENDS DURING OUR CLASS TRIP TO KYOTO IN SECOND YEAR.
OHH!
YEAH.
YUU-CHAN, LEMME HAVE A SIP OF THAT.
OH, SURE.
GO FOR IT!
"YUU-CHAN"......

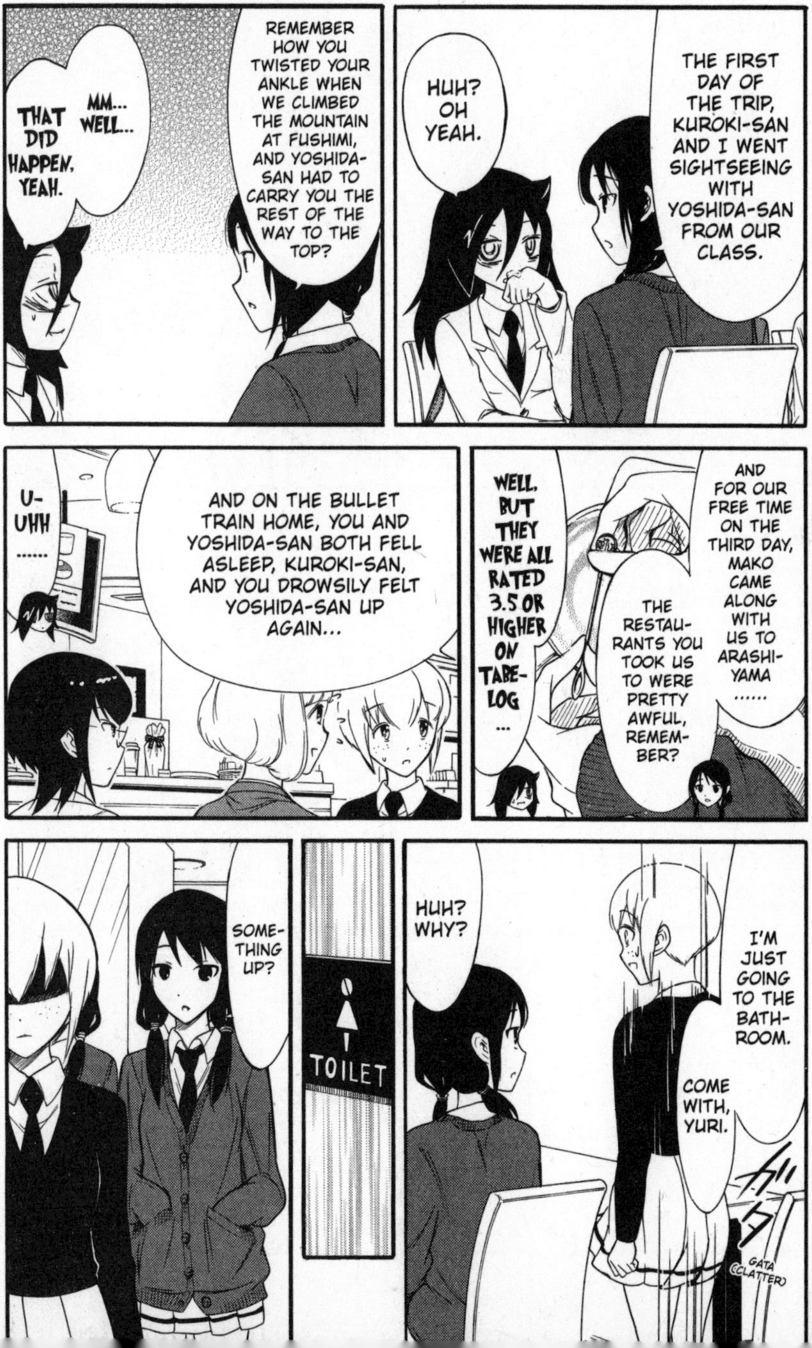
THE FIRST DAY OF THE TRIP, KUROKI-SAN AND I WENT SIGHTSEEING WITH YOSHIDA-SAN FROM OUR CLASS.
HUH? OH YEAH.
REMEMBER HOW YOU TWISTED YOUR ANKLE WHEN WE CLIMBED THE MOUNTAIN AT FUSHIMI, AND YOSHIDA-SAN HAD TO CARRY YOU THE REST OF THE WAY TO THE TOP?
MM... WELL...
THAT DID HAPPEN. YEAH.
AND FOR OUR FREE TIME ON THE THIRD DAY, MAKO CAME ALONG WITH US TO ARASHIYAMA......
THE RESTAURANTS YOU TOOK US TO WERE PRETTY AWFUL, REMEMBER?
WELL, BUT THEY WERE ALL RATED 3.5 OR HIGHER ON TABELOG...
AND ON THE BULLET TRAIN HOME, YOU AND YOSHIDA-SAN BOTH FELL ASLEEP, KUROKI-SAN, AND YOU DROWSILY FELT YOSHIDA-SAN UP AGAIN...
U-UHH......
I'M JUST GOING TO THE BATHROOM.
COME WITH, YURI.
HUH? WHY?
GATA (CLATTER)
TOILET
SOMETHING UP?

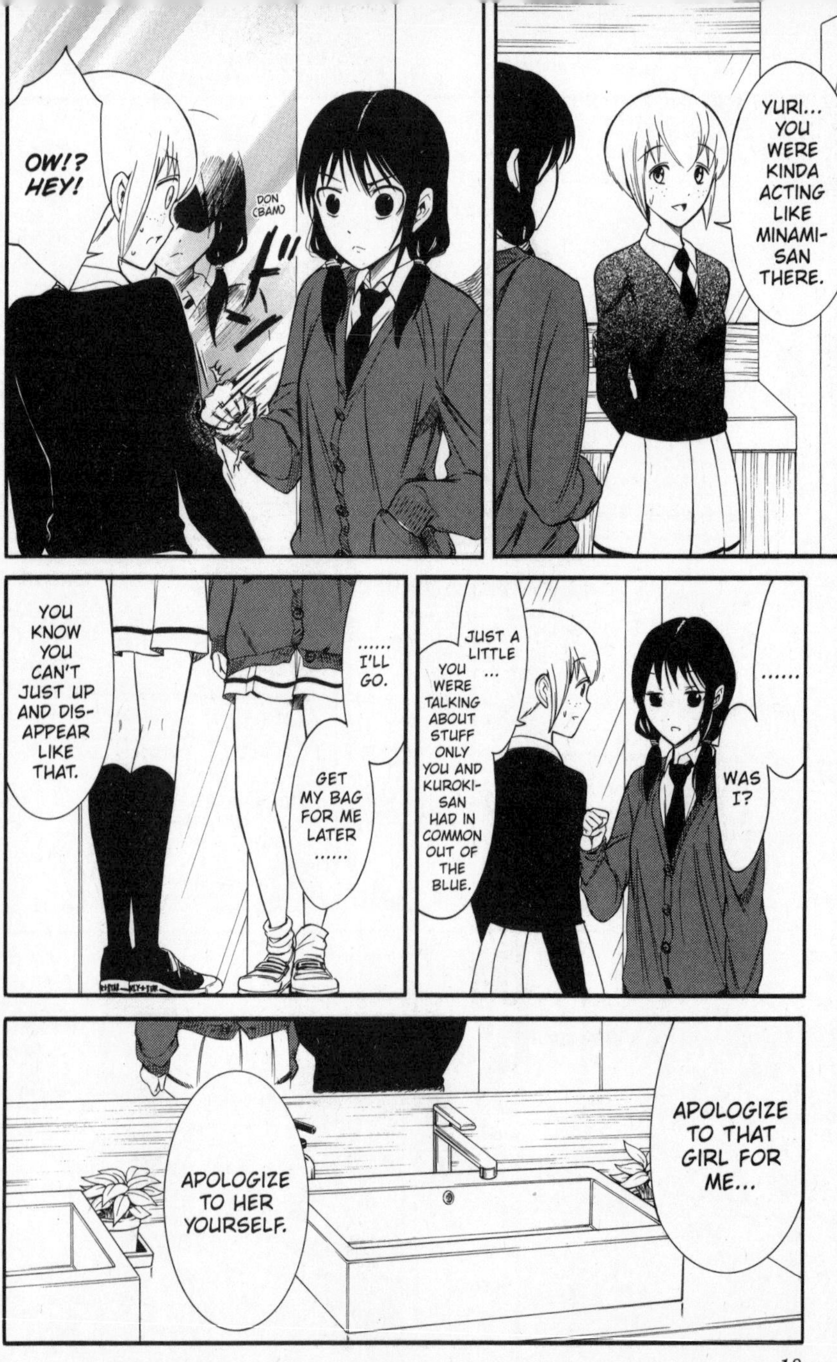
YURI... YOU WERE KINDA ACTING LIKE MINAMI-SAN THERE.
OW!? HEY!
DON (BAM)
......
WAS I?
JUST A LITTLE ... YOU WERE TALKING ABOUT STUFF ONLY YOU AND KUROKI-SAN HAD IN COMMON OUT OF THE BLUE.
...... I'LL GO.
GET MY BAG FOR ME LATER ......
YOU KNOW YOU CAN'T JUST UP AND DISAPPEAR LIKE THAT.
APOLOGIZE TO THAT GIRL FOR ME...
APOLOGIZE TO HER YOURSELF.

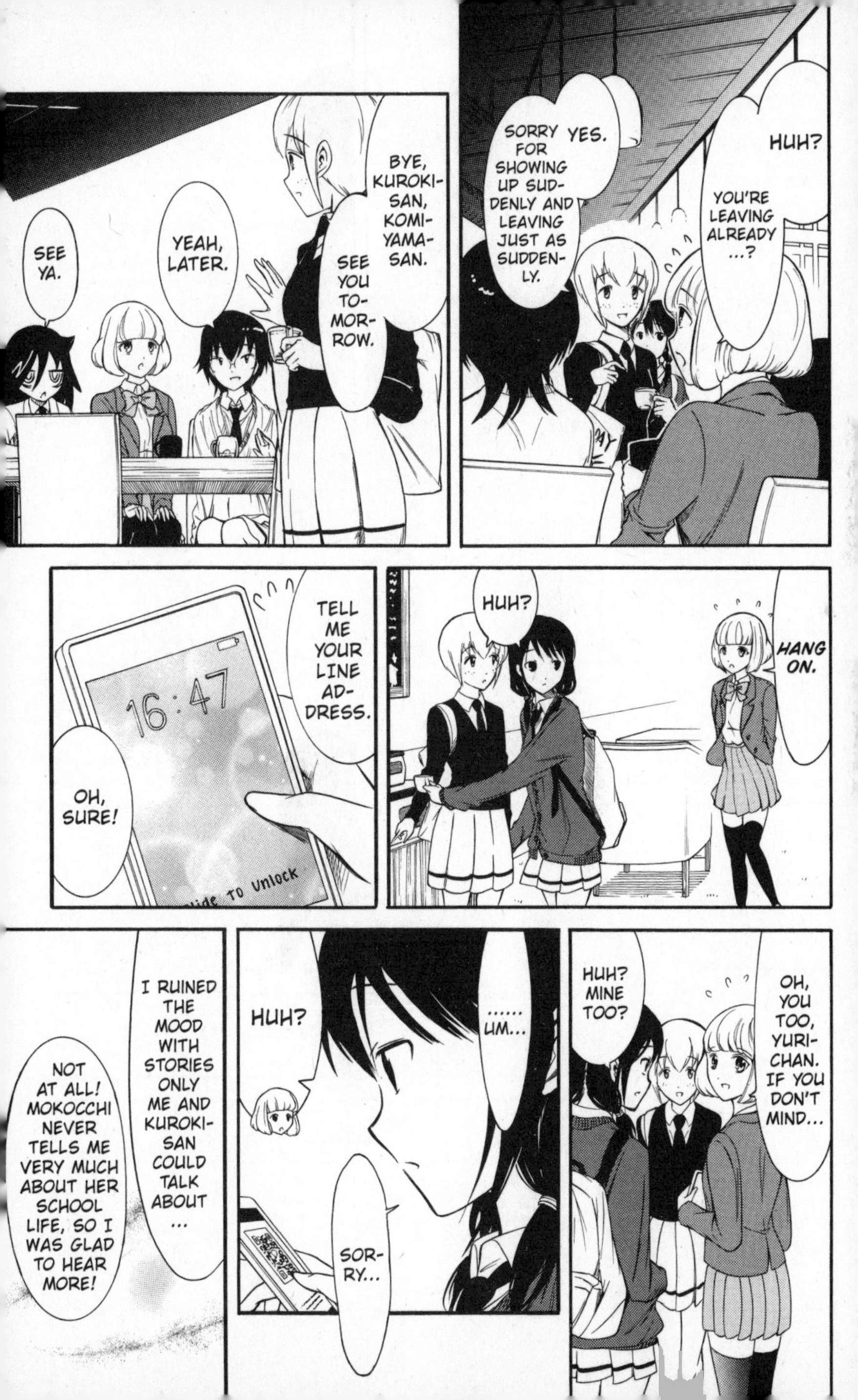
HUH?
YOU'RE LEAVING ALREADY...?
YES.
SORRY FOR SHOWING UP SUDDENLY AND LEAVING JUST AS SUDDENLY.
BYE, KUROKI-SAN, KOMIYAMA-SAN.
SEE YOU TOMORROW.
YEAH, LATER.
SEE YA.
HANG ON.
HUH?
TELL ME YOUR LINE ADDRESS.
16:47
OH, SURE!
lide to unlock
OH, YOU TOO, YURI-CHAN. IF YOU DON'T MIND...
HUH? MINE TOO?
......UM...
HUH?
SORRY...
I RUINED THE MOOD WITH STORIES ONLY ME AND KUROKI-SAN COULD TALK ABOUT...
NOT AT ALL! MOKOCCHI NEVER TELLS ME VERY MUCH ABOUT HER SCHOOL LIFE, SO I WAS GLAD TO HEAR MORE!

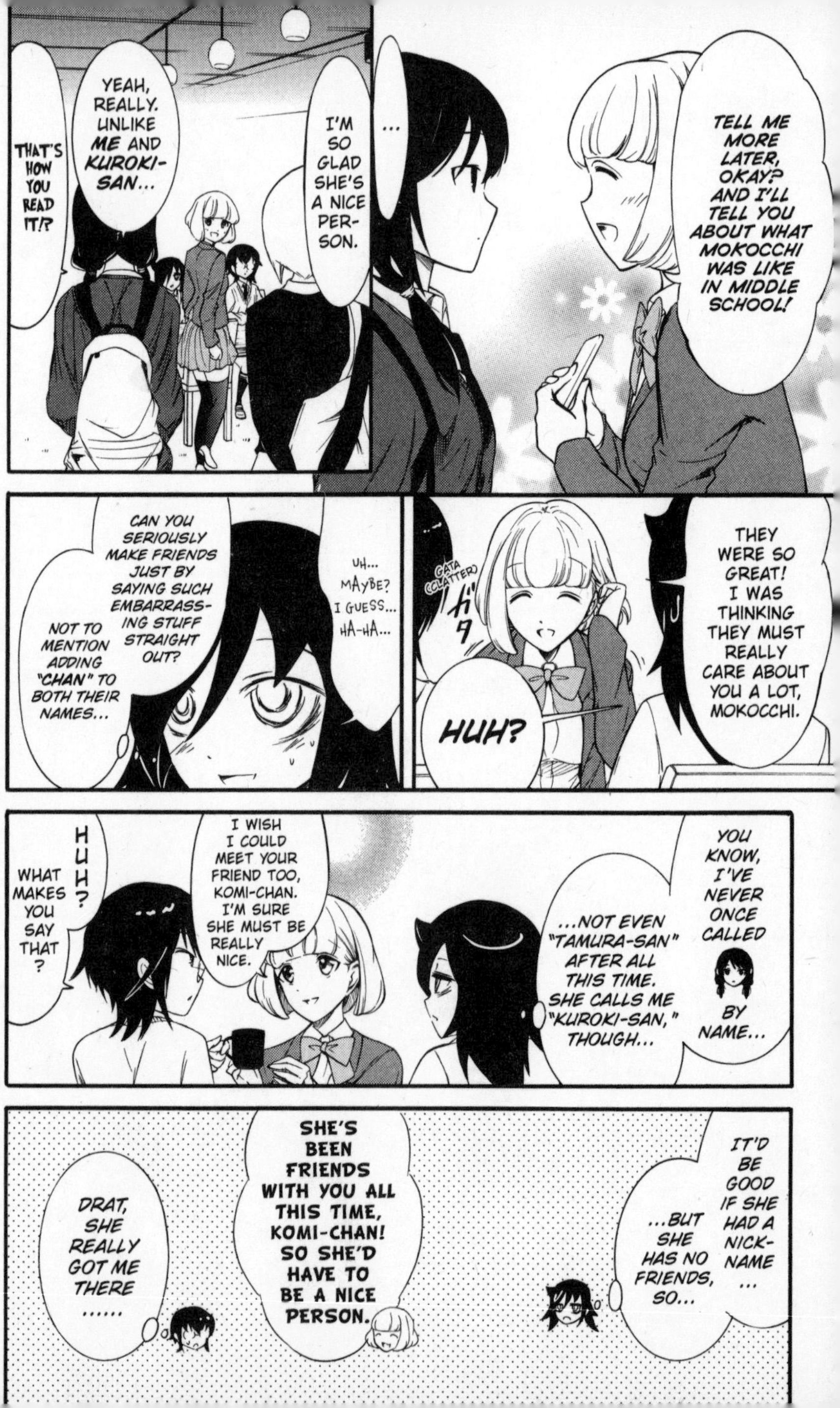
TELL ME MORE LATER, OKAY? AND I'LL TELL YOU ABOUT WHAT MOKOCCHI WAS LIKE IN MIDDLE SCHOOL!
...
I'M SO GLAD SHE'S A NICE PERSON.
YEAH, REALLY. UNLIKE ME AND KUROKI-SAN...
THAT'S HOW YOU READ IT!?
THEY WERE SO GREAT! I WAS THINKING THEY MUST REALLY CARE ABOUT YOU A LOT, MOKOCCHI.
GATA (CLATTER)
ガタ
HUH?
UH... MAYBE? I GUESS... HA-HA...
CAN YOU SERIOUSLY MAKE FRIENDS JUST BY SAYING SUCH EMBARRASSING STUFF STRAIGHT OUT?
NOT TO MENTION ADDING "CHAN" TO BOTH THEIR NAMES...
YOU KNOW, I'VE NEVER ONCE CALLED
BY NAME...
...NOT EVEN "TAMURA-SAN" AFTER ALL THIS TIME. SHE CALLS ME "KUROKI-SAN," THOUGH...
I WISH I COULD MEET YOUR FRIEND TOO, KOMI-CHAN. I'M SURE SHE MUST BE REALLY NICE.
HUH?
WHAT MAKES YOU SAY THAT?
IT'D BE GOOD IF SHE HAD A NICKNAME...
...BUT SHE HAS NO FRIENDS, SO...
SHE'S BEEN FRIENDS WITH YOU ALL THIS TIME, KOMI-CHAN! SO SHE'D HAVE TO BE A NICE PERSON.
DRAT, SHE REALLY GOT ME THERE ......

No Matter How I Look at It, It's You Guys' Fault I'm Not Popular!

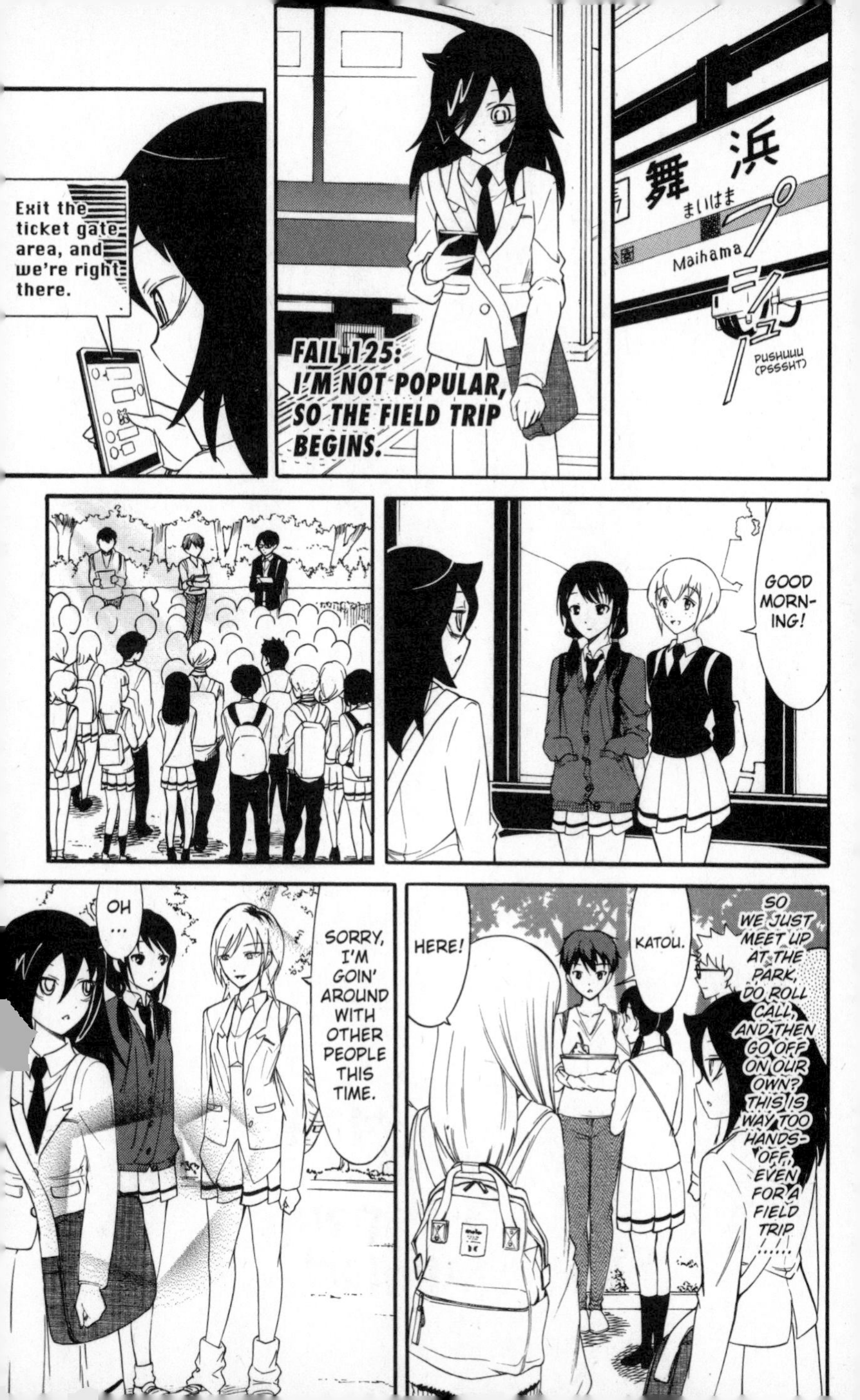

舞浜
まいはま
Maihama
プシュー
PUSHUUU (PSSSHT)
FAIL 125: I'M NOT POPULAR, SO THE FIELD TRIP BEGINS.
Exit the ticket gate area, and we're right there.
GOOD MORNING!
SO WE JUST MEET UP AT THE PARK, DO ROLL CALL, AND THEN GO OFF ON OUR OWN? THIS IS WAY TOO HANDS-OFF, EVEN FOR A FIELD TRIP......
KATOU.
HERE!
SORRY, I'M GOIN' AROUND WITH OTHER PEOPLE THIS TIME.
OH ...

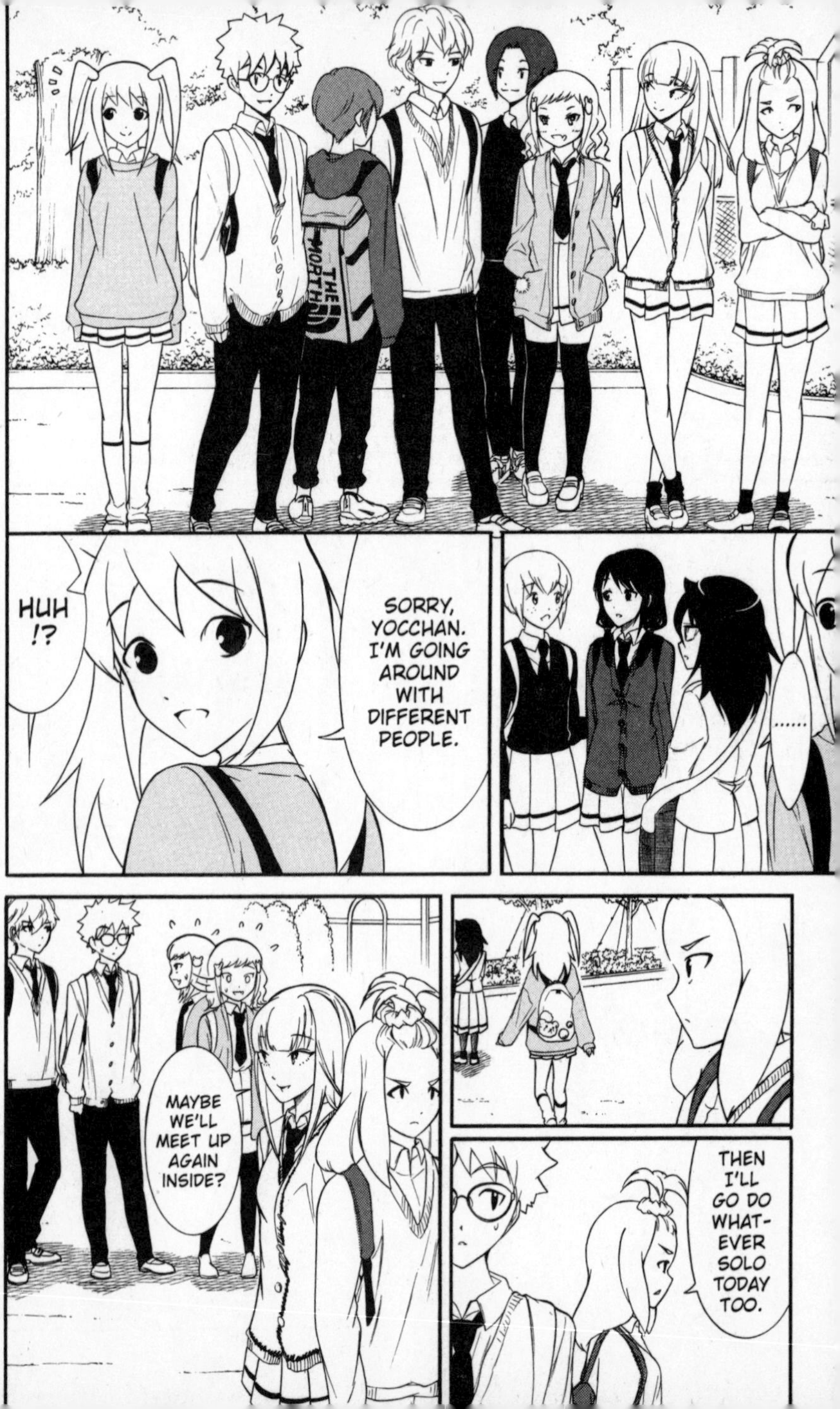
......
SORRY, YOCCHAN. I'M GOING AROUND WITH DIFFERENT PEOPLE.
HUH !?
THEN I'LL GO DO WHAT-EVER SOLO TODAY TOO.
MAYBE WE'LL MEET UP AGAIN INSIDE?

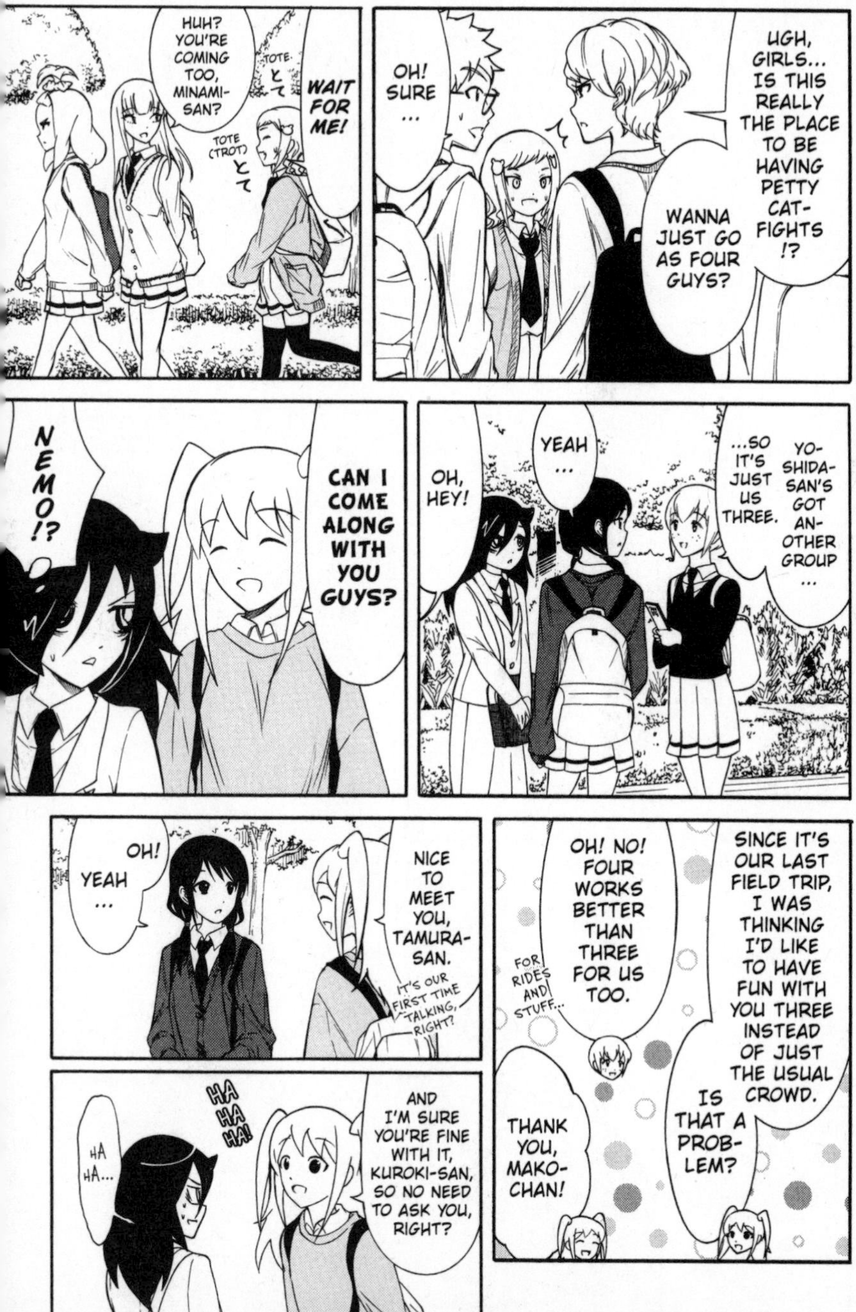
UGH, GIRLS... IS THIS REALLY THE PLACE TO BE HAVING PETTY CAT-FIGHTS!?
WANNA JUST GO AS FOUR GUYS?
OH! SURE ...
WAIT FOR ME!
TOTE とて
HUH? YOU'RE COMING TOO, MINAMI-SAN?
TOTE (TROT) とて
YO-SHIDA-SAN'S GOT AN-OTHER GROUP ...
...SO IT'S JUST US THREE.
YEAH ...
OH, HEY!
CAN I COME ALONG WITH YOU GUYS?
NEMO!?
SINCE IT'S OUR LAST FIELD TRIP, I WAS THINKING I'D LIKE TO HAVE FUN WITH YOU THREE INSTEAD OF JUST THE USUAL CROWD.
IS THAT A PROB-LEM?
OH! NO! FOUR WORKS BETTER THAN THREE FOR US TOO.
FOR RIDES AND STUFF...
THANK YOU, MAKO-CHAN!
NICE TO MEET YOU, TAMURA-SAN.
IT'S OUR FIRST TIME TALKING, RIGHT?
OH! YEAH ...
AND I'M SURE YOU'RE FINE WITH IT, KUROKI-SAN, SO NO NEED TO ASK YOU, RIGHT?
HA HA HA!
HA HA...

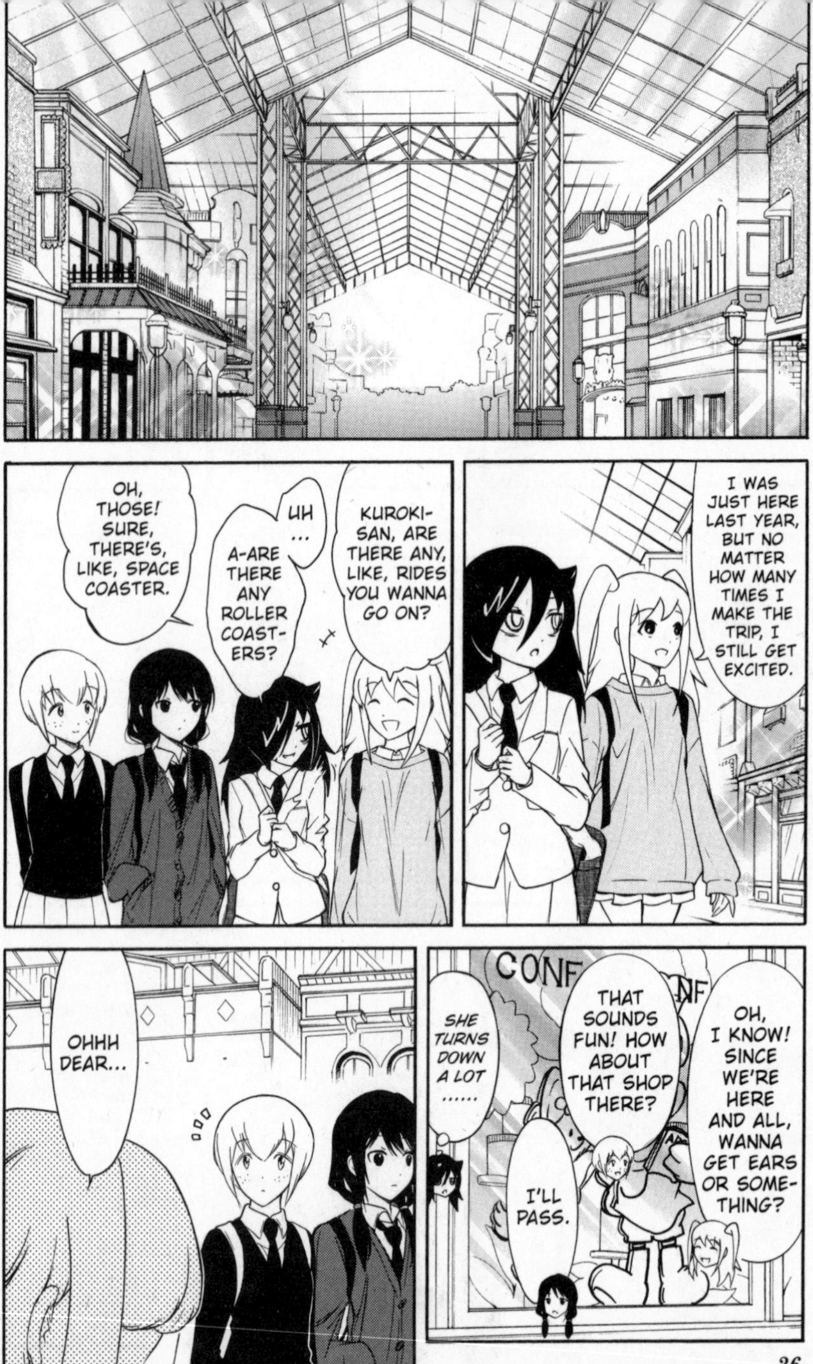
I WAS JUST HERE LAST YEAR, BUT NO MATTER HOW MANY TIMES I MAKE THE TRIP, I STILL GET EXCITED.
KUROKI-SAN, ARE THERE ANY, LIKE, RIDES YOU WANNA GO ON?
UH ...
A-ARE THERE ANY ROLLER COASTERS?
OH, THOSE! SURE, THERE'S, LIKE, SPACE COASTER.
CONF
OH, I KNOW! SINCE WE'RE HERE AND ALL, WANNA GET EARS OR SOMETHING?
THAT SOUNDS FUN! HOW ABOUT THAT SHOP THERE?
SHE TURNS DOWN A LOT ......
I'LL PASS.
OHHH DEAR...

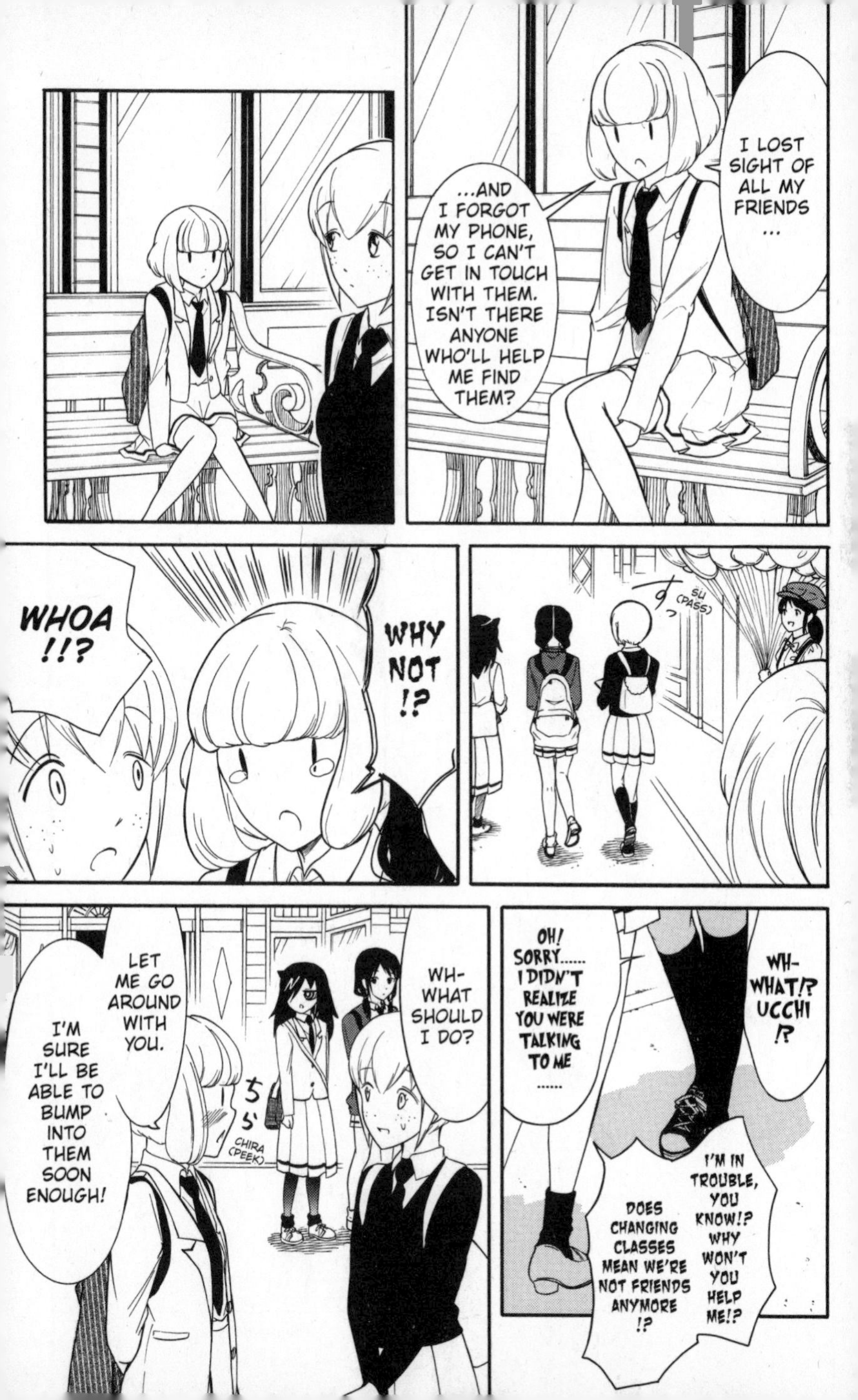
I LOST SIGHT OF ALL MY FRIENDS ...
...AND I FORGOT MY PHONE, SO I CAN'T GET IN TOUCH WITH THEM. ISN'T THERE ANYONE WHO'LL HELP ME FIND THEM?
すっ SU (PASS)
WHY NOT !?
WHOA !!?
WH-WHAT!? UCCHI !?
OH! SORRY...... I DIDN'T REALIZE YOU WERE TALKING TO ME ......
I'M IN TROUBLE, YOU KNOW!? WHY WON'T YOU HELP ME!?
DOES CHANGING CLASSES MEAN WE'RE NOT FRIENDS ANYMORE !?
WH-WHAT SHOULD I DO?
LET ME GO AROUND WITH YOU.
ちら CHIRA (PEEK)
I'M SURE I'LL BE ABLE TO BUMP INTO THEM SOON ENOUGH!

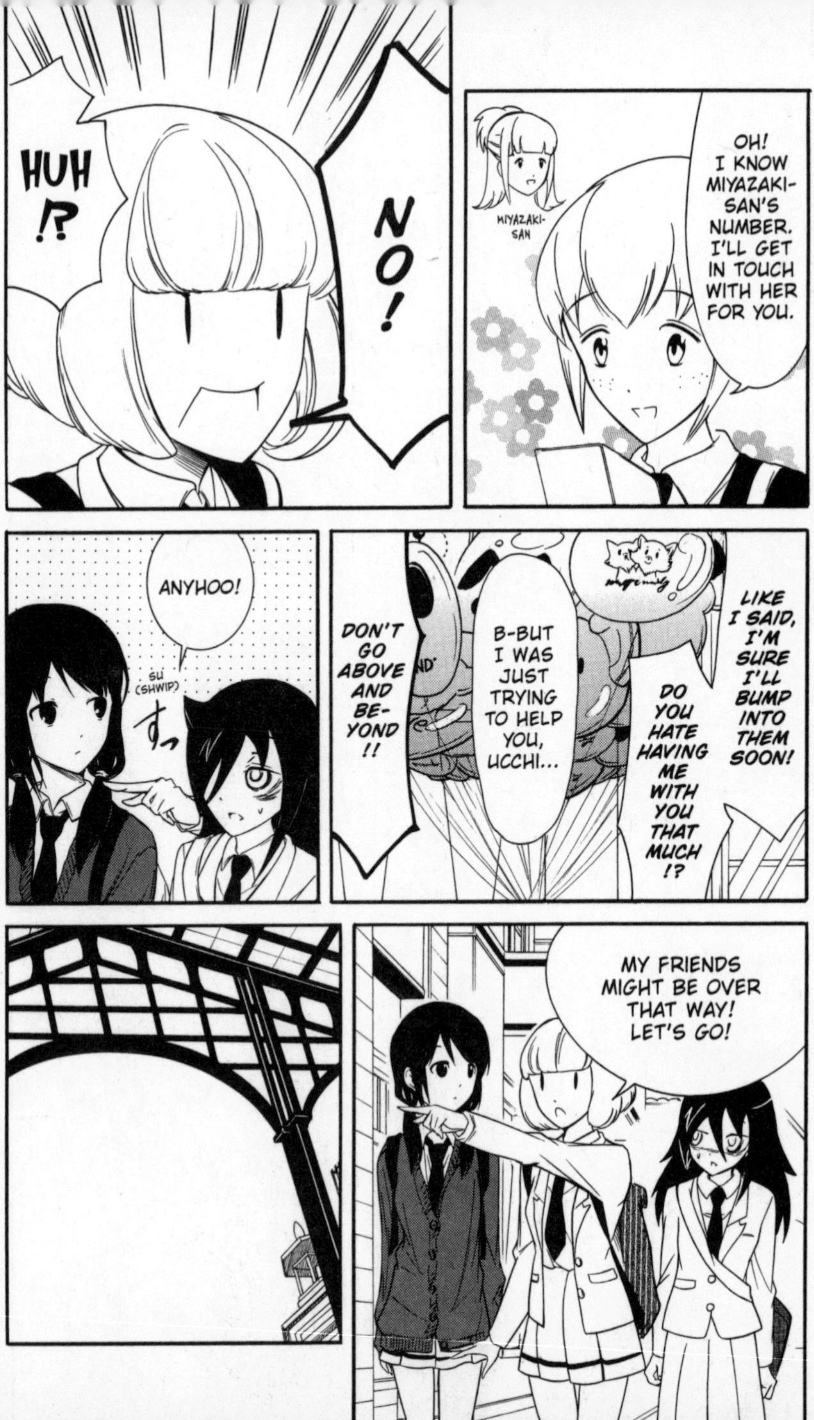
OH! I KNOW MIYAZAKI-SAN'S NUMBER. I'LL GET IN TOUCH WITH HER FOR YOU.
MIYAZAKI-SAN
NO!
HUH !?
LIKE I SAID, I'M SURE I'LL BUMP INTO THEM SOON!
DO YOU HATE HAVING ME WITH YOU THAT MUCH !?
B-BUT I WAS JUST TRYING TO HELP YOU, UCCHI...
DON'T GO ABOVE AND BE-YOND !!
ANYHOO!
SU (SHWIP)
すっ
MY FRIENDS MIGHT BE OVER THAT WAY! LET'S GO!

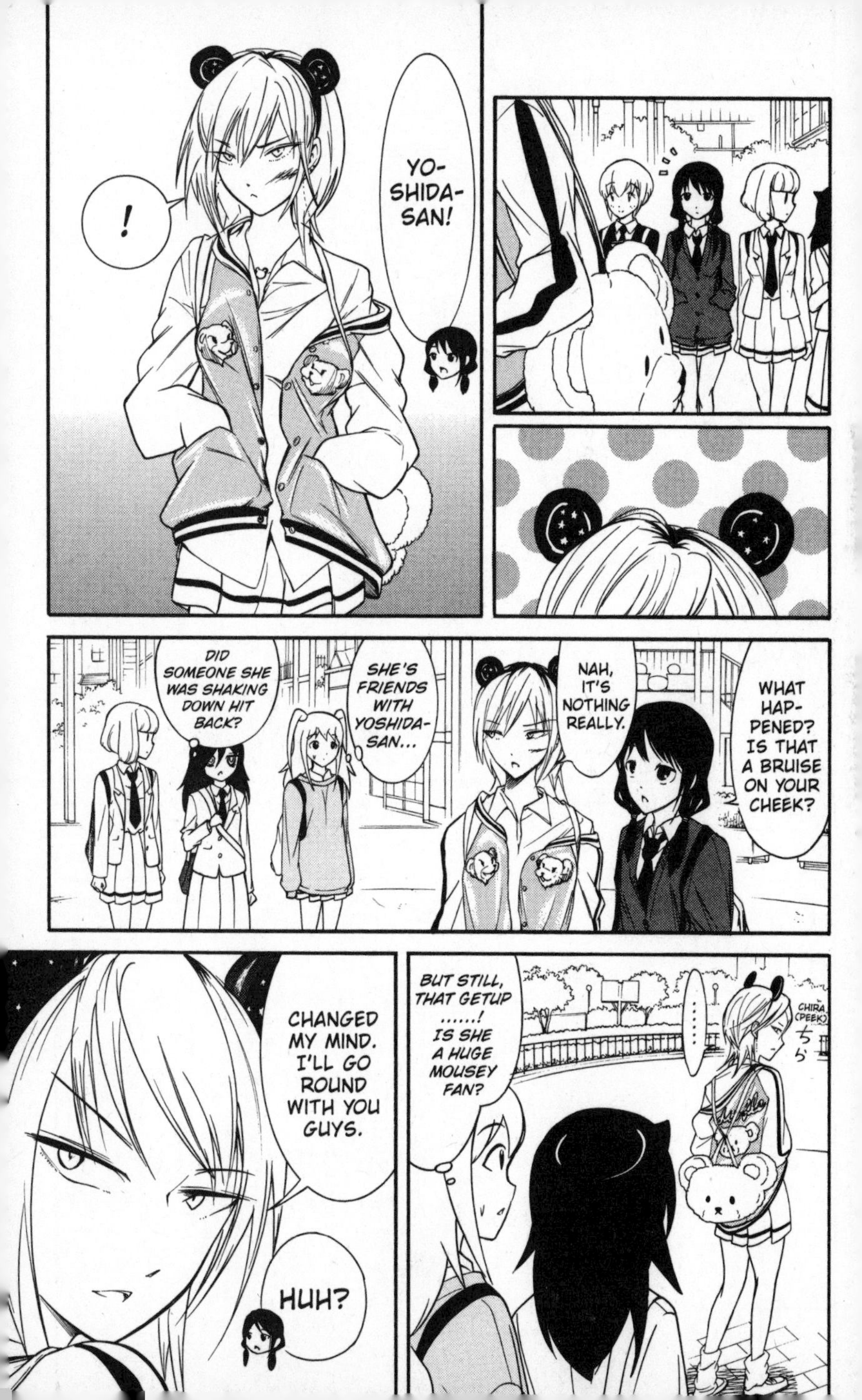
YO-SHIDA-SAN!
!
WHAT HAP-PENED? IS THAT A BRUISE ON YOUR CHEEK?
NAH, IT'S NOTHING REALLY.
SHE'S FRIENDS WITH YOSHIDA-SAN...
DID SOMEONE SHE WAS SHAKING DOWN HIT BACK?
CHIRA (PEEK)
ちら
......
BUT STILL, THAT GETUP ......! IS SHE A HUGE MOUSEY FAN?
CHANGED MY MIND. I'LL GO ROUND WITH YOU GUYS.
HUH?

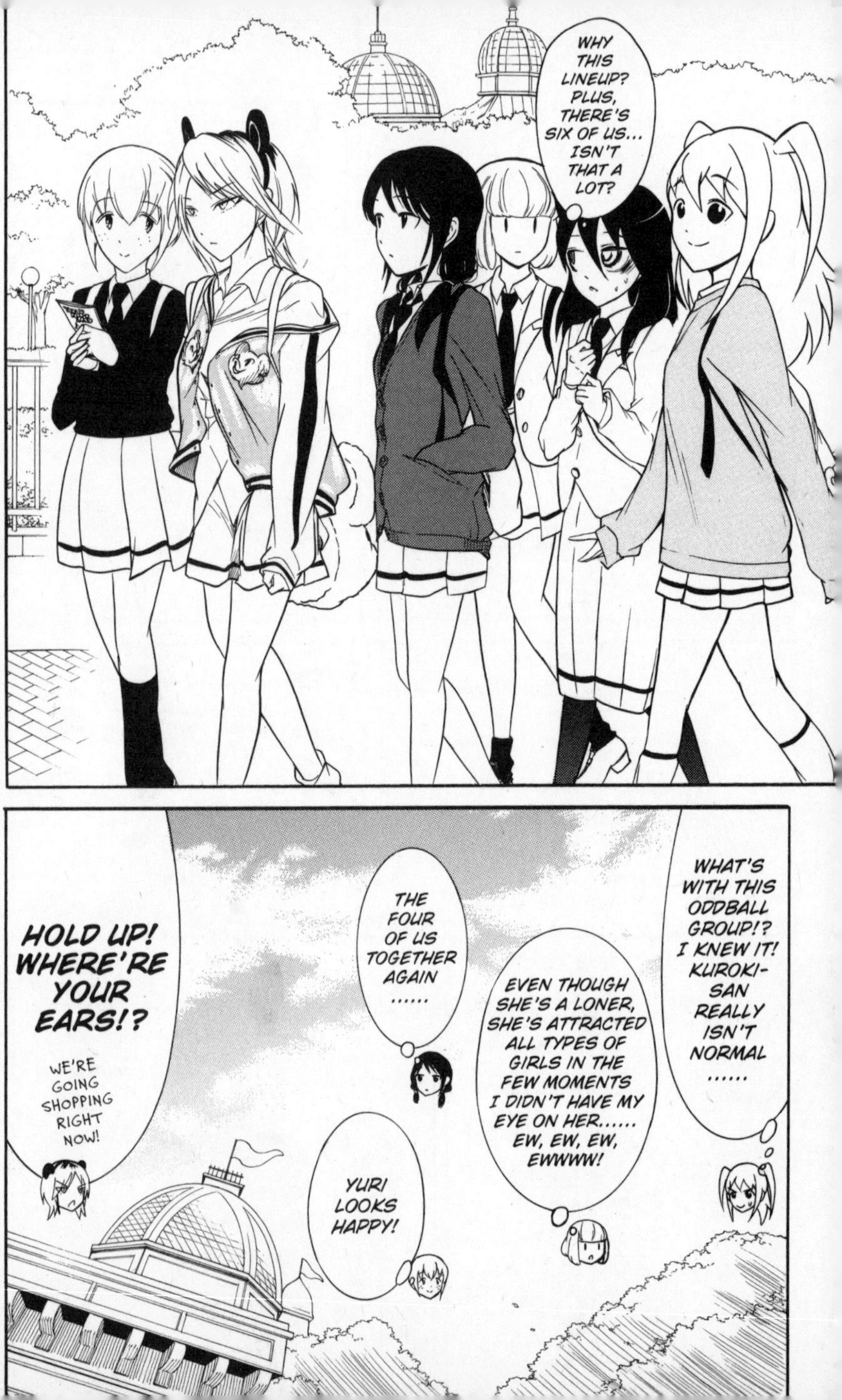
WHY THIS LINEUP? PLUS, THERE'S SIX OF US... ISN'T THAT A LOT?
WHAT'S WITH THIS ODDBALL GROUP!? I KNEW IT! KUROKI-SAN REALLY ISN'T NORMAL......
EVEN THOUGH SHE'S A LONER, SHE'S ATTRACTED ALL TYPES OF GIRLS IN THE FEW MOMENTS I DIDN'T HAVE MY EYE ON HER...... EW, EW, EW, EWWWW!
THE FOUR OF US TOGETHER AGAIN......
YURI LOOKS HAPPY!
HOLD UP! WHERE'RE YOUR EARS!?
WE'RE GOING SHOPPING RIGHT NOW!

No Matter How I Look at It, It's You Guys' Fault I'm Not Popular!

FAIL 126: I'M NOT POPULAR, SO I'LL GET CALLED BY A NICKNAME.

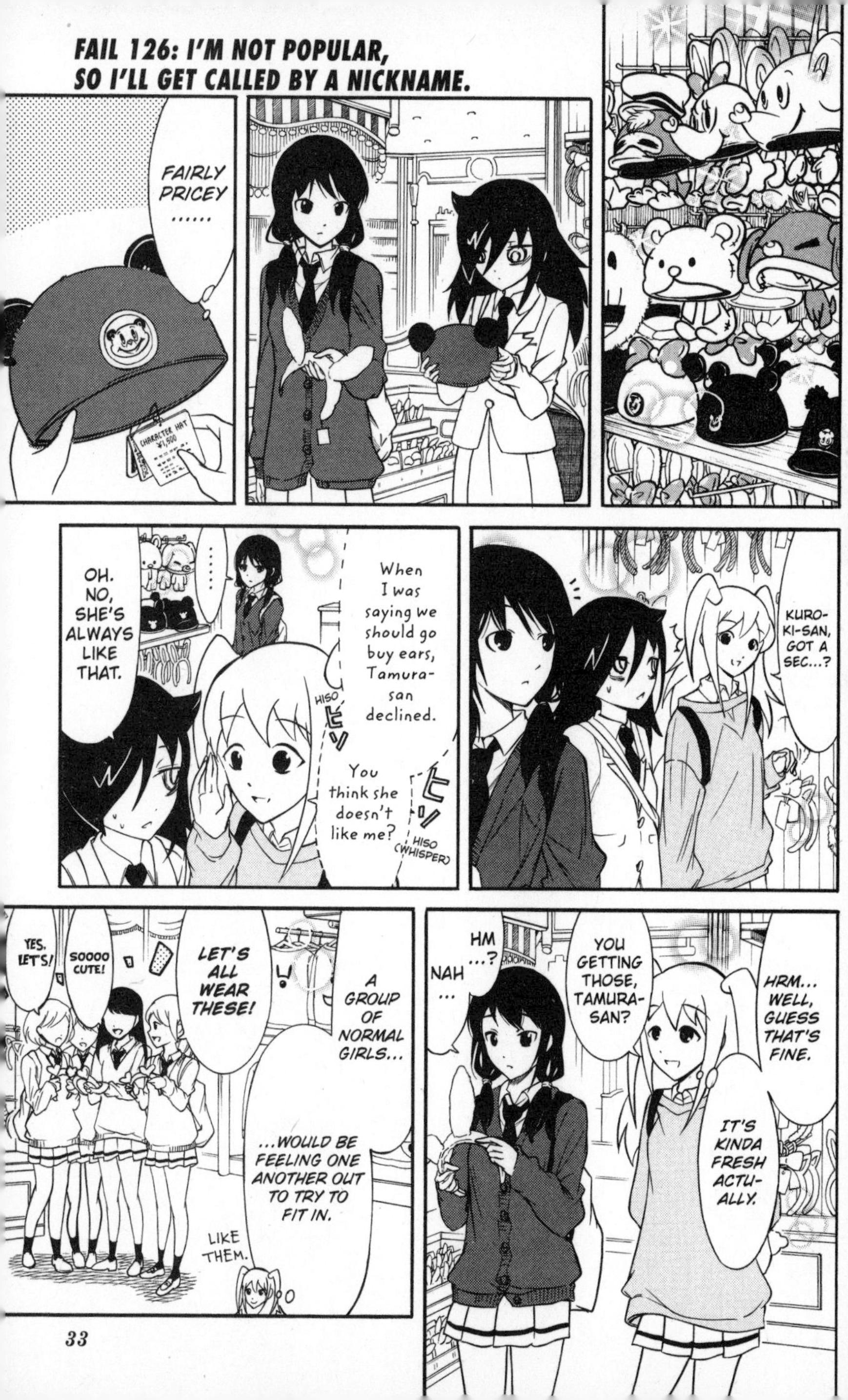
FAIRLY PRICEY ......
CHARACTER HAT ¥1,500
KURO-KI-SAN, GOT A SEC...?
When I was saying we should go buy ears, Tamura-san declined.
You think she doesn't like me?
HISO (WHISPER)
HISO
......
OH. NO, SHE'S ALWAYS LIKE THAT.
YOU GETTING THOSE, TAMURA-SAN?
HM ...?
NAH ...
HRM... WELL, GUESS THAT'S FINE.
IT'S KINDA FRESH ACTU-ALLY.
A GROUP OF NORMAL GIRLS...
LET'S ALL WEAR THESE!
SOOOO CUTE!
YES. LET'S!
...WOULD BE FEELING ONE ANOTHER OUT TO TRY TO FIT IN.
LIKE THEM.

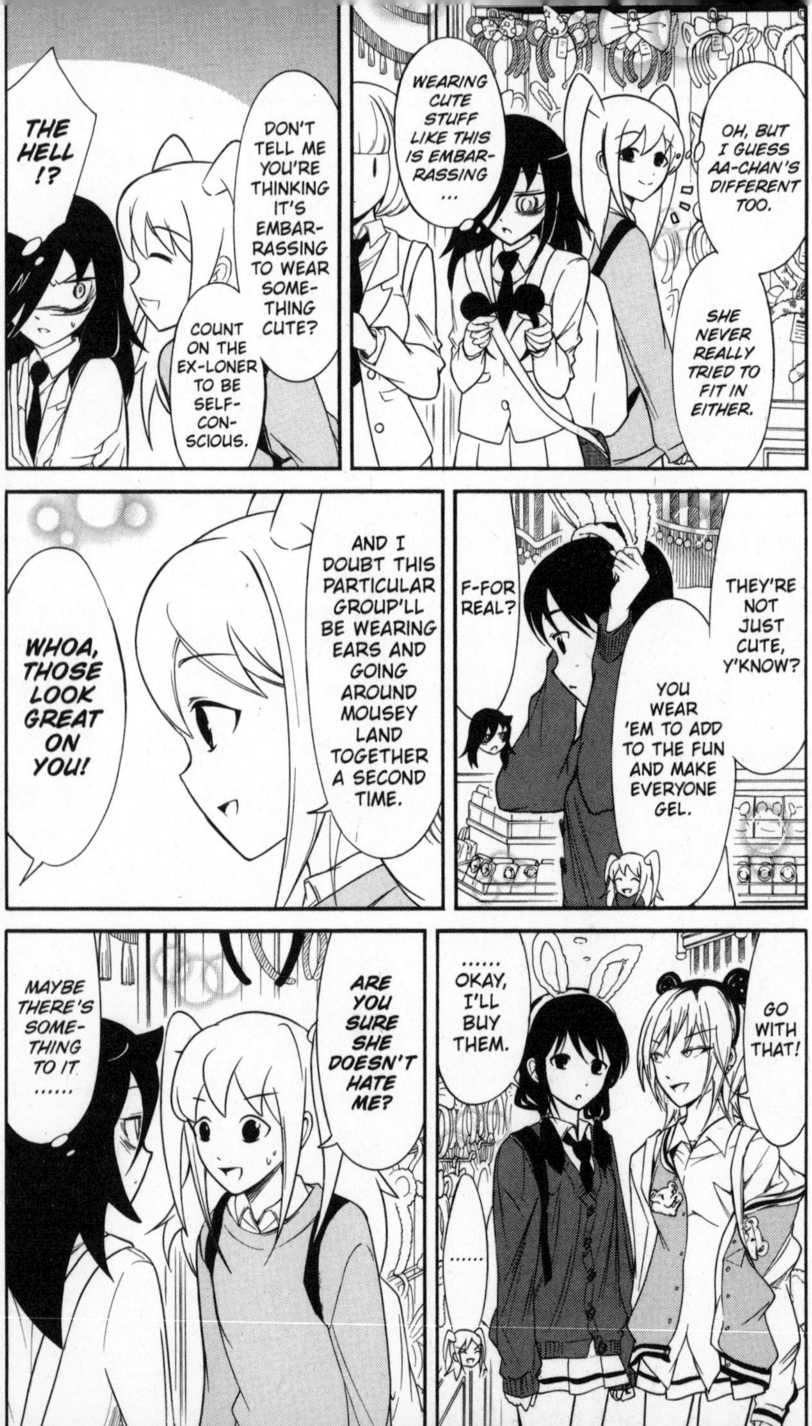
OH, BUT I GUESS AA-CHAN'S DIFFERENT TOO.
SHE NEVER REALLY TRIED TO FIT IN EITHER.
WEARING CUTE STUFF LIKE THIS IS EMBARRASSING...
DON'T TELL ME YOU'RE THINKING IT'S EMBARRASSING TO WEAR SOMETHING CUTE?
COUNT ON THE EX-LONER TO BE SELF-CONSCIOUS.
THE HELL!?
THEY'RE NOT JUST CUTE, Y'KNOW?
YOU WEAR 'EM TO ADD TO THE FUN AND MAKE EVERYONE GEL.
F-FOR REAL?
AND I DOUBT THIS PARTICULAR GROUP'LL BE WEARING EARS AND GOING AROUND MOUSEY LAND TOGETHER A SECOND TIME.
WHOA, THOSE LOOK GREAT ON YOU!
GO WITH THAT!
......OKAY, I'LL BUY THEM.
......
ARE YOU SURE SHE DOESN'T HATE ME?
MAYBE THERE'S SOMETHING TO IT......

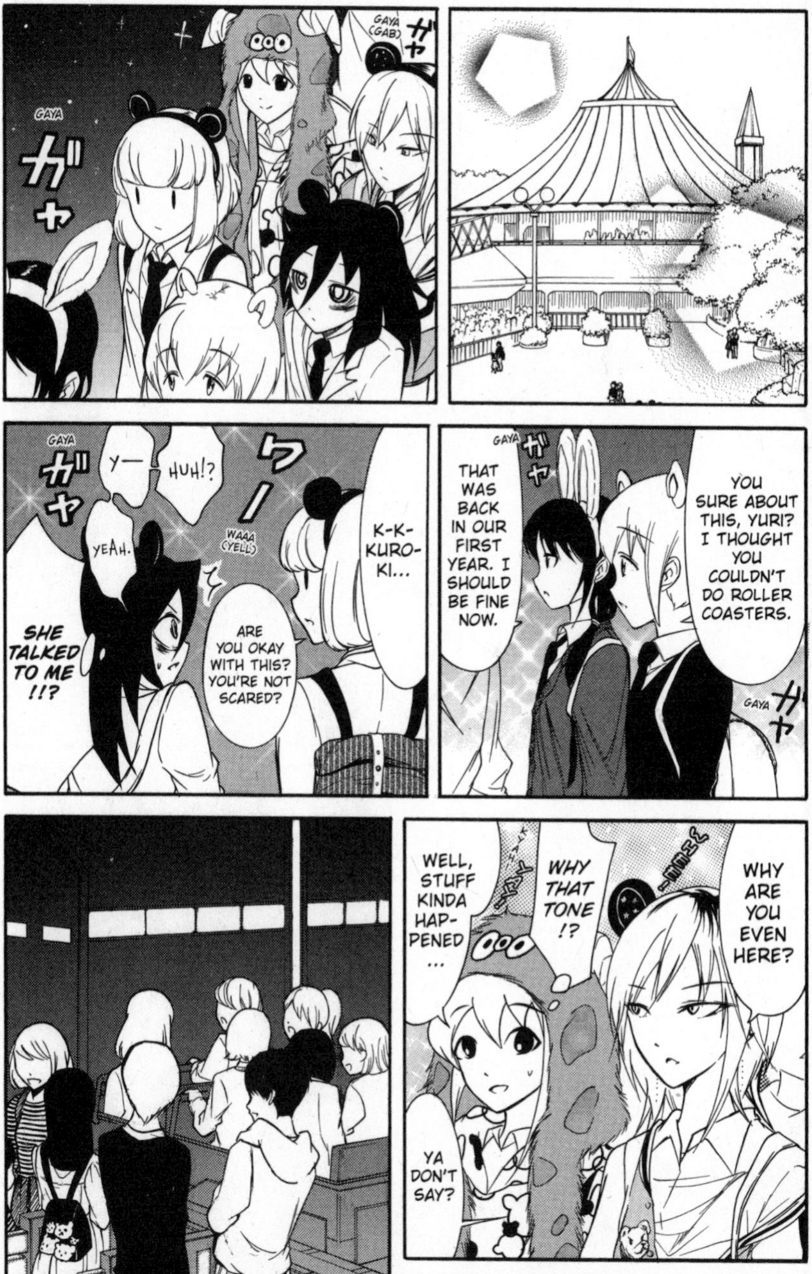
GAYA (GAB)
ガヤ
GAYA
ガヤ
GAYA
ガヤ
YOU SURE ABOUT THIS, YURI? I THOUGHT YOU COULDN'T DO ROLLER COASTERS.
THAT WAS BACK IN OUR FIRST YEAR. I SHOULD BE FINE NOW.
GAYA
ガヤ
K-K-KURO-KI...
WAAA (YELL)
ワー
ARE YOU OKAY WITH THIS? YOU'RE NOT SCARED?
HUH!?
Y—
YEAH.
SHE TALKED TO ME!!?
GAYA
ガヤ
WHY ARE YOU EVEN HERE?
WHY THAT TONE!?
WELL, STUFF KINDA HAPPENED...
YA DON'T SAY?

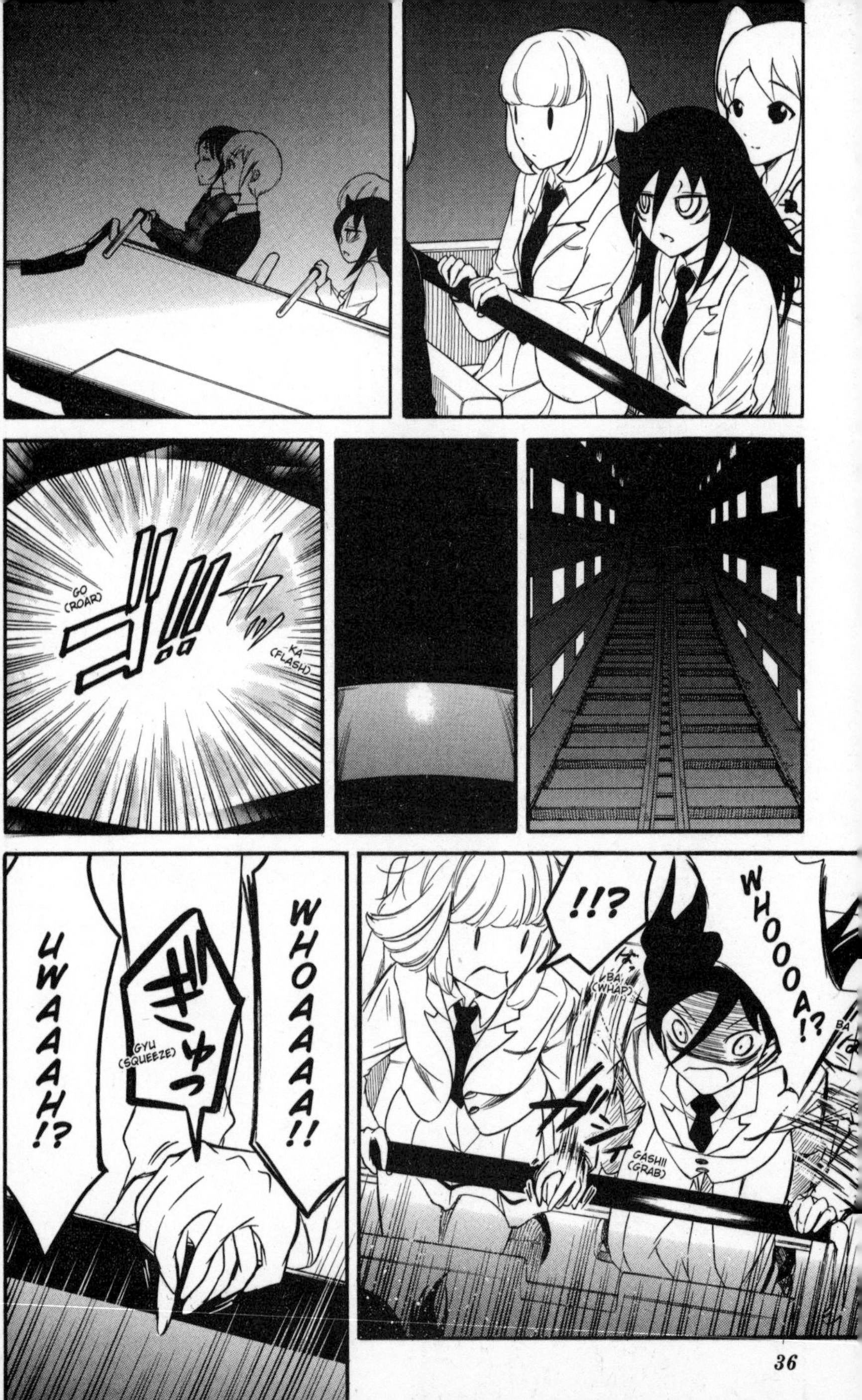
GO (ROAR)
KA (FLASH)
WHOOOOA!?
!!?
BA (WHAP)
BA
GASHI! (GRAB)
WHOAAAAAA!!
GYU (SQUEEZE)
UWAAAAAH!?

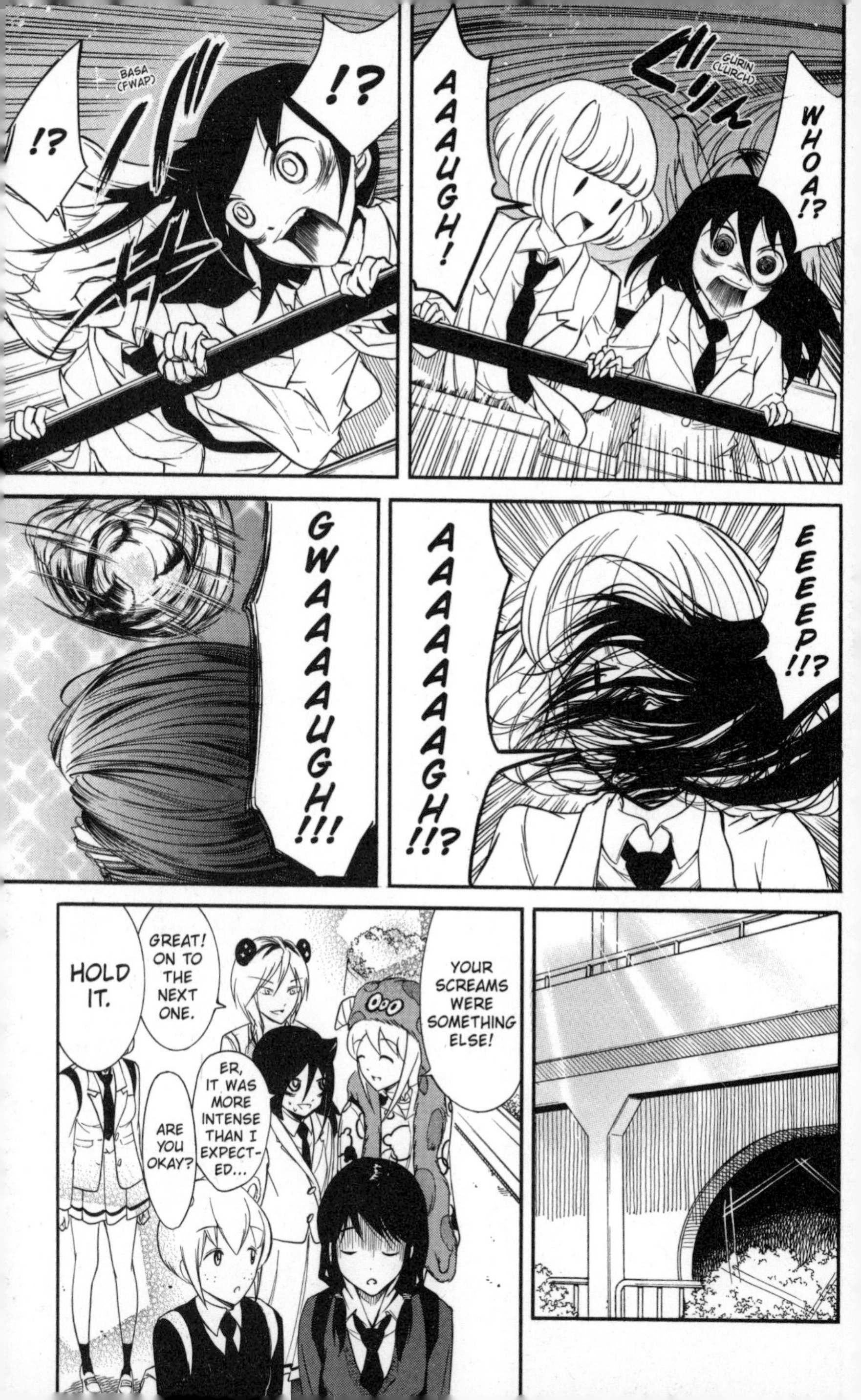

GURIN (LURCH)
WHOA!?
AAAAUGH!
!?
BASA (FWAP)
!?
EEEEP!!?
AAAAAAAGH!!?
GWAAAAUGH!!!
YOUR SCREAMS WERE SOMETHING ELSE!
GREAT! ON TO THE NEXT ONE.
HOLD IT.
ER, IT WAS MORE INTENSE THAN I EXPECTED...
ARE YOU OKAY?

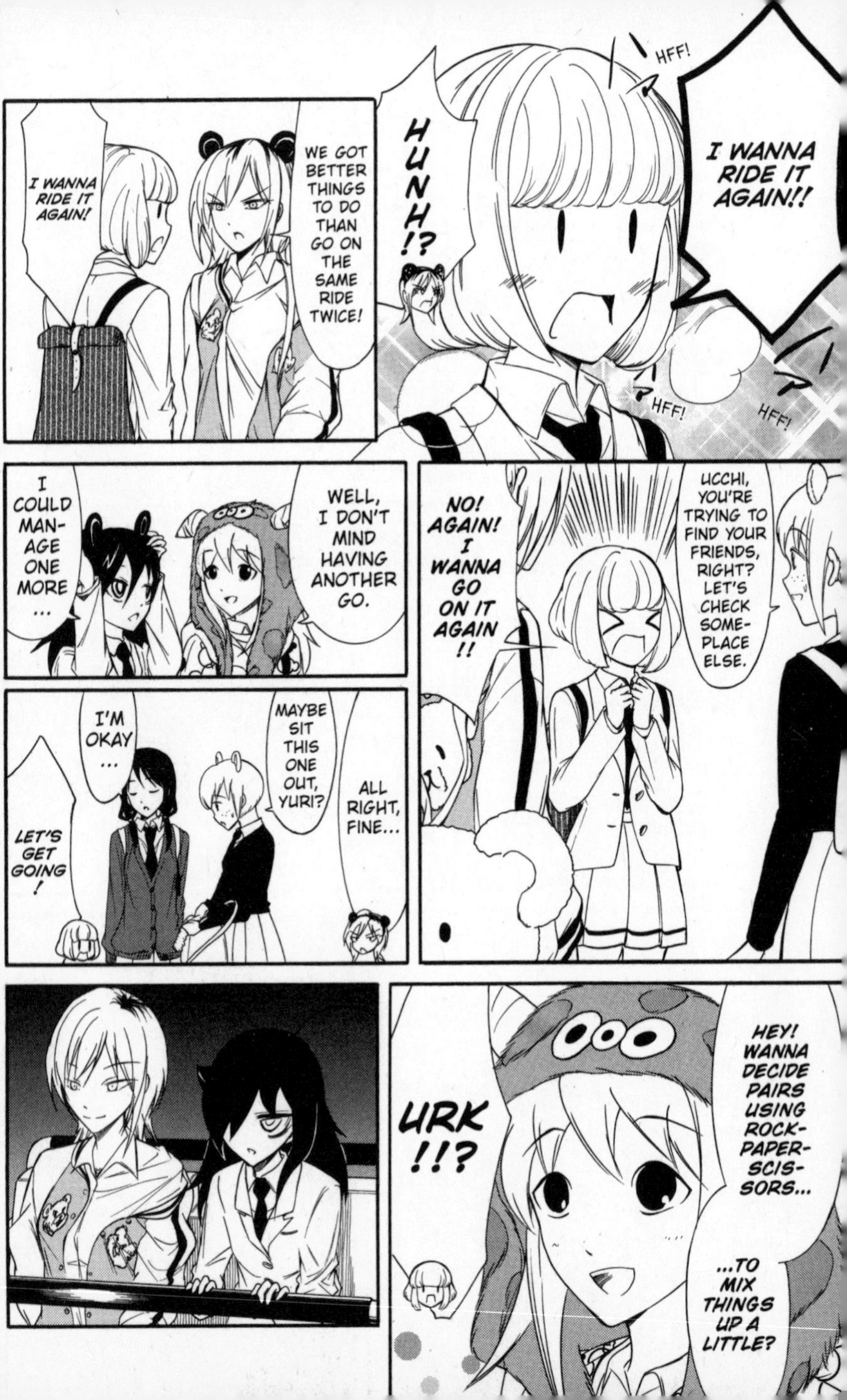
HFF!
I WANNA RIDE IT AGAIN!!
HUNH!?
HFF!
HFF!
I WANNA RIDE IT AGAIN!
WE GOT BETTER THINGS TO DO THAN GO ON THE SAME RIDE TWICE!
UCCHI, YOU'RE TRYING TO FIND YOUR FRIENDS, RIGHT? LET'S CHECK SOMEPLACE ELSE.
NO! AGAIN! I WANNA GO ON IT AGAIN!!
WELL, I DON'T MIND HAVING ANOTHER GO.
I COULD MANAGE ONE MORE...
MAYBE SIT THIS ONE OUT, YURI?
I'M OKAY...
ALL RIGHT, FINE...
LET'S GET GOING!
HEY! WANNA DECIDE PAIRS USING ROCK-PAPER-SCISSORS...
...TO MIX THINGS UP A LITTLE?
URK!!?

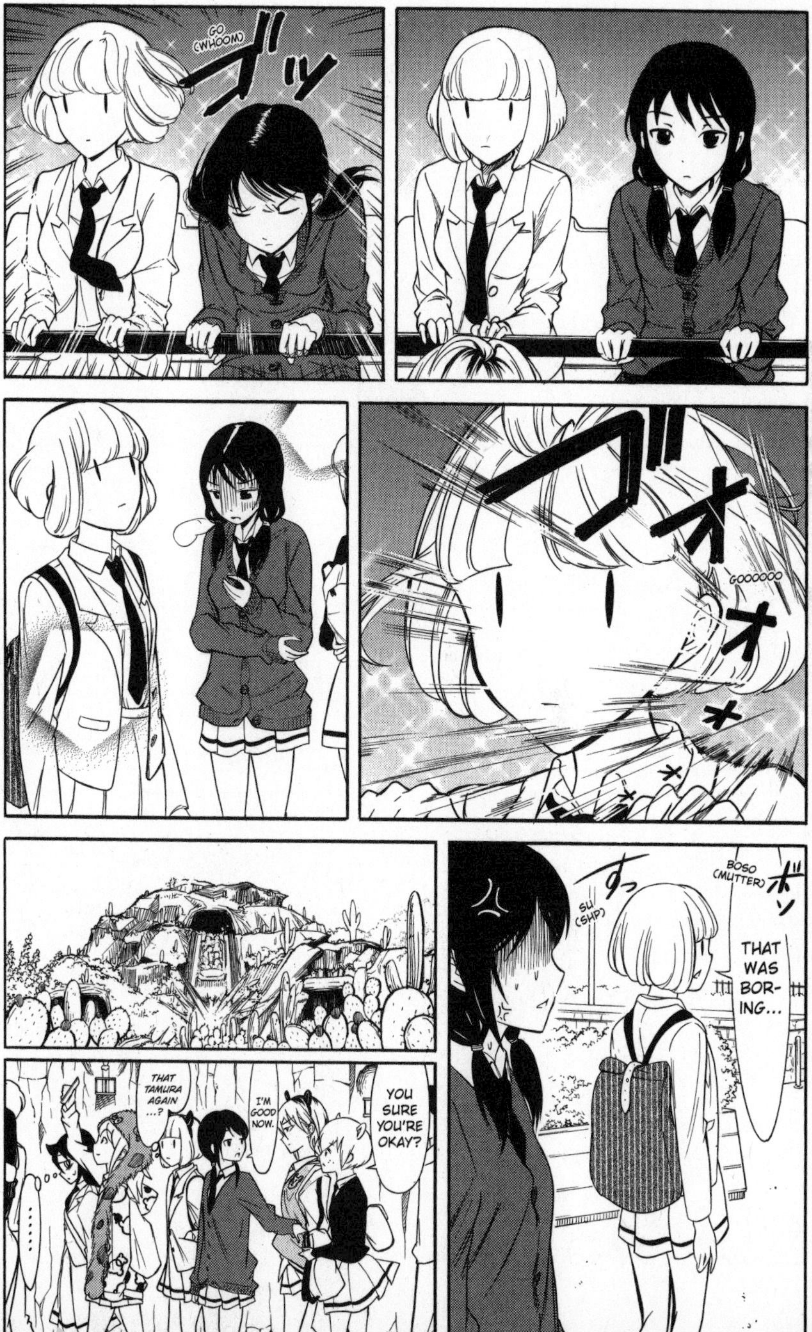
GO (WHOOM)
GOOOOOO
BOSO (MUTTER)
THAT WAS BOR-ING...
SU (SHP)
YOU SURE YOU'RE OKAY?
I'M GOOD NOW.
THAT TAMURA AGAIN ...?
......

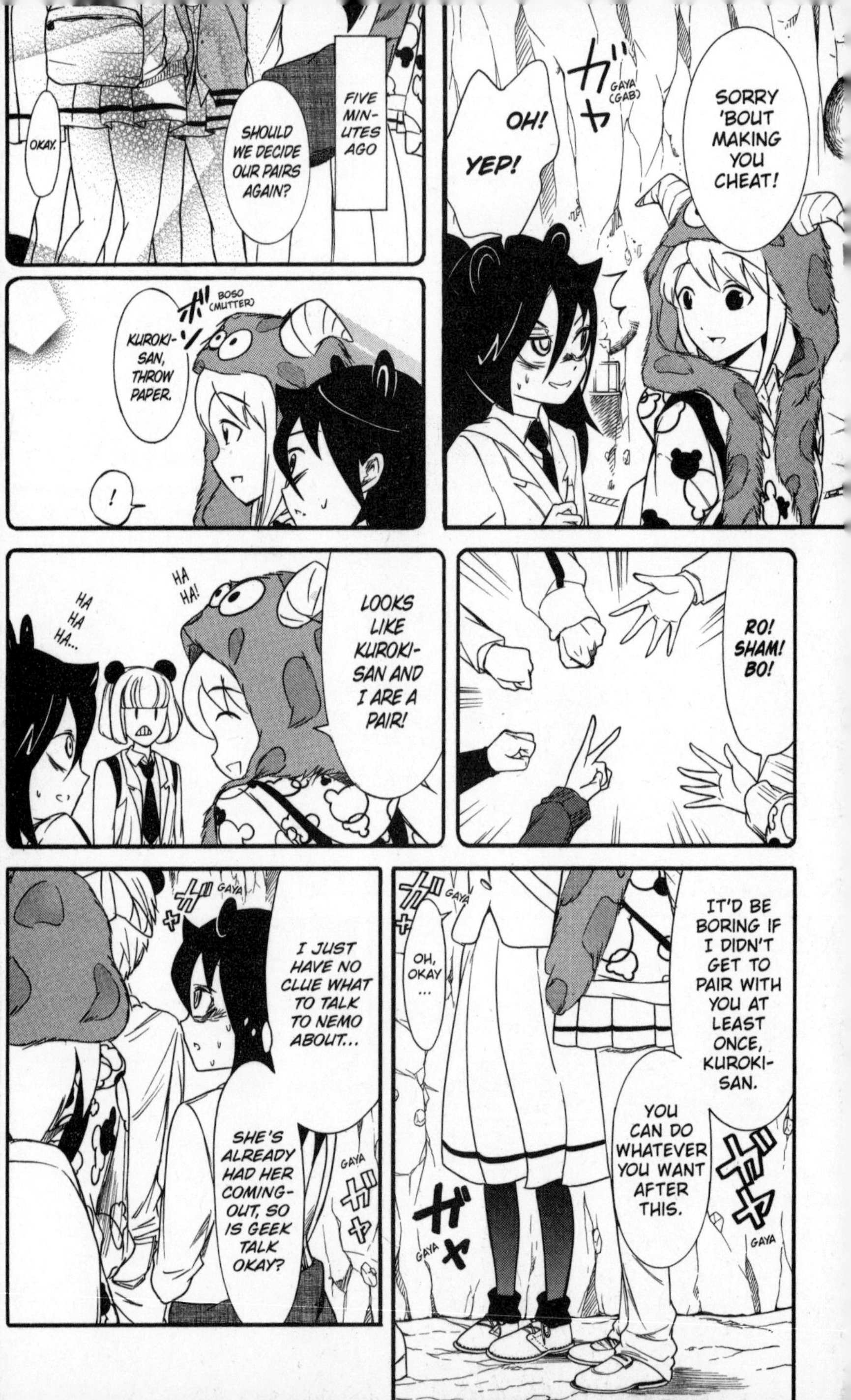
SORRY 'BOUT MAKING YOU CHEAT!
GAYA (GAB)
OH!
YEP!
FIVE MIN-UTES AGO
SHOULD WE DECIDE OUR PAIRS AGAIN?
OKAY.
BOSO (MUTTER)
KUROKI-SAN, THROW PAPER.
!
RO! SHAM! BO!
LOOKS LIKE KUROKI-SAN AND I ARE A PAIR!
HA HA!
HA HA HA...
IT'D BE BORING IF I DIDN'T GET TO PAIR WITH YOU AT LEAST ONCE, KUROKI-SAN.
YOU CAN DO WHATEVER YOU WANT AFTER THIS.
GAYA
GAYA
OH, OKAY ...
GAYA
GAYA
I JUST HAVE NO CLUE WHAT TO TALK TO NEMO ABOUT...
GAYA
SHE'S ALREADY HAD HER COMING-OUT, SO IS GEEK TALK OKAY?

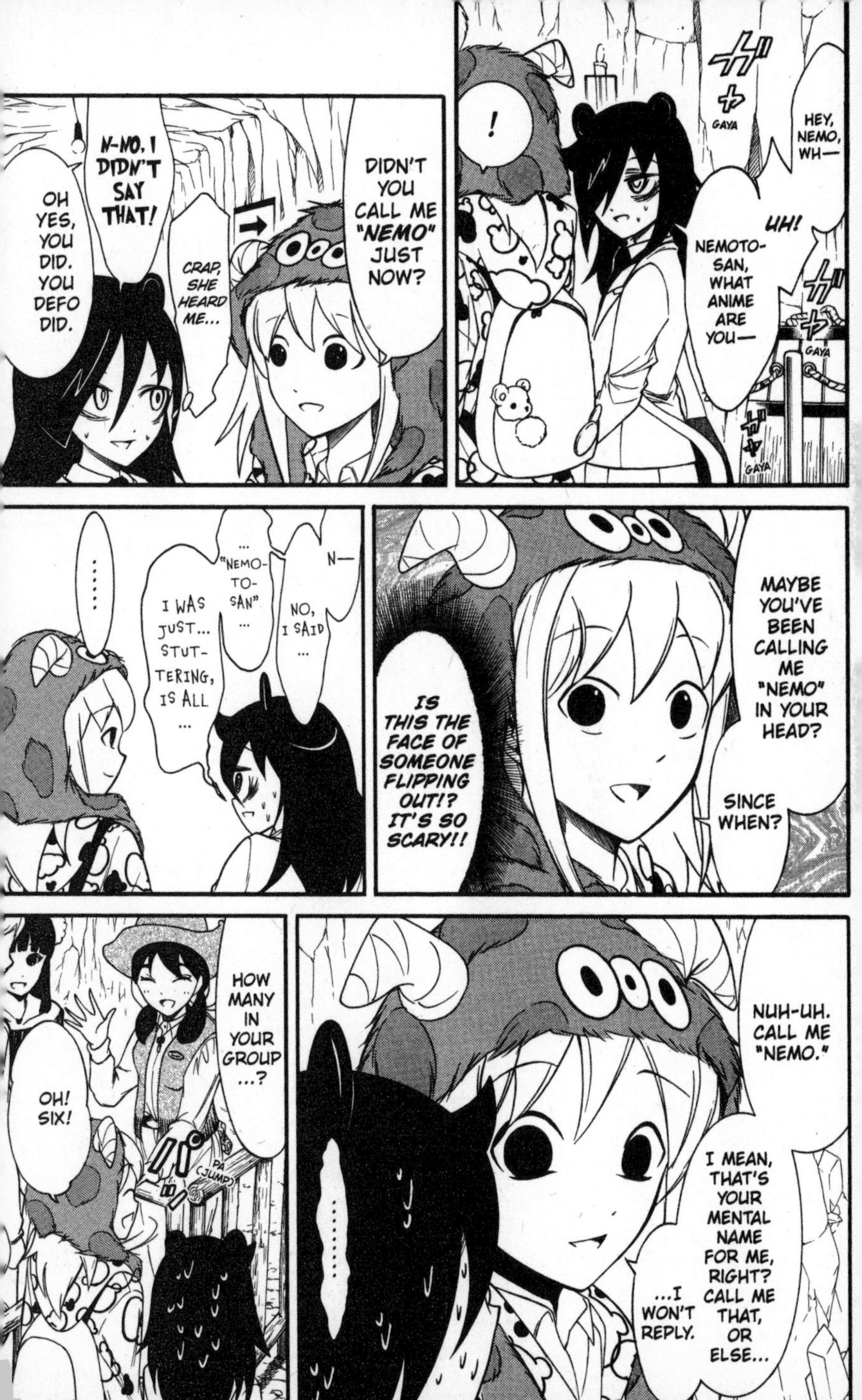
HEY, NEMO, WH—
GAYA
!
UH!
NEMOTO-SAN, WHAT ANIME ARE YOU—
GAYA
GAYA
DIDN'T YOU CALL ME "NEMO" JUST NOW?
N-NO. I DIDN'T SAY THAT!
CRAP, SHE HEARD ME...
OH YES, YOU DID. YOU DEFO DID.
MAYBE YOU'VE BEEN CALLING ME "NEMO" IN YOUR HEAD?
SINCE WHEN?
IS THIS THE FACE OF SOMEONE FLIPPING OUT!? IT'S SO SCARY!!
N—
NO, I SAID ...
... "NEMO-TO-SAN" ...
I WAS JUST... STUT-TERING, IS ALL ...
......
NUH-UH. CALL ME "NEMO."
I MEAN, THAT'S YOUR MENTAL NAME FOR ME, RIGHT? CALL ME THAT, OR ELSE...
...I WON'T REPLY.
......
HOW MANY IN YOUR GROUP ...?
PA (JUMP)
OH! SIX!

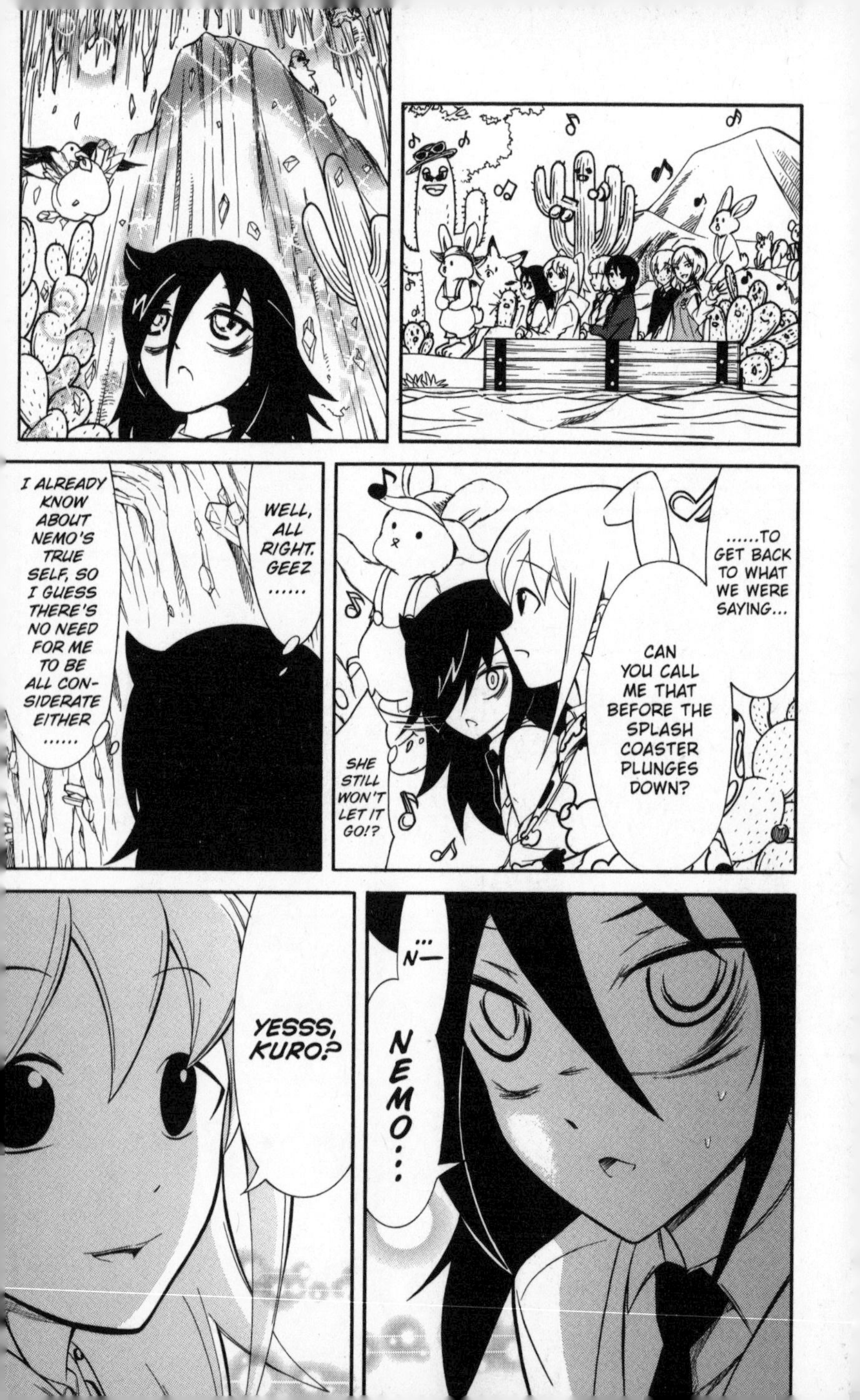
......TO GET BACK TO WHAT WE WERE SAYING...
CAN YOU CALL ME THAT BEFORE THE SPLASH COASTER PLUNGES DOWN?
SHE STILL WON'T LET IT GO!?
WELL, ALL RIGHT. GEEZ ......
I ALREADY KNOW ABOUT NEMO'S TRUE SELF, SO I GUESS THERE'S NO NEED FOR ME TO BE ALL CON-SIDERATE EITHER ......
...N—
NEMO...
YESSS, KURO?

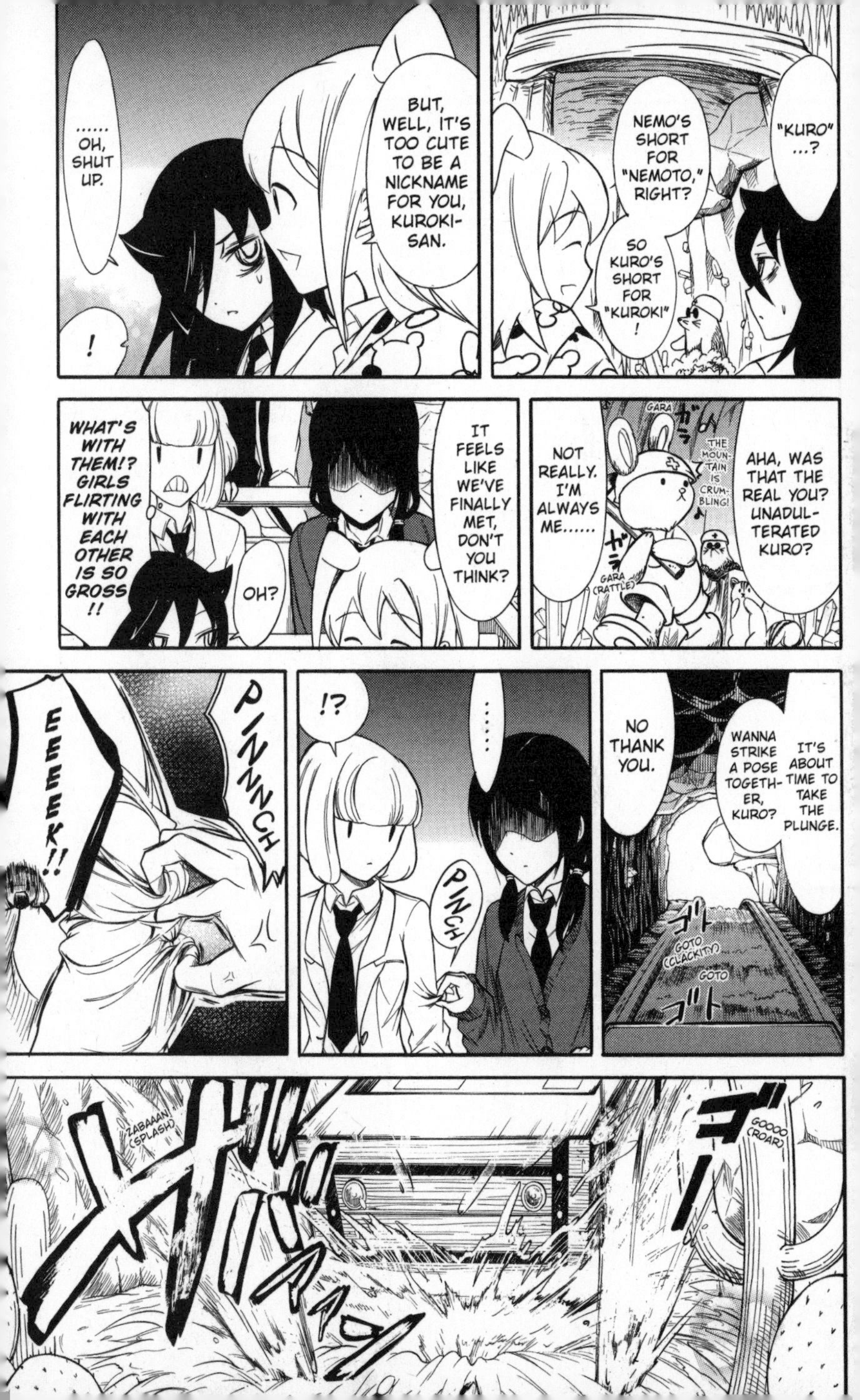
"KURO" ...?
NEMO'S SHORT FOR "NEMOTO," RIGHT?
SO KURO'S SHORT FOR "KUROKI"!
BUT, WELL, IT'S TOO CUTE TO BE A NICKNAME FOR YOU, KUROKI-SAN.
...... OH, SHUT UP.
!
AHA, WAS THAT THE REAL YOU? UNADULTERATED KURO?
GARA
THE MOUNTAIN IS CRUMBLING!
GARA (RATTLE)
NOT REALLY. I'M ALWAYS ME......
IT FEELS LIKE WE'VE FINALLY MET, DON'T YOU THINK?
OH?
WHAT'S WITH THEM!? GIRLS FLIRTING WITH EACH OTHER IS SO GROSS!!
IT'S ABOUT TIME TO TAKE THE PLUNGE.
WANNA STRIKE A POSE TOGETHER, KURO?
NO THANK YOU.
GOTO (CLACKITY)
GOTO
......
!?
PINCH
PINNNCH
EEEEEK!!
GOOOO (ROAR)
ZABAAAN! (SPLASH)

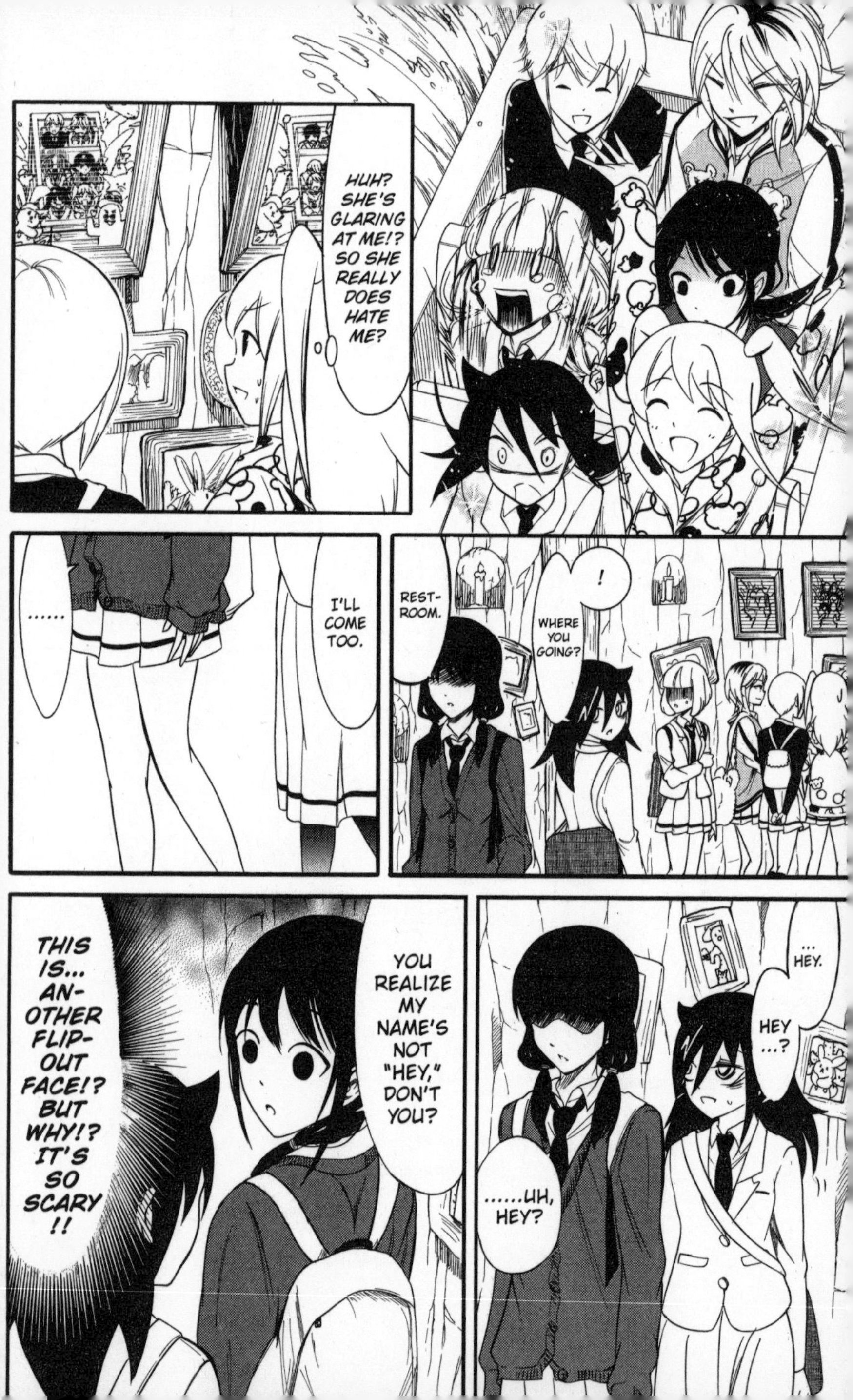
HUH? SHE'S GLARING AT ME!? SO SHE REALLY DOES HATE ME?
!
WHERE YOU GOING?
REST-ROOM.
I'LL COME TOO.
......
...HEY.
HEY ...?
......UH, HEY?
YOU REALIZE MY NAME'S NOT "HEY," DON'T YOU?
THIS IS... AN-OTHER FLIP-OUT FACE!? BUT WHY!? IT'S SO SCARY!!

No Matter How I Look at It, It's You Guys' Fault I'm Not Popular!

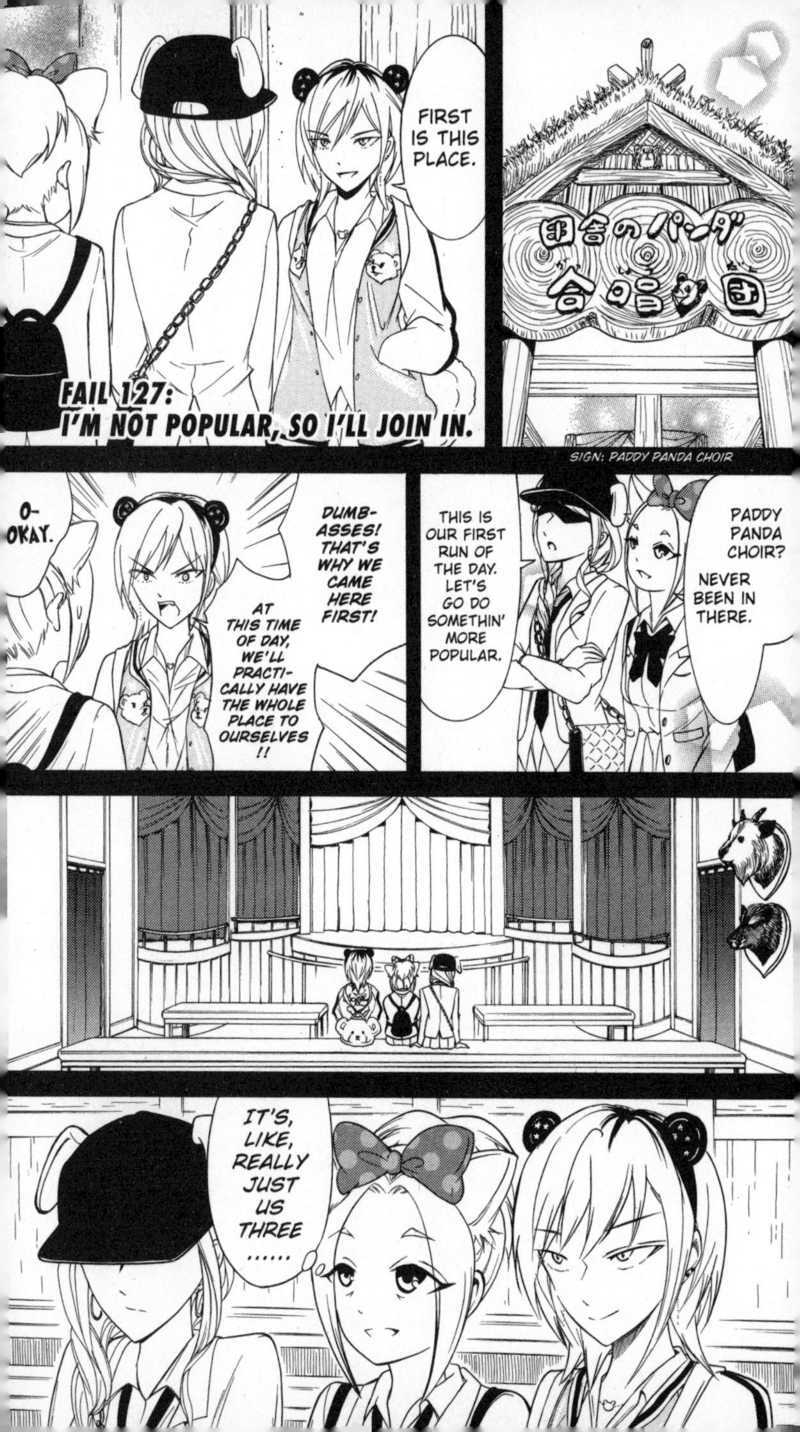
田舎のパンダ合唱団
SIGN: PADDY PANDA CHOIR
FIRST IS THIS PLACE.
FAIL 127: I'M NOT POPULAR, SO I'LL JOIN IN.
PADDY PANDA CHOIR? NEVER BEEN IN THERE.
THIS IS OUR FIRST RUN OF THE DAY. LET'S GO DO SOMETHIN' MORE POPULAR.
DUMB-ASSES! THAT'S WHY WE CAME HERE FIRST!
AT THIS TIME OF DAY, WE'LL PRACTI-CALLY HAVE THE WHOLE PLACE TO OURSELVES !!
O-OKAY.
IT'S, LIKE, REALLY JUST US THREE ......

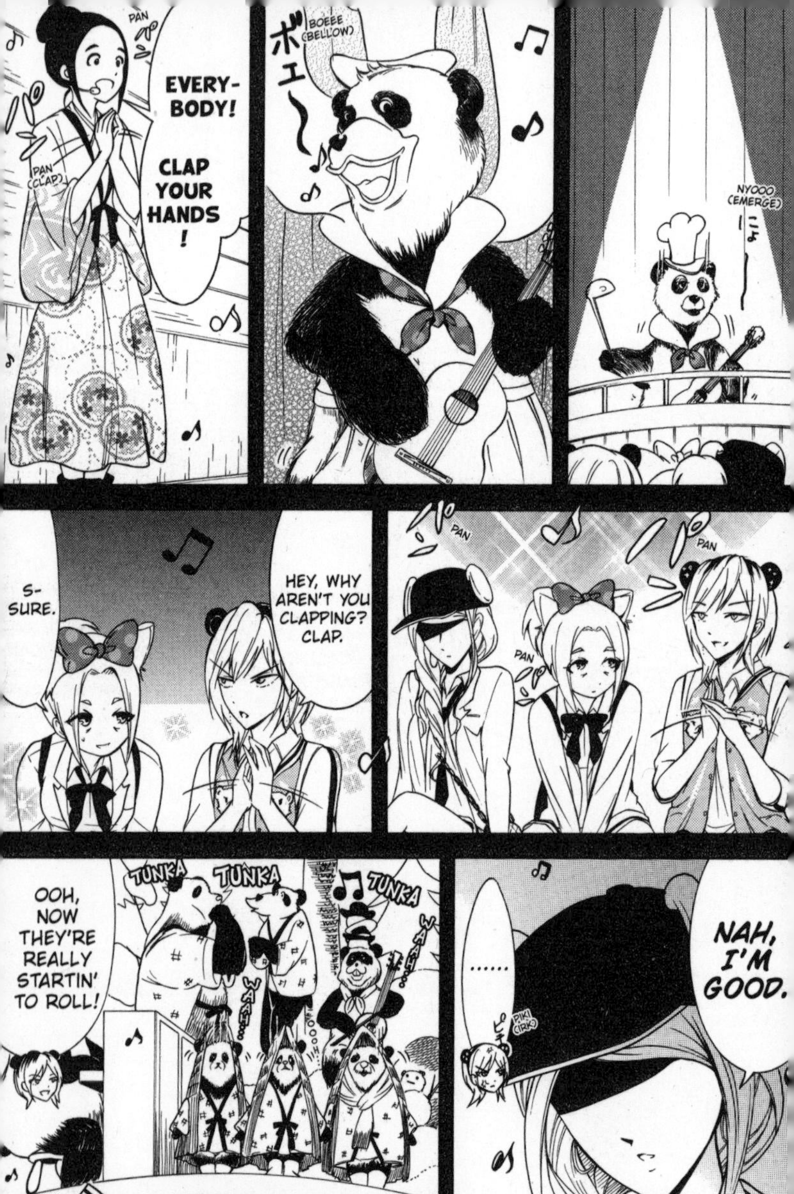

NYOOO (EMERGE)
にょ〜
ボエ〜
BOEEE (BELLOW)
PAN
パ
EVERY-BODY!
CLAP YOUR HANDS!
パ
PAN (CLAP)
パ
PAN
パ
PAN
PAN
HEY, WHY AREN'T YOU CLAPPING? CLAP.
S-SURE.
NAH, I'M GOOD.
......
ピキ
PIKI (IRK)
TUNKA
TUNKA
TUNKA
WAAAH...
WAAAH...
OOOH...
OOH, NOW THEY'RE REALLY STARTIN' TO ROLL!

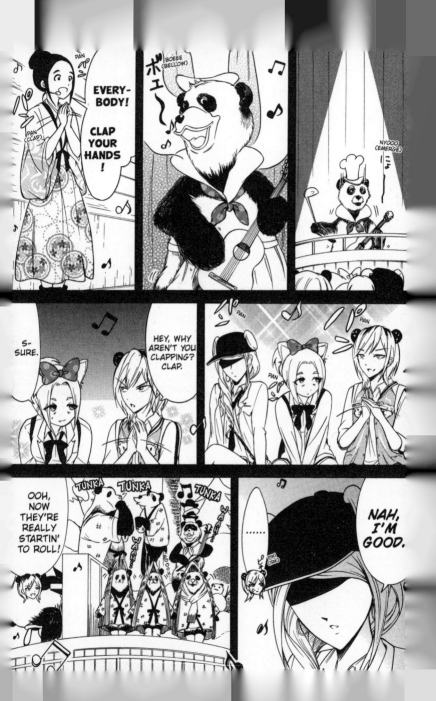

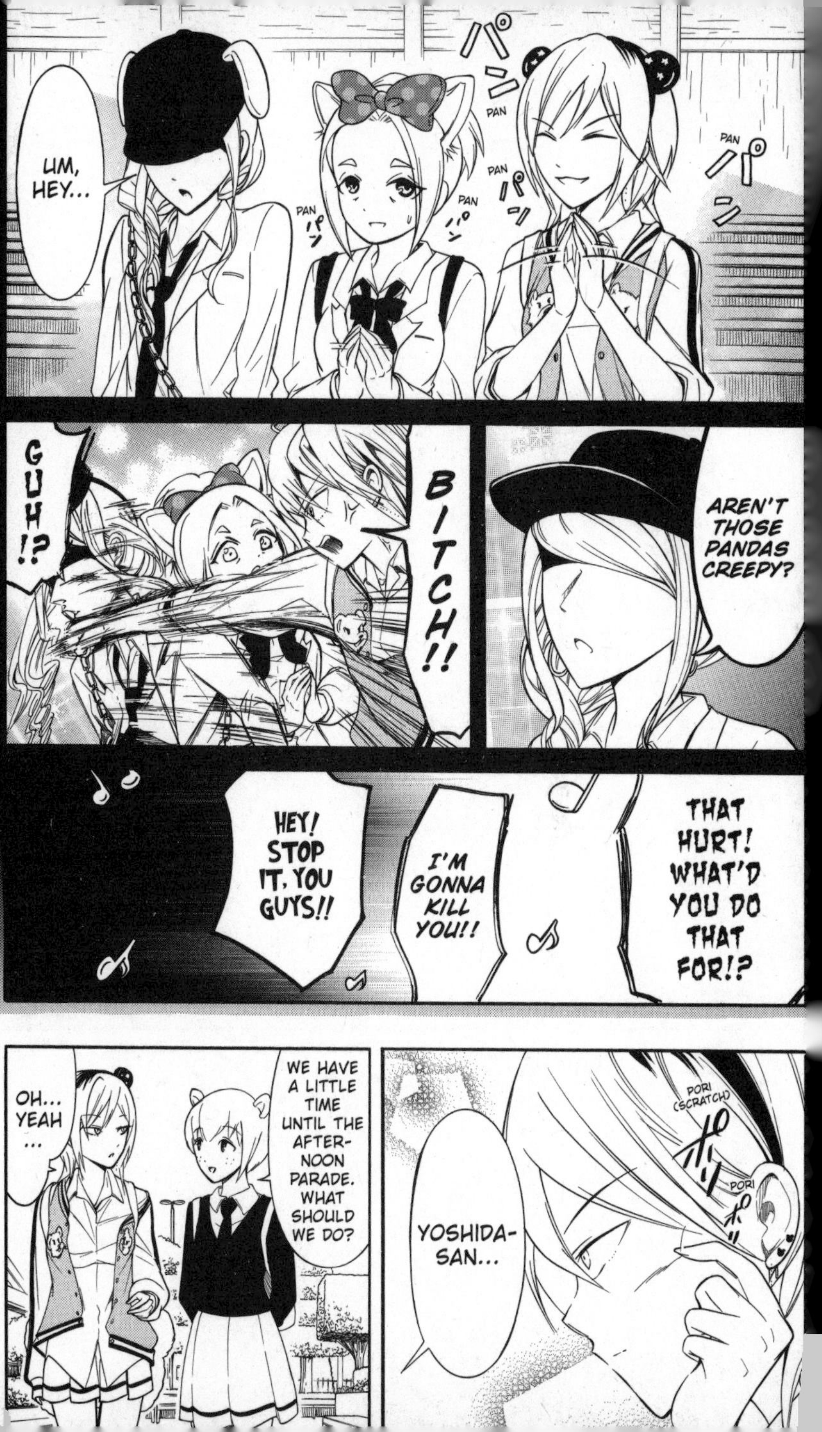
PAN
PAN
PAN
PAN
PAN
UM, HEY...
AREN'T THOSE PANDAS CREEPY?
BITCH!!
GUH!?
THAT HURT! WHAT'D YOU DO THAT FOR!?
I'M GONNA KILL YOU!!
HEY! STOP IT, YOU GUYS!!
PORI (SCRATCH)
PORI
YOSHIDA-SAN...
WE HAVE A LITTLE TIME UNTIL THE AFTERNOON PARADE. WHAT SHOULD WE DO?
OH... YEAH...

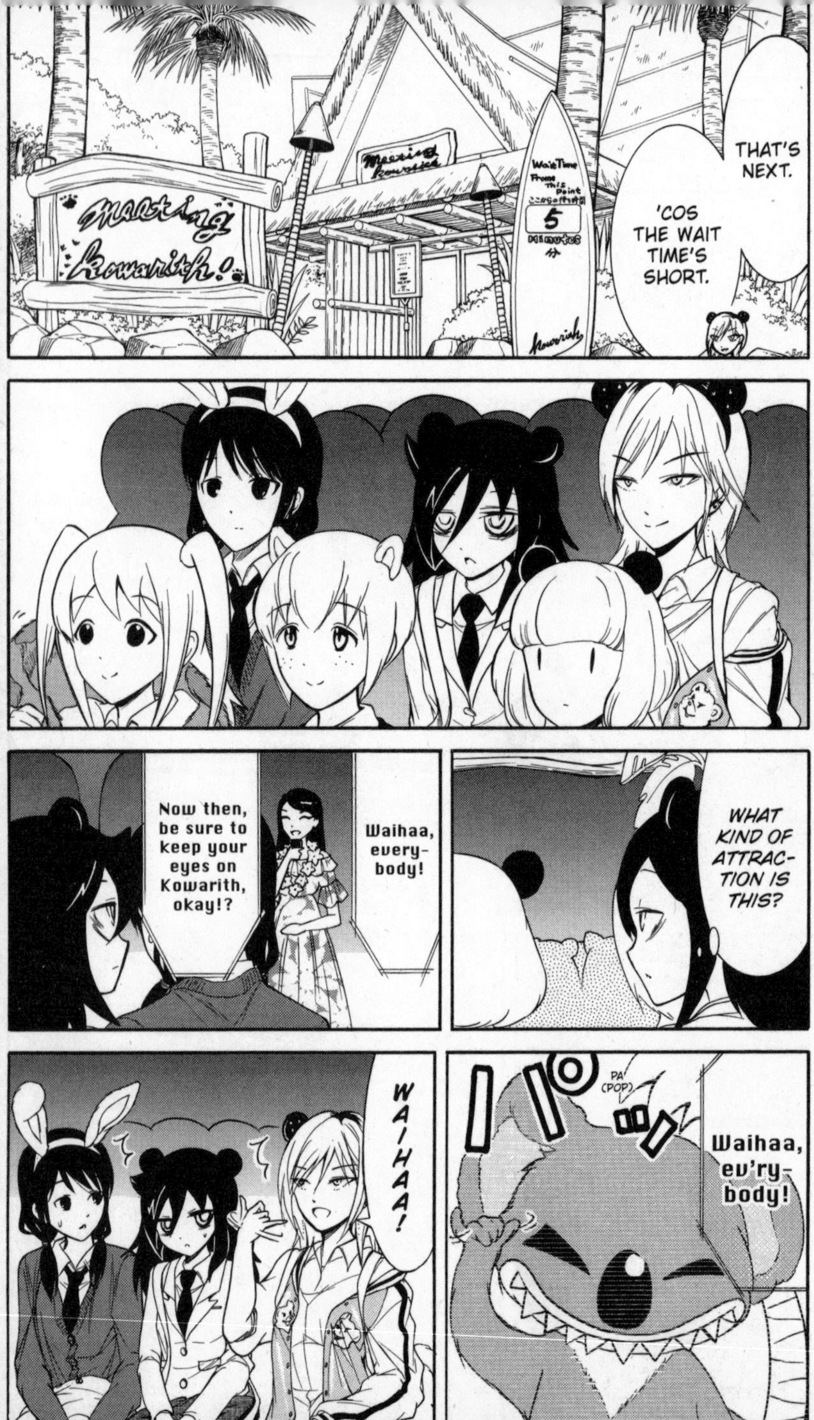
Meeting Kowarith!
Wait Time From This Point
ここからの待ち時間
5
Minutes
分
THAT'S NEXT.
'COS THE WAIT TIME'S SHORT.
WHAT KIND OF ATTRACTION IS THIS?
Waihaa, every-body!
Now then, be sure to keep your eyes on Kowarith, okay!?
PA (POP)
Waihaa, ev'ry-body!
WAIHAA!

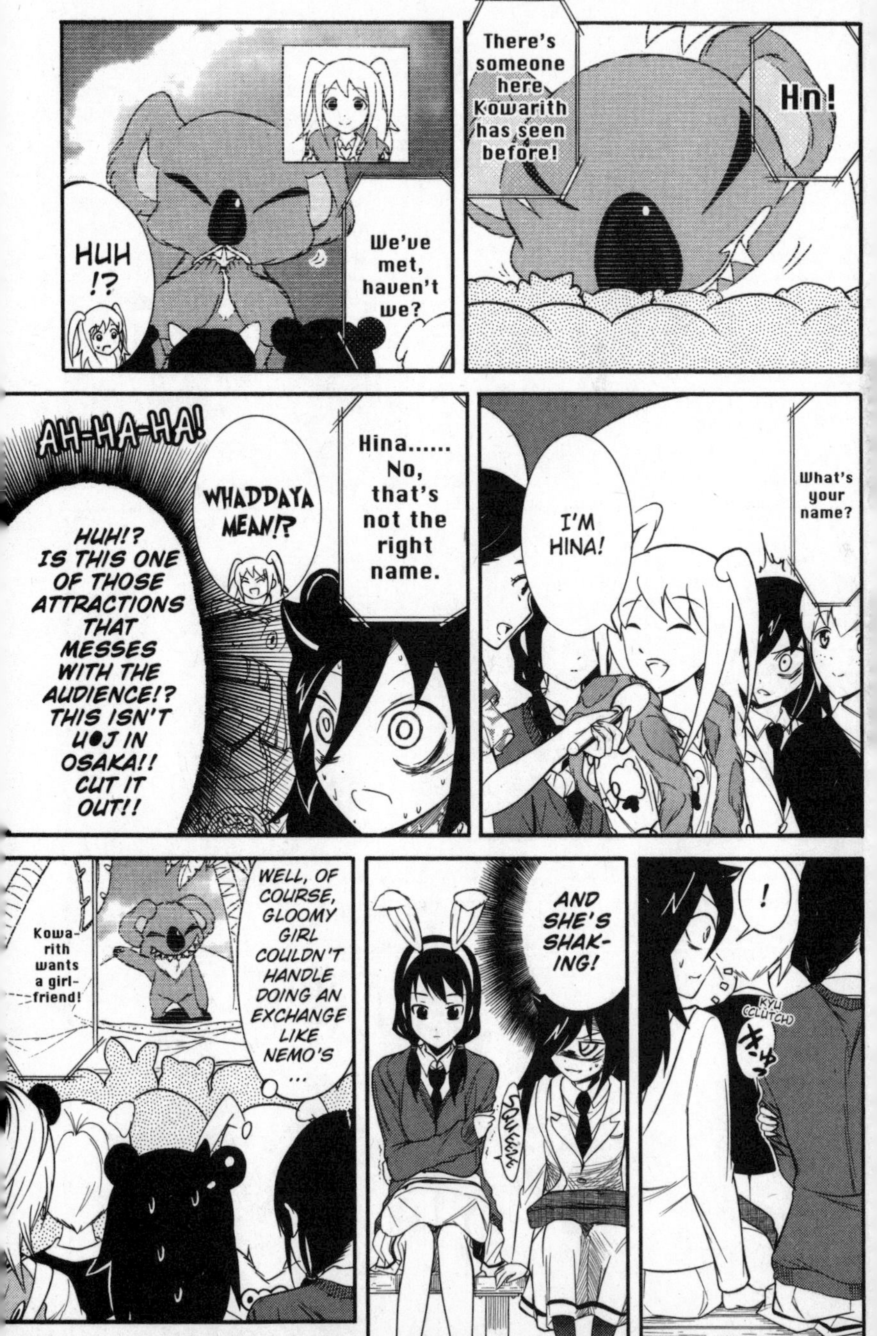
There's someone here Kowarith has seen before!
Hn!
We've met, haven't we?
HUH !?
What's your name?
I'M HINA!
Hina...... No, that's not the right name.
WHADDAYA MEAN!?
AH-HA-HA!
HUH!? IS THIS ONE OF THOSE ATTRACTIONS THAT MESSES WITH THE AUDIENCE!? THIS ISN'T U●J IN OSAKA!! CUT IT OUT!!
!
KYU (CLUTCH)
AND SHE'S SHAK-ING!
WELL, OF COURSE, GLOOMY GIRL COULDN'T HANDLE DOING AN EXCHANGE LIKE NEMO'S ...
Kowa-rith wants a girl-friend!

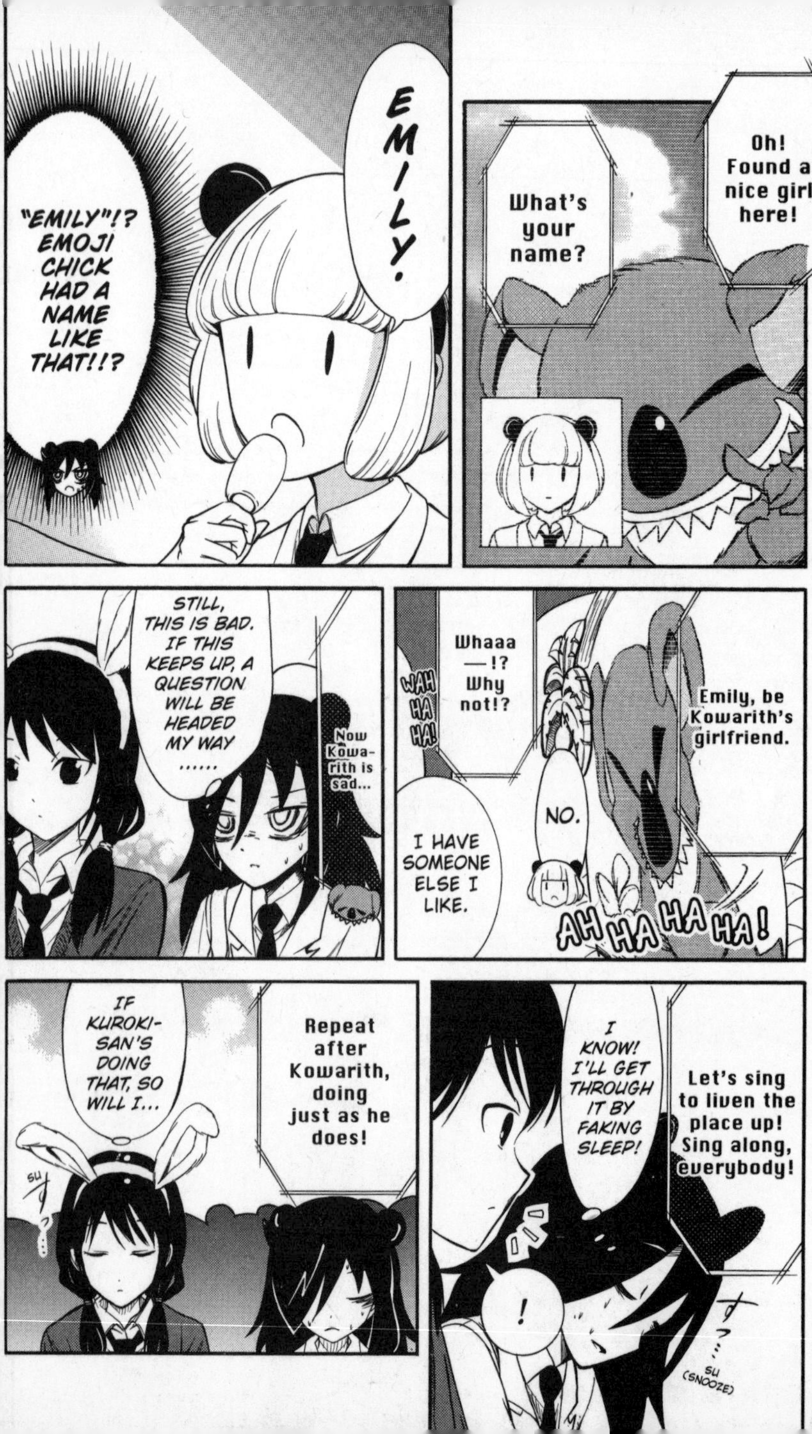
Oh! Found a nice girl here!
What's your name?
EMILY.
"EMILY"!? EMOJI CHICK HAD A NAME LIKE THAT!!?
Emily, be Kowarith's girlfriend.
AH HA HA HA!
NO.
I HAVE SOMEONE ELSE I LIKE.
Whaaa—!? Why not!?
WAH HA HA!
STILL, THIS IS BAD. IF THIS KEEPS UP, A QUESTION WILL BE HEADED MY WAY ......
Now Kowarith is sad...
Let's sing to liven the place up! Sing along, everybody!
I KNOW! I'LL GET THROUGH IT BY FAKING SLEEP!
!
SU (SNOOZE)
Repeat after Kowarith, doing just as he does!
IF KUROKI-SAN'S DOING THAT, SO WILL I...
SU
?...

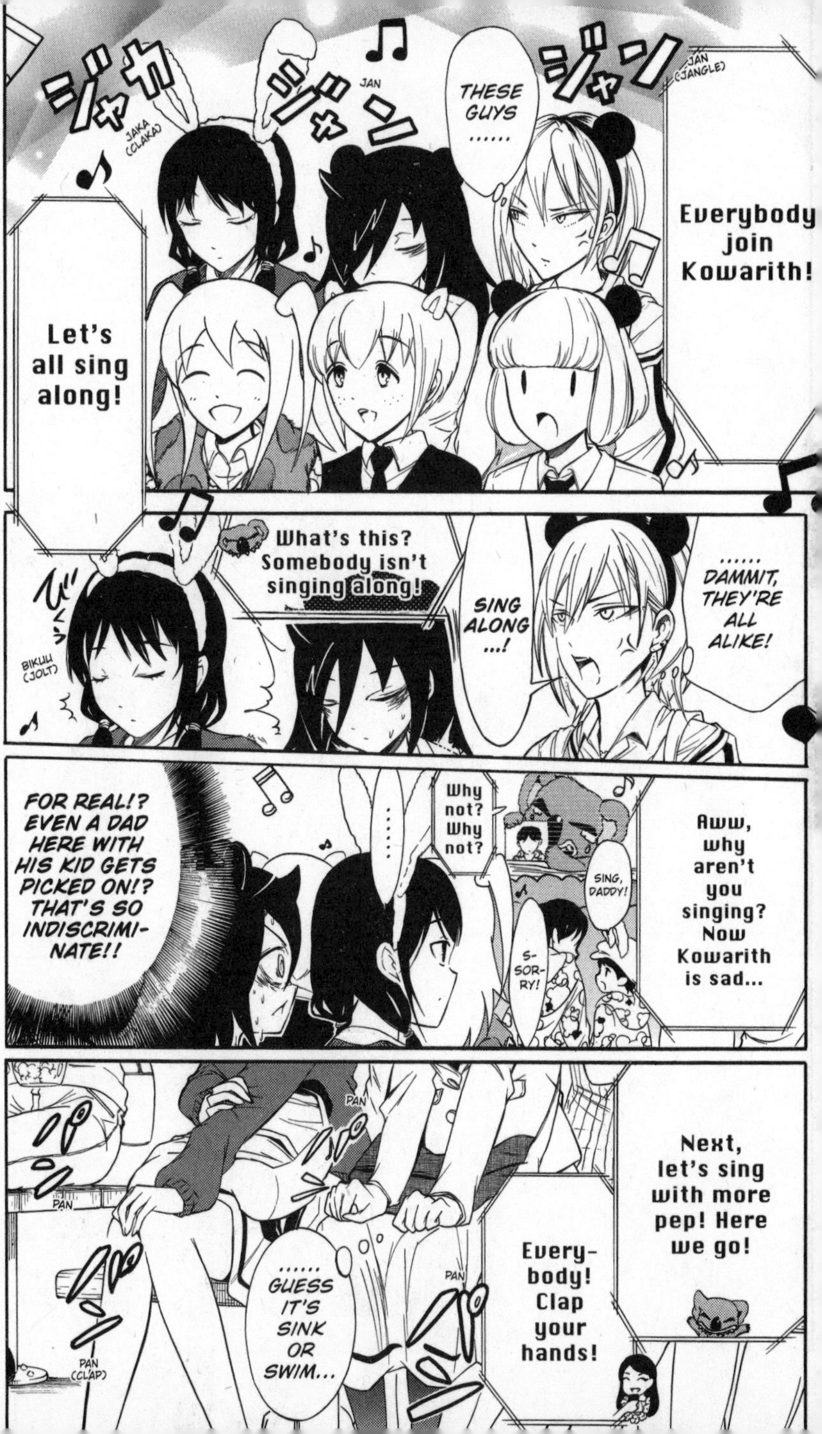
JAN (JANGLE)
Everybody join Kowarith!
THESE GUYS ......
JAN
JAKA (CLAKA)
Let's all sing along!
...... DAMMIT, THEY'RE ALL ALIKE!
SING ALONG ...!
What's this? Somebody isn't singing along!
BIKUU (JOLT)
Aww, why aren't you singing? Now Kowarith is sad...
SING, DADDY!
S-SORRY!
Why not? Why not?
......
FOR REAL!? EVEN A DAD HERE WITH HIS KID GETS PICKED ON!? THAT'S SO INDISCRIMINATE!!
Next, let's sing with more pep! Here we go!
Every-body! Clap your hands!
PAN
...... GUESS IT'S SINK OR SWIM...
PAN
PAN
PAN (CLAP)

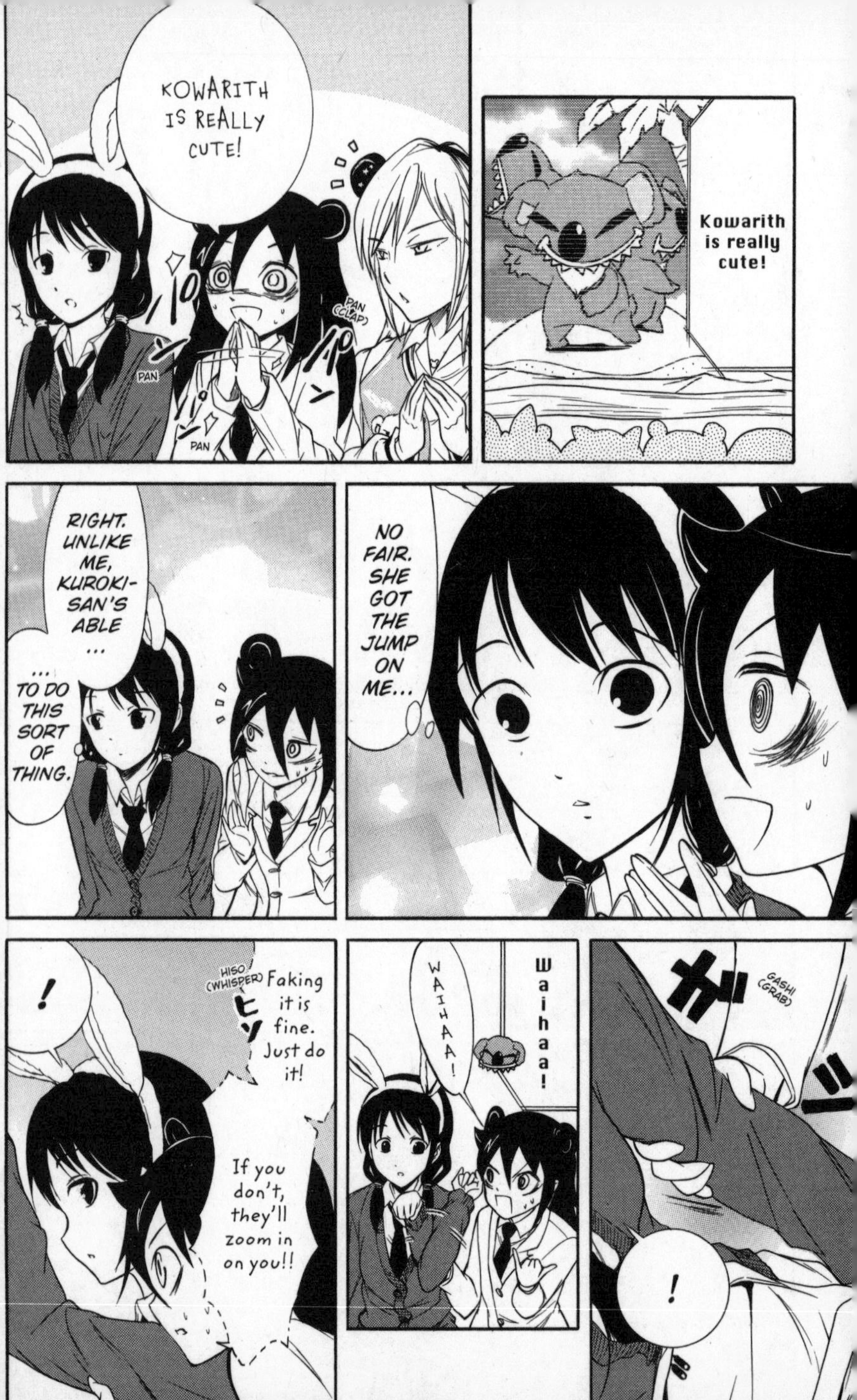
Kowarith is really cute!
KOWARITH IS REALLY CUTE!
PAN (CLAP)
PAN
PAN
NO FAIR. SHE GOT THE JUMP ON ME...
RIGHT. UNLIKE ME, KUROKI-SAN'S ABLE ...
... TO DO THIS SORT OF THING.
GASHI (GRAB)
!
Waihaa!
WAIHAA!
HISO (WHISPER)
Faking it is fine. Just do it!
If you don't, they'll zoom in on you!!
!

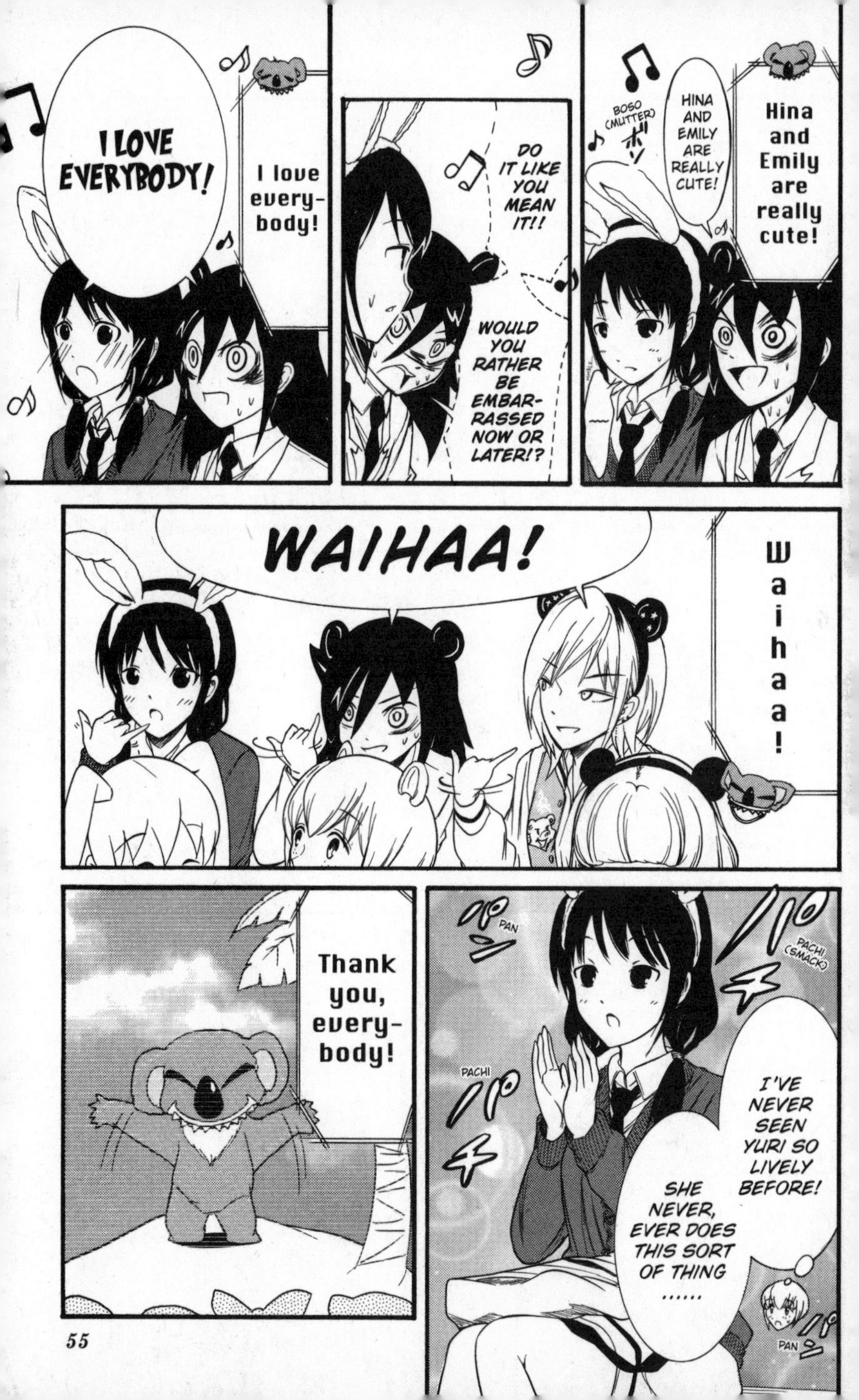
Hina and Emily are really cute!
HINA AND EMILY ARE REALLY CUTE!
BOSO (MUTTER)
DO IT LIKE YOU MEAN IT!!
WOULD YOU RATHER BE EMBARRASSED NOW OR LATER!?
I love every-body!
I LOVE EVERYBODY!
Waihaa!
WAIHAA!
PACHI (SMACK)
PAN
I'VE NEVER SEEN YURI SO LIVELY BEFORE!
SHE NEVER, EVER DOES THIS SORT OF THING ......
PACHI
PAN
Thank you, every-body!

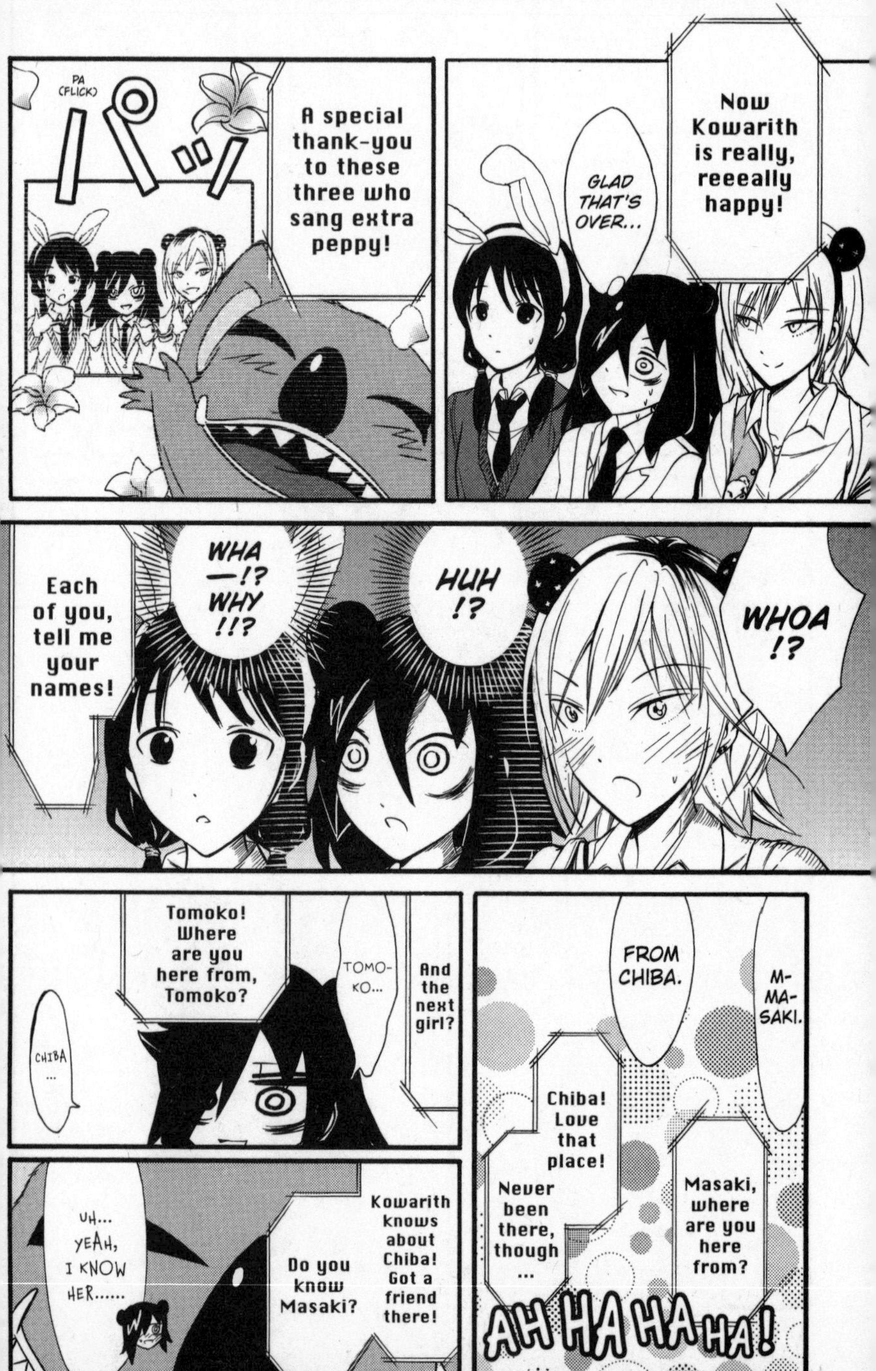
Now Kowarith is really, reeeally happy!
GLAD THAT'S OVER...
A special thank-you to these three who sang extra peppy!
PA (FLICK)
WHOA !?
HUH !?
WHA—!? WHY !!?
Each of you, tell me your names!
M-MA-SAKI.
FROM CHIBA.
Masaki, where are you here from?
Chiba! Love that place!
Never been there, though ...
AH HA HA HA HA!
And the next girl?
TOMO-KO...
Tomoko! Where are you here from, Tomoko?
CHIBA ...
Kowarith knows about Chiba! Got a friend there!
Do you know Masaki?
UH... YEAH, I KNOW HER......

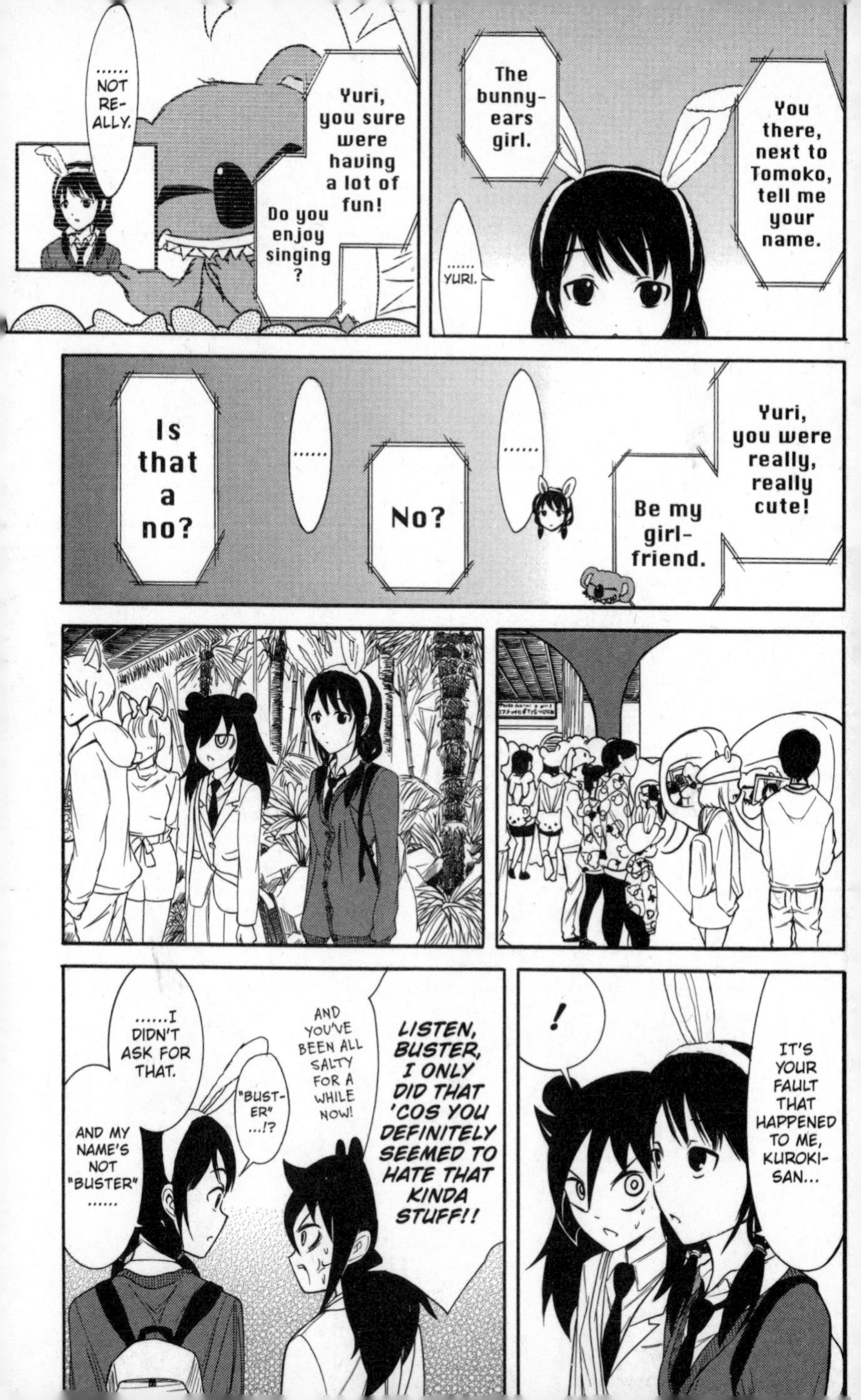
You there, next to Tomoko, tell me your name.
The bunny-ears girl.
......YURI.
Yuri, you sure were having a lot of fun!
Do you enjoy singing?
......NOT REALLY.
Yuri, you were really, really cute!
Be my girlfriend.
......
No?
......
Is that a no?
!
IT'S YOUR FAULT THAT HAPPENED TO ME, KUROKI-SAN...
LISTEN, BUSTER, I ONLY DID THAT 'COS YOU DEFINITELY SEEMED TO HATE THAT KINDA STUFF!!
AND YOU'VE BEEN ALL SALTY FOR A WHILE NOW!
"BUSTER" ...!?
......I DIDN'T ASK FOR THAT.
AND MY NAME'S NOT "BUSTER"......

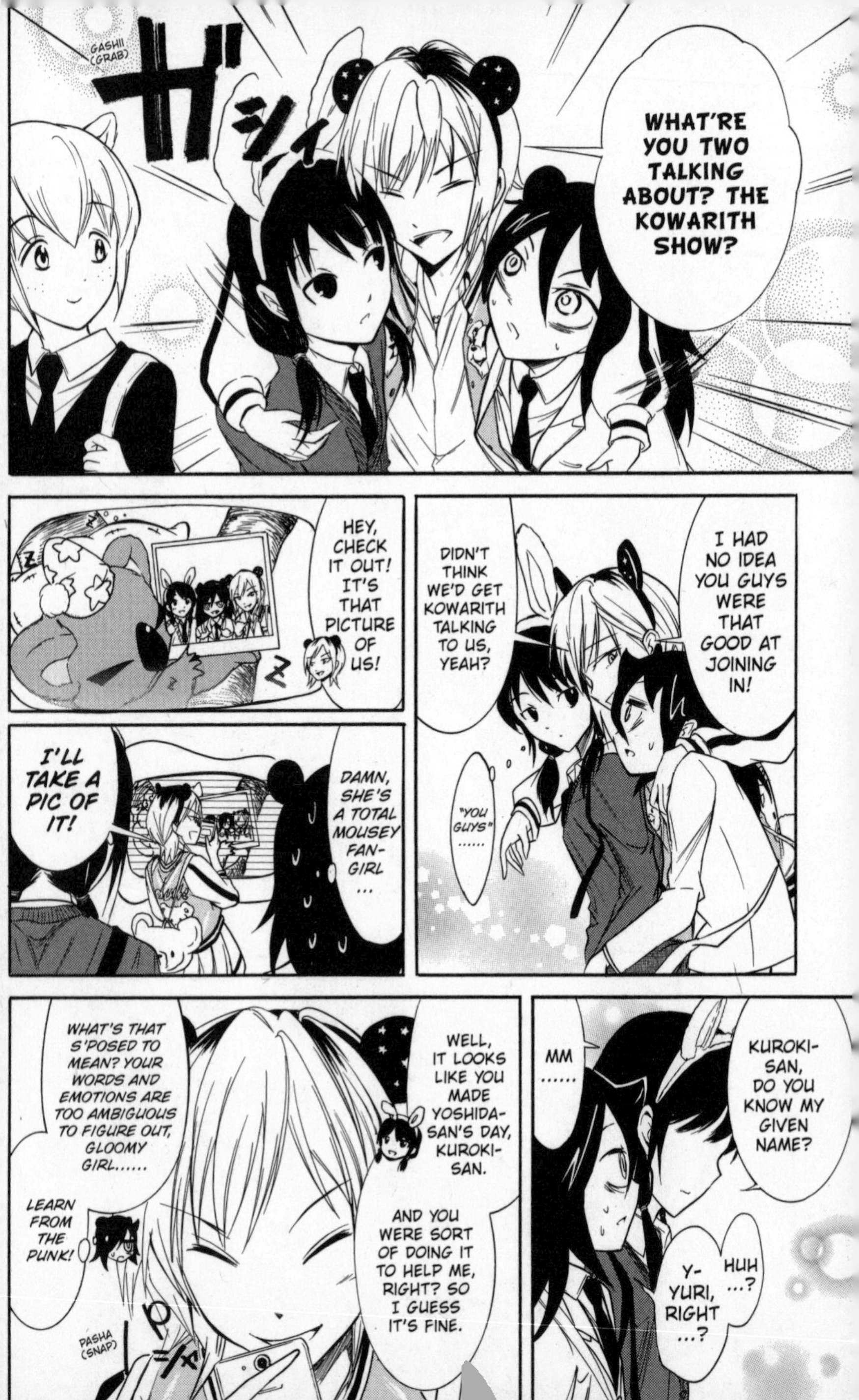
WHAT'RE YOU TWO TALKING ABOUT? THE KOWARITH SHOW?
GASHII (GRAB)
I HAD NO IDEA YOU GUYS WERE THAT GOOD AT JOINING IN!
DIDN'T THINK WE'D GET KOWARITH TALKING TO US, YEAH?
"YOU GUYS"......
HEY, CHECK IT OUT! IT'S THAT PICTURE OF US!
DAMN, SHE'S A TOTAL MOUSEY FAN-GIRL...
I'LL TAKE A PIC OF IT!
KUROKI-SAN, DO YOU KNOW MY GIVEN NAME?
MM......
HUH...?
Y-YURI, RIGHT...?
WELL, IT LOOKS LIKE YOU MADE YOSHIDA-SAN'S DAY, KUROKI-SAN.
AND YOU WERE SORT OF DOING IT TO HELP ME, RIGHT? SO I GUESS IT'S FINE.
WHAT'S THAT S'POSED TO MEAN? YOUR WORDS AND EMOTIONS ARE TOO AMBIGUOUS TO FIGURE OUT, GLOOMY GIRL......
LEARN FROM THE PUNK!
PASHA (SNAP)

No Matter How I Look at It, It's You Guys' Fault I'm Not Popular!

FAIL 128: I'M NOT POPULAR, SO I'LL MAKE THE ROUNDS.

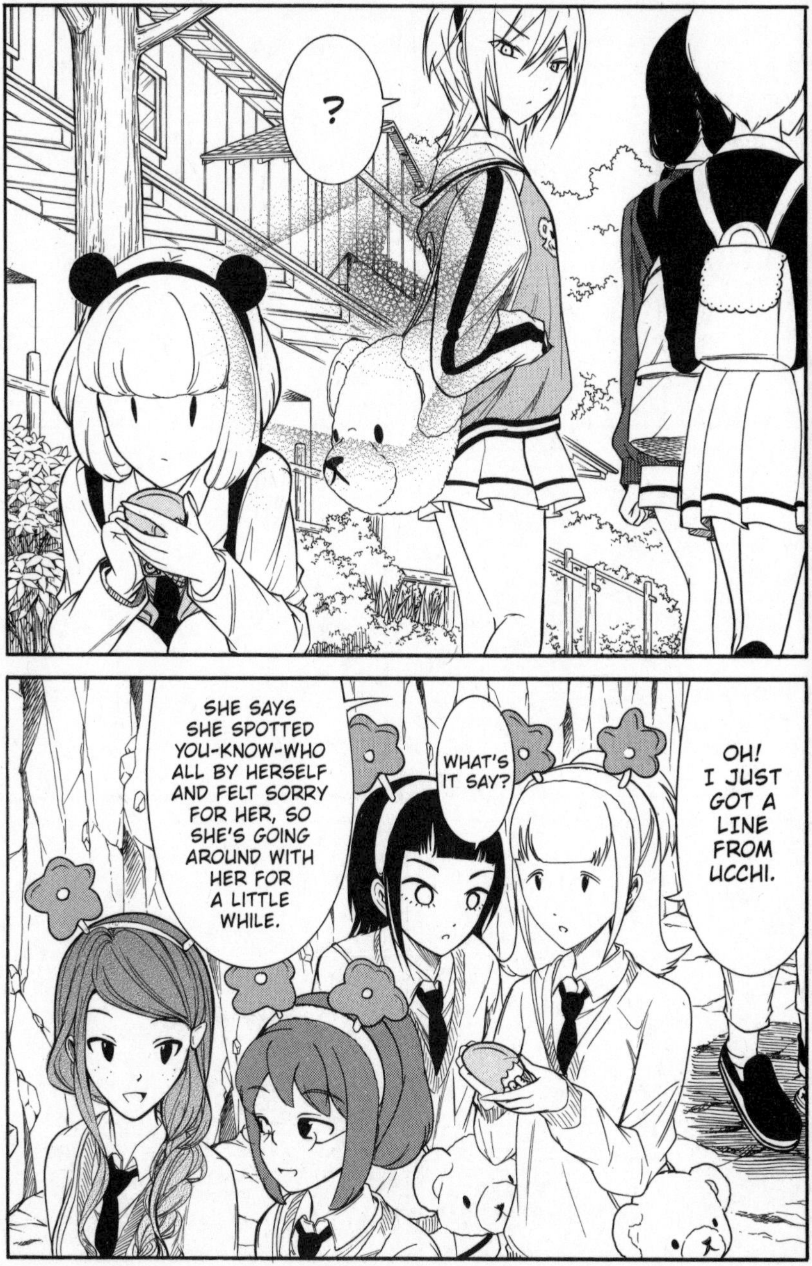
?
OH! I JUST GOT A LINE FROM UCCHI.
WHAT'S IT SAY?
SHE SAYS SHE SPOTTED YOU-KNOW-WHO ALL BY HERSELF AND FELT SORRY FOR HER, SO SHE'S GOING AROUND WITH HER FOR A LITTLE WHILE.

I THOUGHT THAT WAS A GIVEN

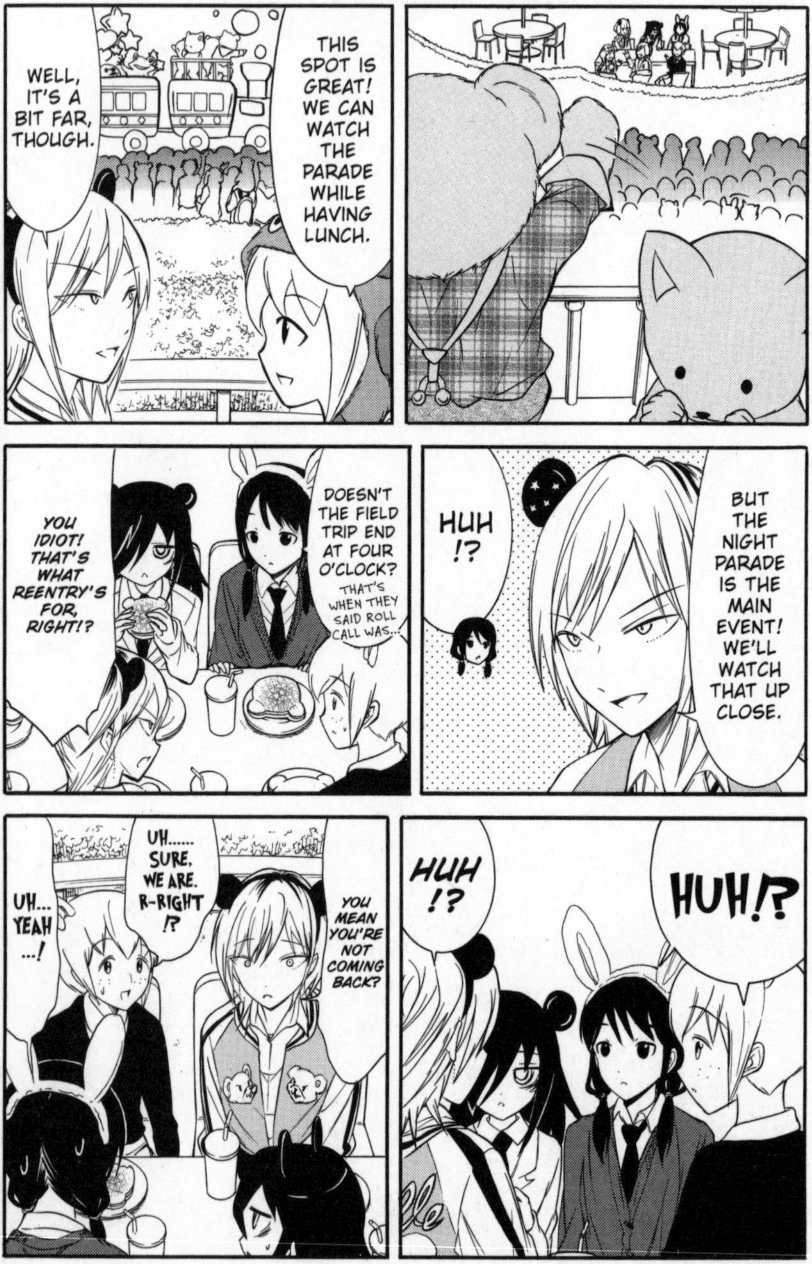

THIS SPOT IS GREAT! WE CAN WATCH THE PARADE WHILE HAVING LUNCH.
WELL, IT'S A BIT FAR, THOUGH.
BUT THE NIGHT PARADE IS THE MAIN EVENT! WE'LL WATCH THAT UP CLOSE.
HUH !?
DOESN'T THE FIELD TRIP END AT FOUR O'CLOCK?
THAT'S WHEN THEY SAID ROLL CALL WAS...
YOU IDIOT! THAT'S WHAT REENTRY'S FOR, RIGHT!?
HUH!?
HUH !?
YOU MEAN YOU'RE NOT COMING BACK?
UH...... SURE, WE ARE. R-RIGHT !?
UH... YEAH ...!

GET A PICTURE TOGETHER

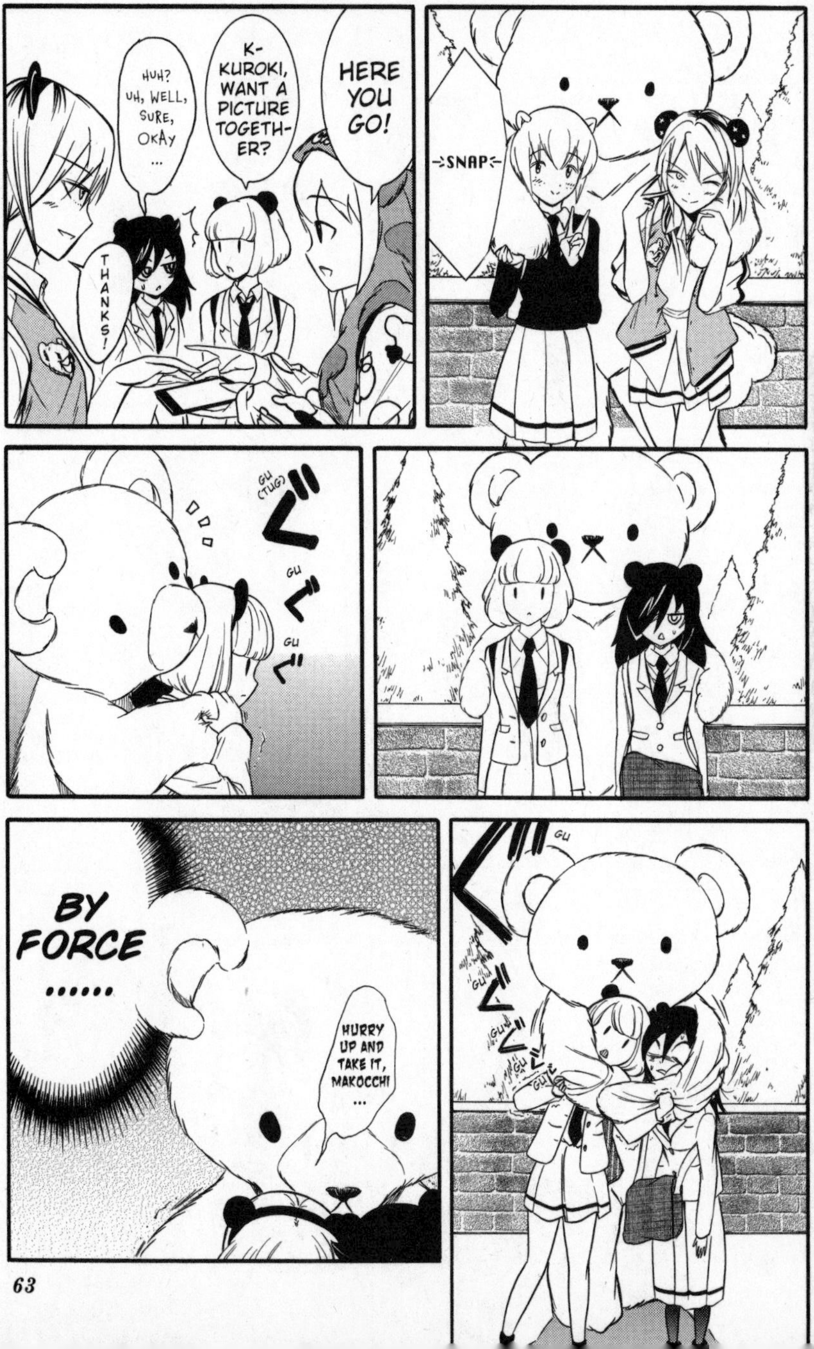

SNAP
HERE YOU GO!
K-KUROKI, WANT A PICTURE TOGETH-ER?
HUH? UH, WELL, SURE, OKAY ...
THANKS!
GU (TUG)
GU
GU
GU
GU
GU
GU
GU
BY FORCE ......
HURRY UP AND TAKE IT, MAKOCCHI ...

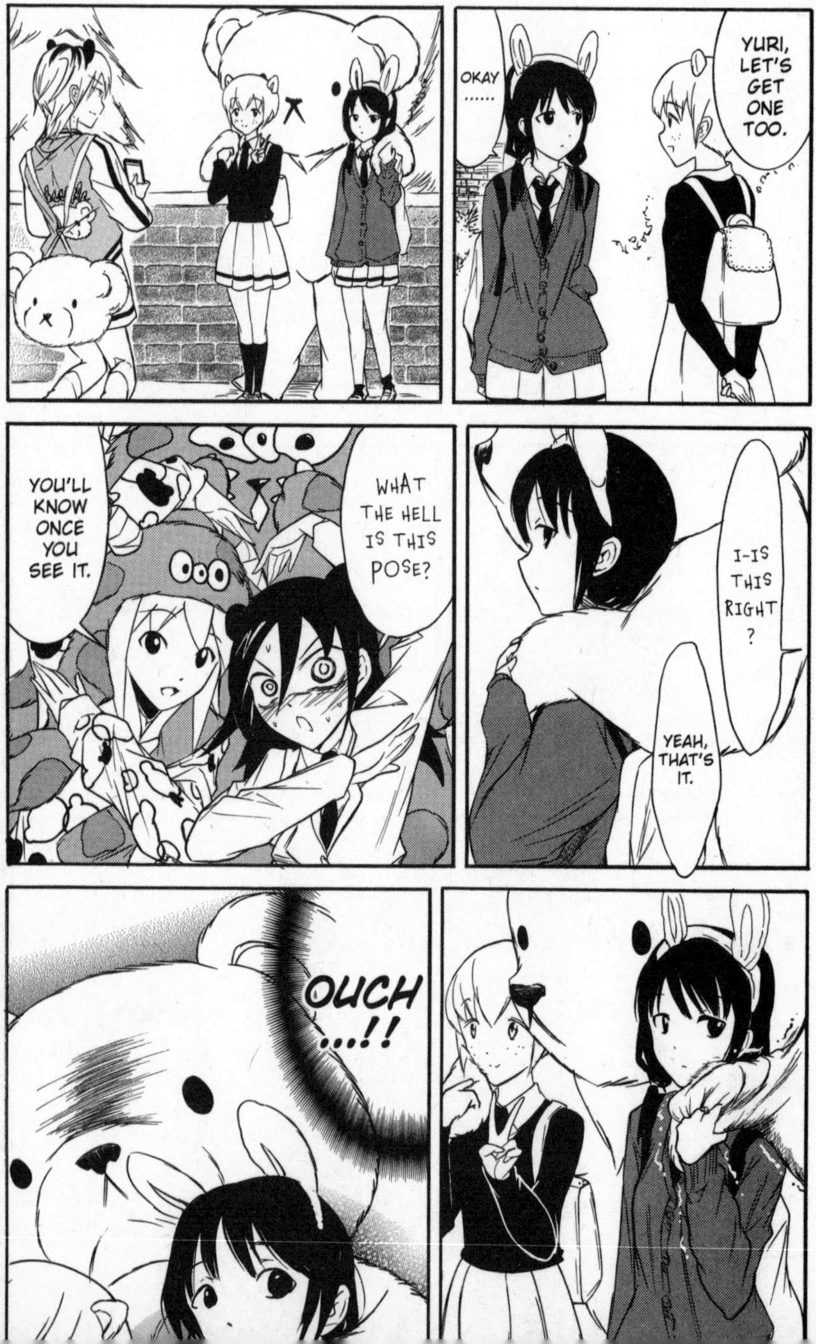
YURI, LET'S GET ONE TOO.
OKAY ......
I-IS THIS RIGHT?
YEAH, THAT'S IT.
WHAT THE HELL IS THIS POSE?
YOU'LL KNOW ONCE YOU SEE IT.
OUCH ...!!

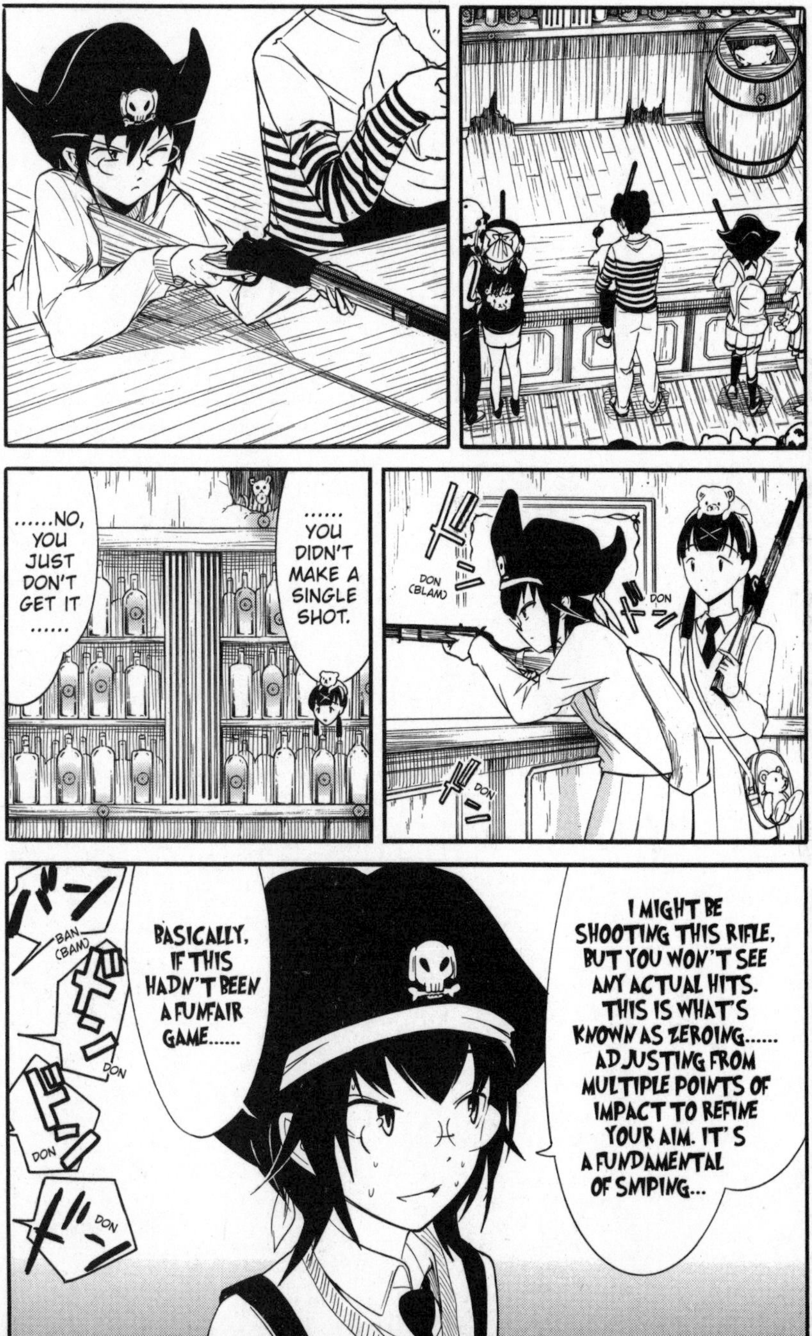
DON (BLAM)
DON
DON
......YOU DIDN'T MAKE A SINGLE SHOT.
......NO, YOU JUST DON'T GET IT......
I MIGHT BE SHOOTING THIS RIFLE, BUT YOU WON'T SEE ANY ACTUAL HITS. THIS IS WHAT'S KNOWN AS ZEROING...... ADJUSTING FROM MULTIPLE POINTS OF IMPACT TO REFINE YOUR AIM. IT'S A FUNDAMENTAL OF SNIPING...
BASICALLY, IF THIS HADN'T BEEN A FUNFAIR GAME......
BAN (BAM)
DON
DON
DON

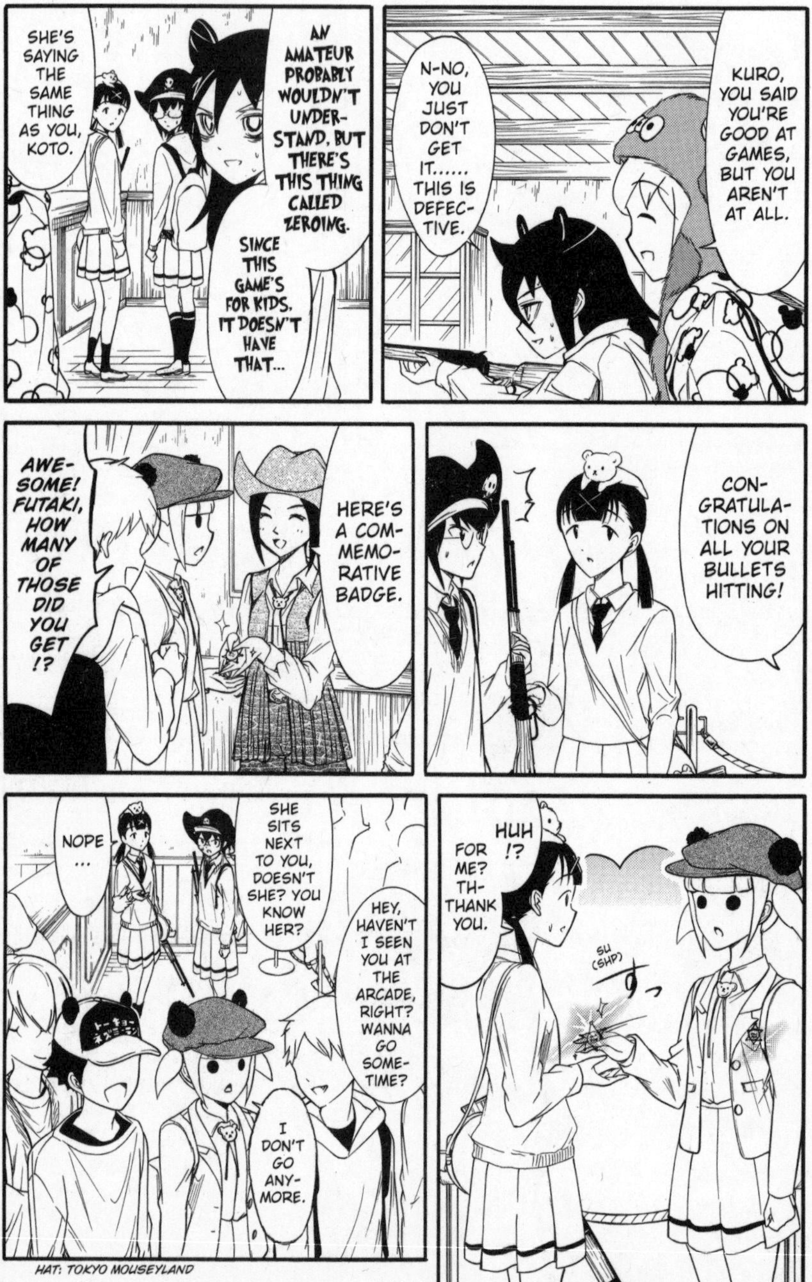
KURO, YOU SAID YOU'RE GOOD AT GAMES, BUT YOU AREN'T AT ALL.
N-NO, YOU JUST DON'T GET IT...... THIS IS DEFEC-TIVE.
AN AMATEUR PROBABLY WOULDN'T UNDER-STAND, BUT THERE'S THIS THING CALLED ZEROING.
SINCE THIS GAME'S FOR KIDS, IT DOESN'T HAVE THAT...
SHE'S SAYING THE SAME THING AS YOU, KOTO.
CON-GRATULA-TIONS ON ALL YOUR BULLETS HITTING!
HERE'S A COM-MEMO-RATIVE BADGE.
AWE-SOME! FUTAKI, HOW MANY OF THOSE DID YOU GET !?
HUH !?
FOR ME? TH-THANK YOU.
SU (SHP)
HEY, HAVEN'T I SEEN YOU AT THE ARCADE, RIGHT? WANNA GO SOME-TIME?
I DON'T GO ANY-MORE.
SHE SITS NEXT TO YOU, DOESN'T SHE? YOU KNOW HER?
NOPE ...

HAT: TOKYO MOUSEYLAND

BROKEN UP

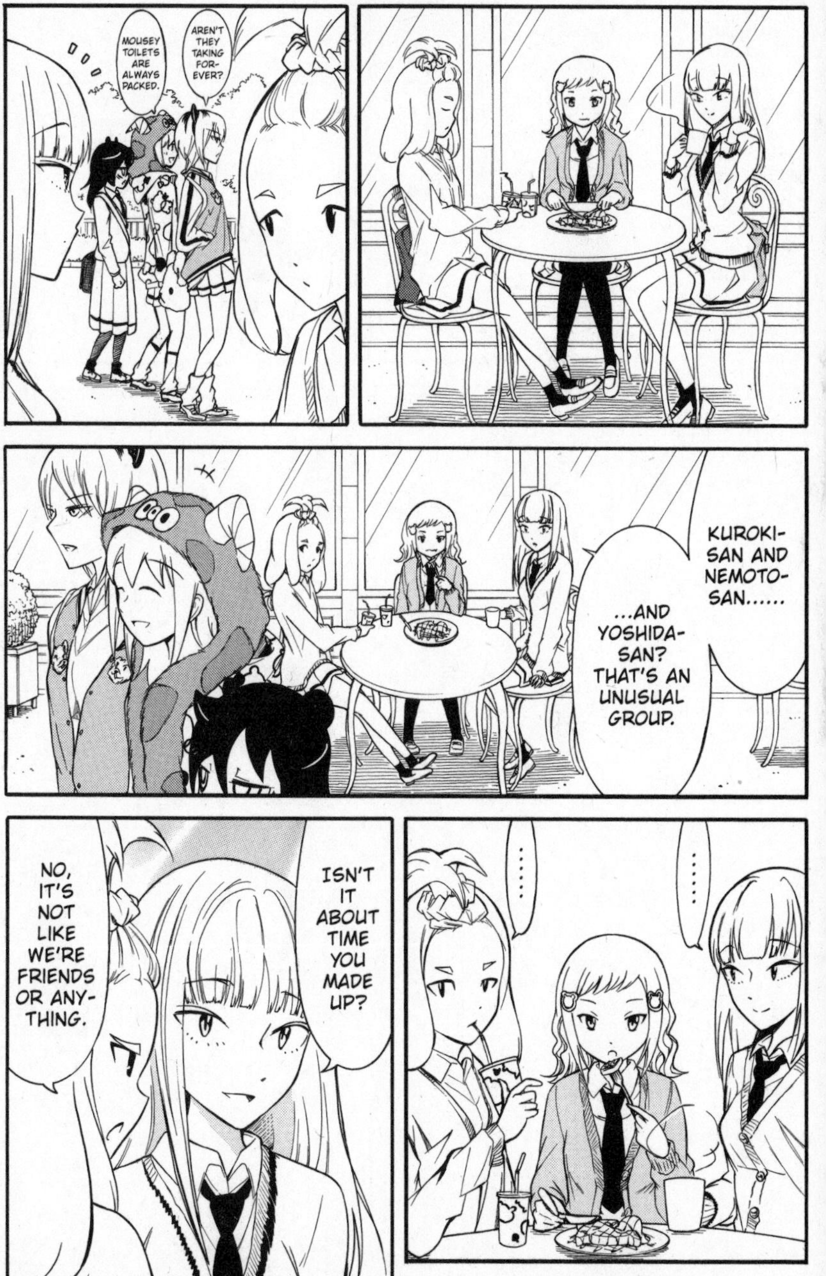
AREN'T THEY TAKING FOR-EVER?
MOUSEY TOILETS ARE ALWAYS PACKED.
KUROKI-SAN AND NEMOTO-SAN......
...AND YOSHIDA-SAN? THAT'S AN UNUSUAL GROUP.
......
......
ISN'T IT ABOUT TIME YOU MADE UP?
NO, IT'S NOT LIKE WE'RE FRIENDS OR ANYTHING.

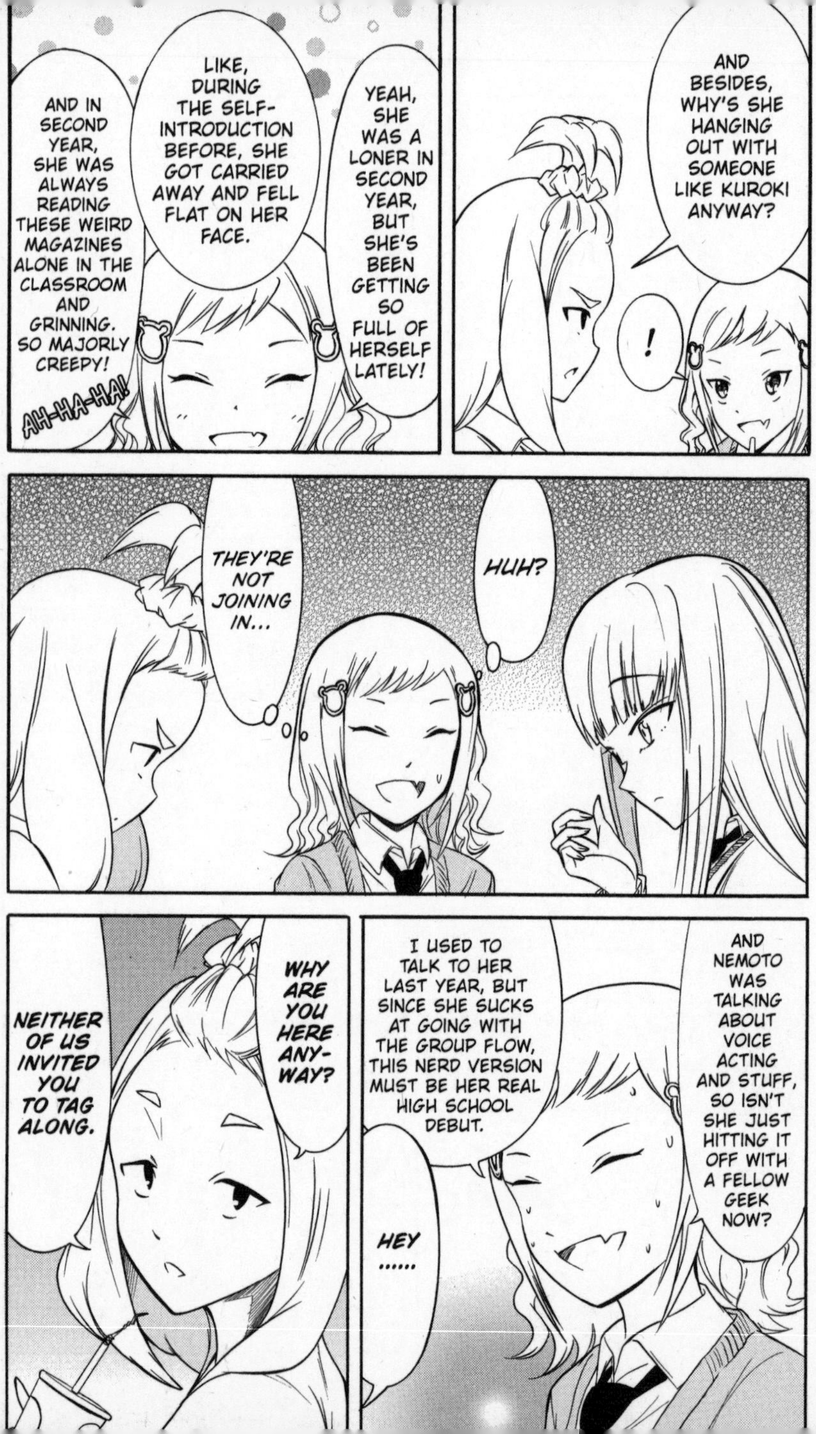

AND BESIDES, WHY'S SHE HANGING OUT WITH SOMEONE LIKE KUROKI ANYWAY?
!
YEAH, SHE WAS A LONER IN SECOND YEAR, BUT SHE'S BEEN GETTING SO FULL OF HERSELF LATELY!
LIKE, DURING THE SELF-INTRODUCTION BEFORE, SHE GOT CARRIED AWAY AND FELL FLAT ON HER FACE.
AND IN SECOND YEAR, SHE WAS ALWAYS READING THESE WEIRD MAGAZINES ALONE IN THE CLASSROOM AND GRINNING. SO MAJORLY CREEPY!
AH-HA-HA!
HUH?
THEY'RE NOT JOINING IN...
AND NEMOTO WAS TALKING ABOUT VOICE ACTING AND STUFF, SO ISN'T SHE JUST HITTING IT OFF WITH A FELLOW GEEK NOW?
I USED TO TALK TO HER LAST YEAR, BUT SINCE SHE SUCKS AT GOING WITH THE GROUP FLOW, THIS NERD VERSION MUST BE HER REAL HIGH SCHOOL DEBUT.
HEY ......
WHY ARE YOU HERE ANYWAY?
NEITHER OF US INVITED YOU TO TAG ALONG.

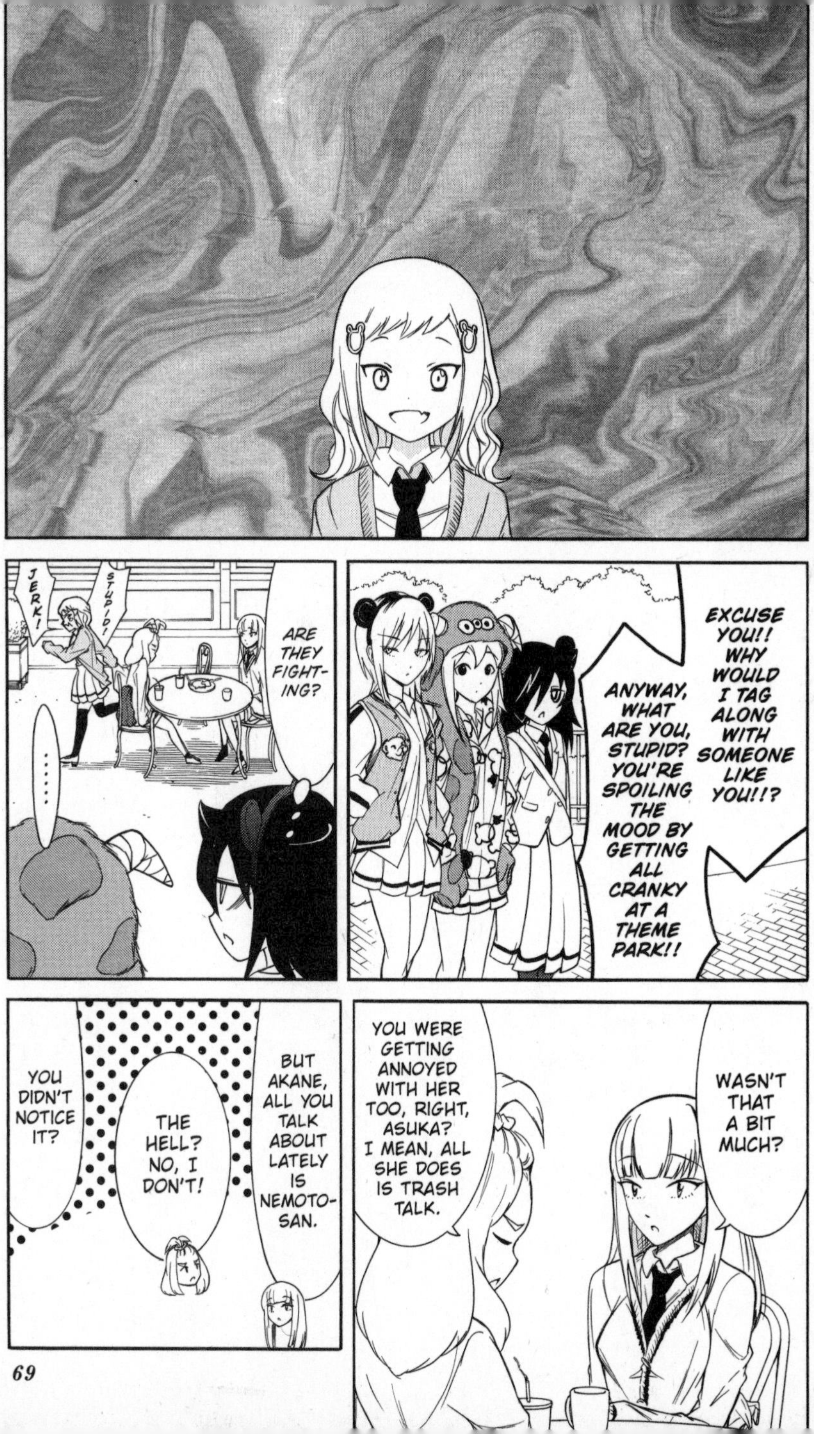
EXCUSE YOU!! WHY WOULD I TAG ALONG WITH SOMEONE LIKE YOU!!?
ANYWAY, WHAT ARE YOU, STUPID? YOU'RE SPOILING THE MOOD BY GETTING ALL CRANKY AT A THEME PARK!!
STUPID!
JERK!
ARE THEY FIGHTING?
......
WASN'T THAT A BIT MUCH?
YOU WERE GETTING ANNOYED WITH HER TOO, RIGHT, ASUKA? I MEAN, ALL SHE DOES IS TRASH TALK.
BUT AKANE, ALL YOU TALK ABOUT LATELY IS NEMOTO-SAN.
THE HELL? NO, I DON'T!
YOU DIDN'T NOTICE IT?

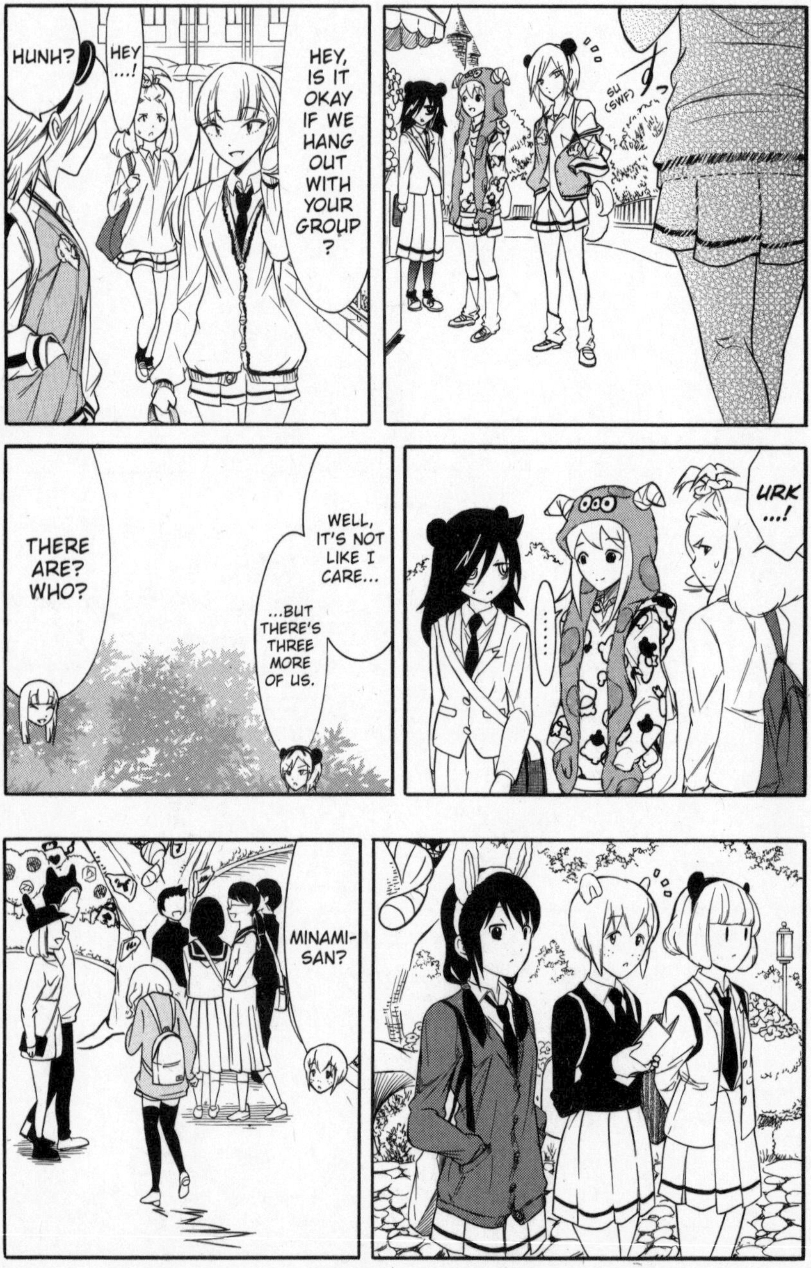
SU (SWF)
HEY, IS IT OKAY IF WE HANG OUT WITH YOUR GROUP?
HEY ...!
HUNH?
URK ...!
......
WELL, IT'S NOT LIKE I CARE...
...BUT THERE'S THREE MORE OF US.
THERE ARE? WHO?
MINAMI-SAN?

No Matter How I
Look at It, It's You
Guys' Fault I'm Not
Popular!

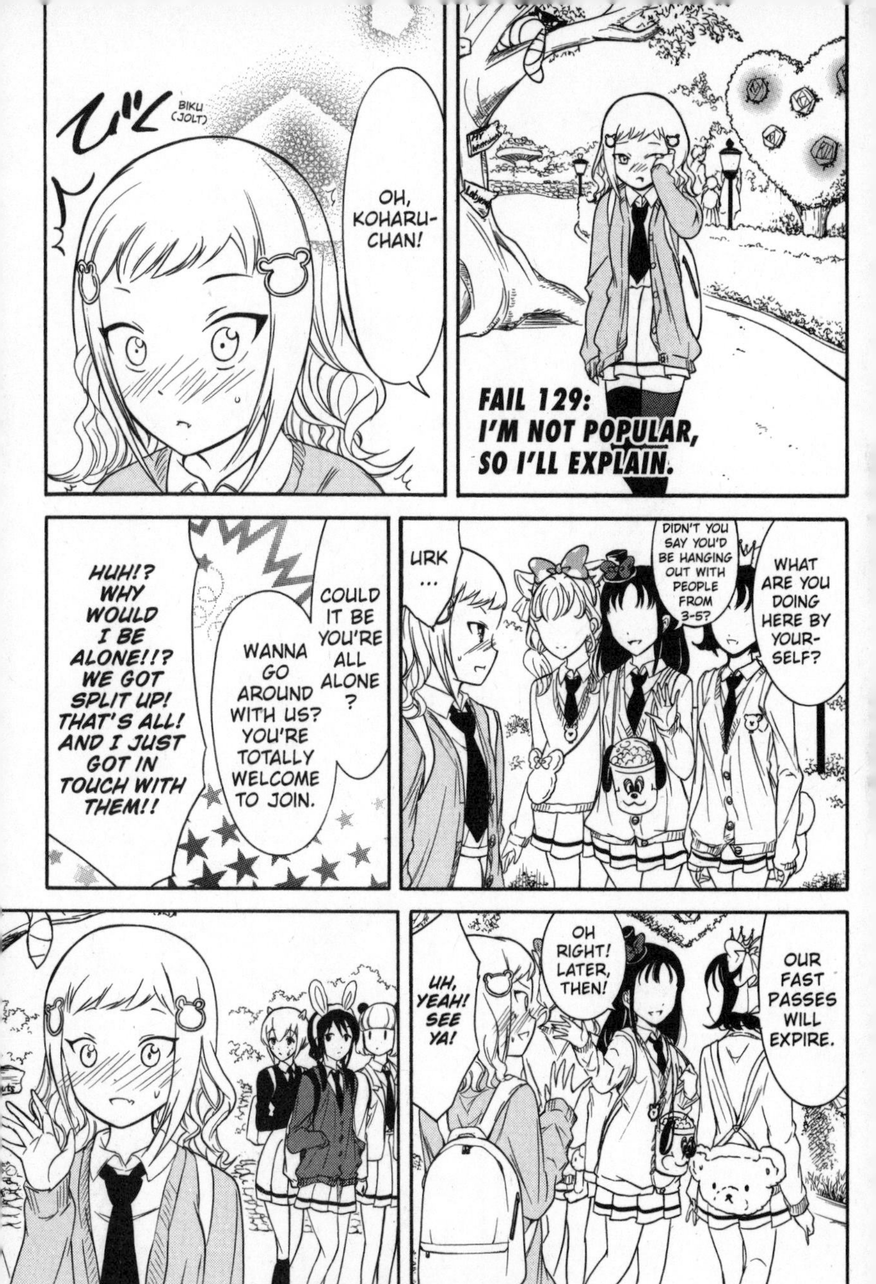
FAIL 129:
I'M NOT POPULAR, SO I'LL EXPLAIN.
OH, KOHARU-CHAN!
BIKU (JOLT)
WHAT ARE YOU DOING HERE BY YOURSELF?
DIDN'T YOU SAY YOU'D BE HANGING OUT WITH PEOPLE FROM 3-5?
URK ...
COULD IT BE YOU'RE ALL ALONE?
WANNA GO AROUND WITH US? YOU'RE TOTALLY WELCOME TO JOIN.
HUH!? WHY WOULD I BE ALONE!!? WE GOT SPLIT UP! THAT'S ALL! AND I JUST GOT IN TOUCH WITH THEM!!
OUR FAST PASSES WILL EXPIRE.
OH RIGHT! LATER, THEN!
UH, YEAH! SEE YA!

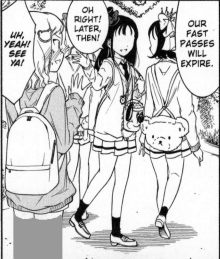

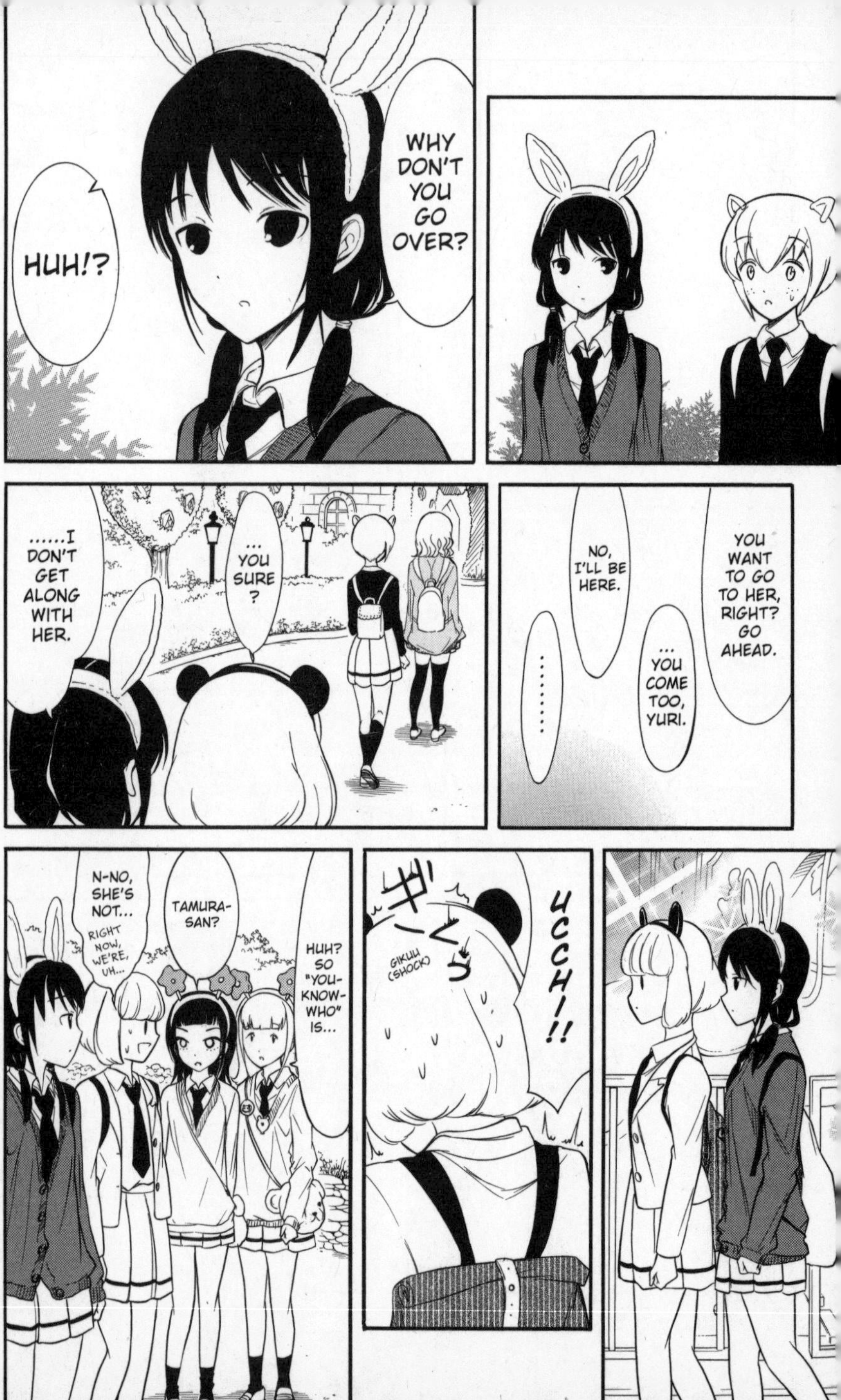
WHY DON'T YOU GO OVER?
HUH!?
YOU WANT TO GO TO HER, RIGHT? GO AHEAD.
NO, I'LL BE HERE.
... YOU COME TOO, YURI.
....
... YOU SURE?
......I DON'T GET ALONG WITH HER.
UCCHI!!
GIKUU (SHOCK)
HUH? SO "YOU-KNOW-WHO" IS...
TAMURA-SAN?
N-NO, SHE'S NOT...
RIGHT NOW, WE'RE, UH...

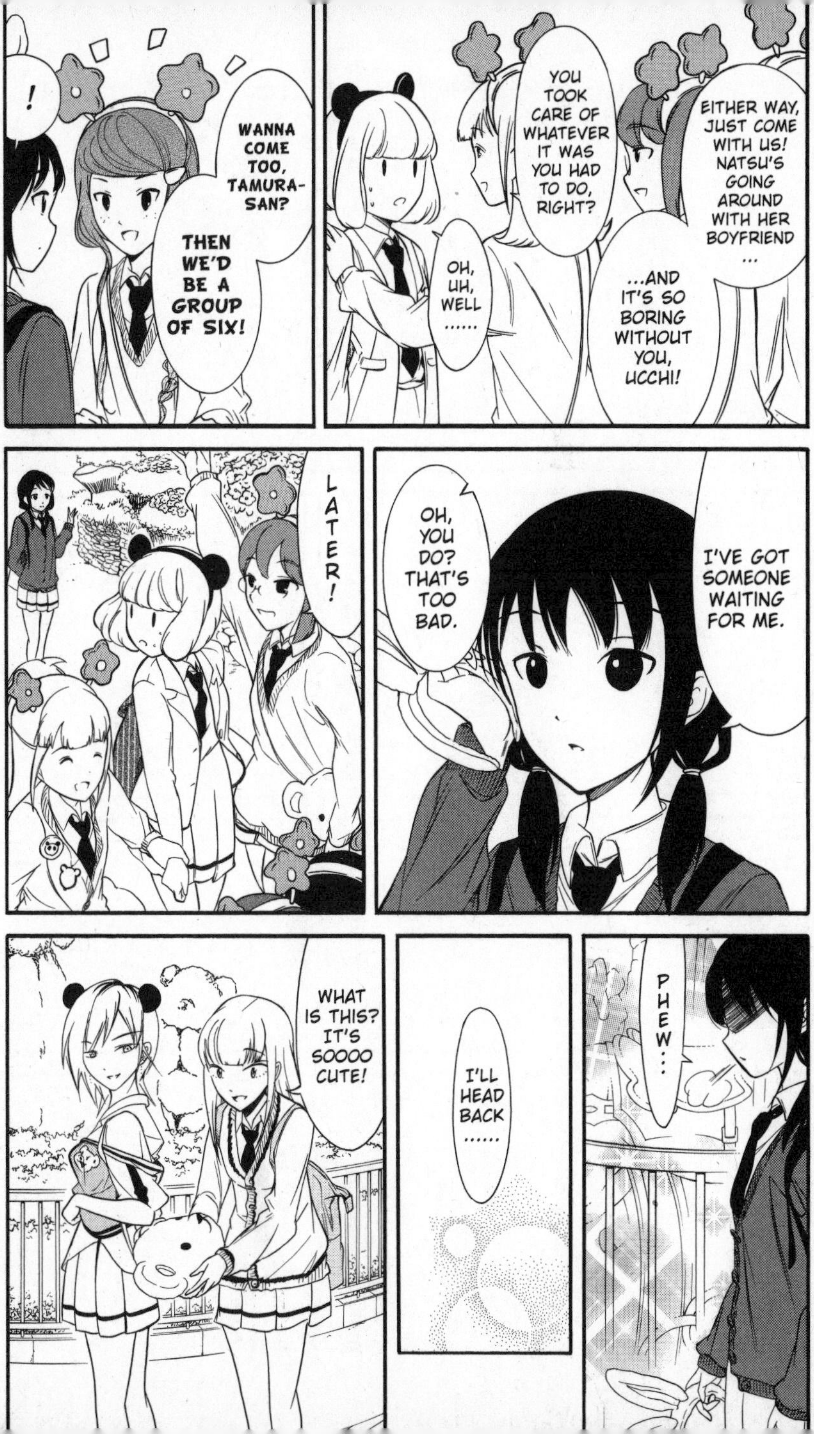
YOU TOOK CARE OF WHATEVER IT WAS YOU HAD TO DO, RIGHT?
OH, UH, WELL ......
EITHER WAY, JUST COME WITH US! NATSU'S GOING AROUND WITH HER BOYFRIEND ...
...AND IT'S SO BORING WITHOUT YOU, UCCHI!
!
WANNA COME TOO, TAMURA-SAN?
THEN WE'D BE A GROUP OF SIX!
I'VE GOT SOMEONE WAITING FOR ME.
OH, YOU DO? THAT'S TOO BAD.
LATER!
PHEW...
I'LL HEAD BACK ......
WHAT IS THIS? IT'S SOOOO CUTE!

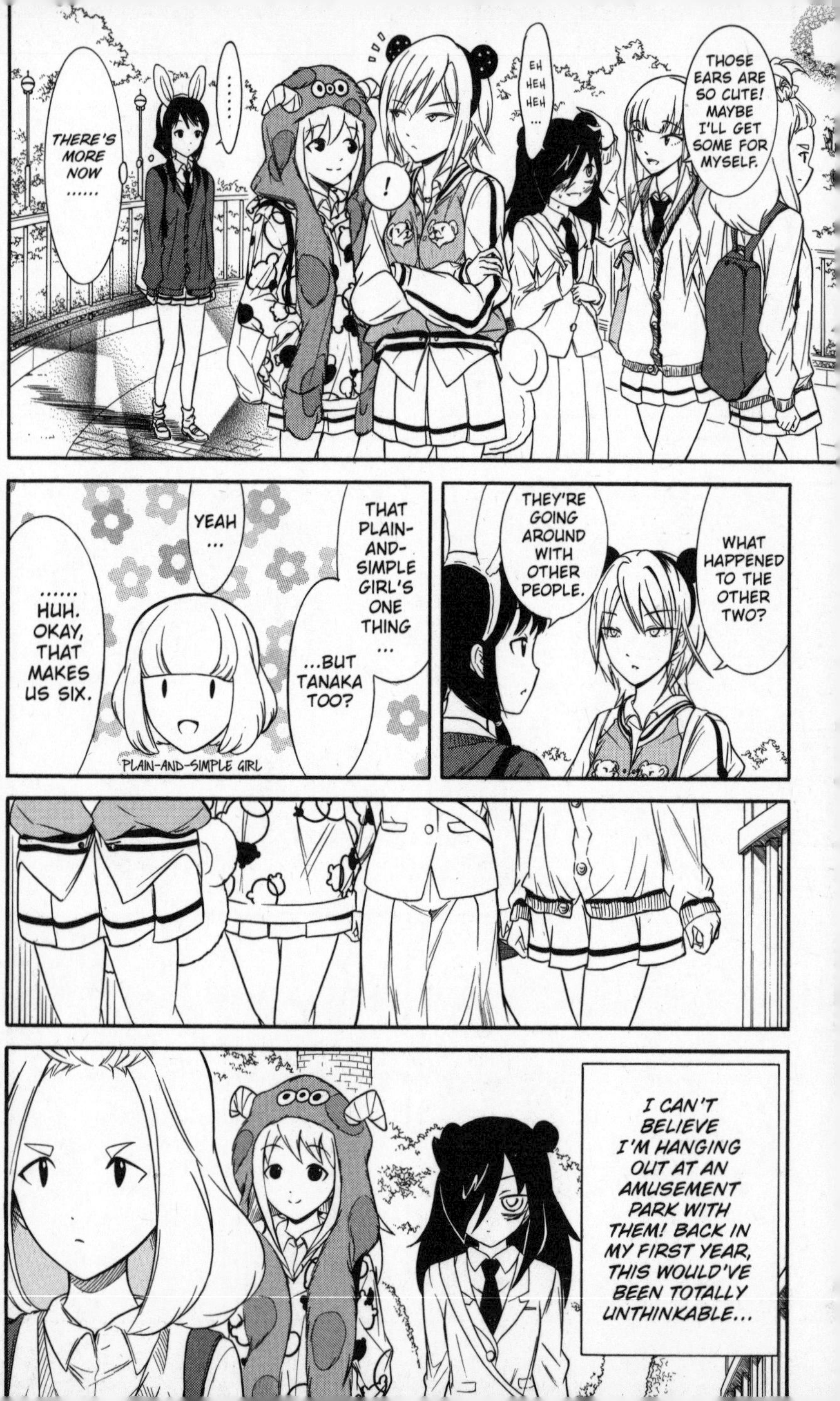
THOSE EARS ARE SO CUTE! MAYBE I'LL GET SOME FOR MYSELF.
EH HEH HEH ...
!
......
THERE'S MORE NOW ......
WHAT HAPPENED TO THE OTHER TWO?
THEY'RE GOING AROUND WITH OTHER PEOPLE.
THAT PLAIN-AND-SIMPLE GIRL'S ONE THING ...
YEAH ...
...BUT TANAKA TOO?
...... HUH. OKAY, THAT MAKES US SIX.
PLAIN-AND-SIMPLE GIRL
I CAN'T BELIEVE I'M HANGING OUT AT AN AMUSEMENT PARK WITH THEM! BACK IN MY FIRST YEAR, THIS WOULD'VE BEEN TOTALLY UNTHINKABLE...

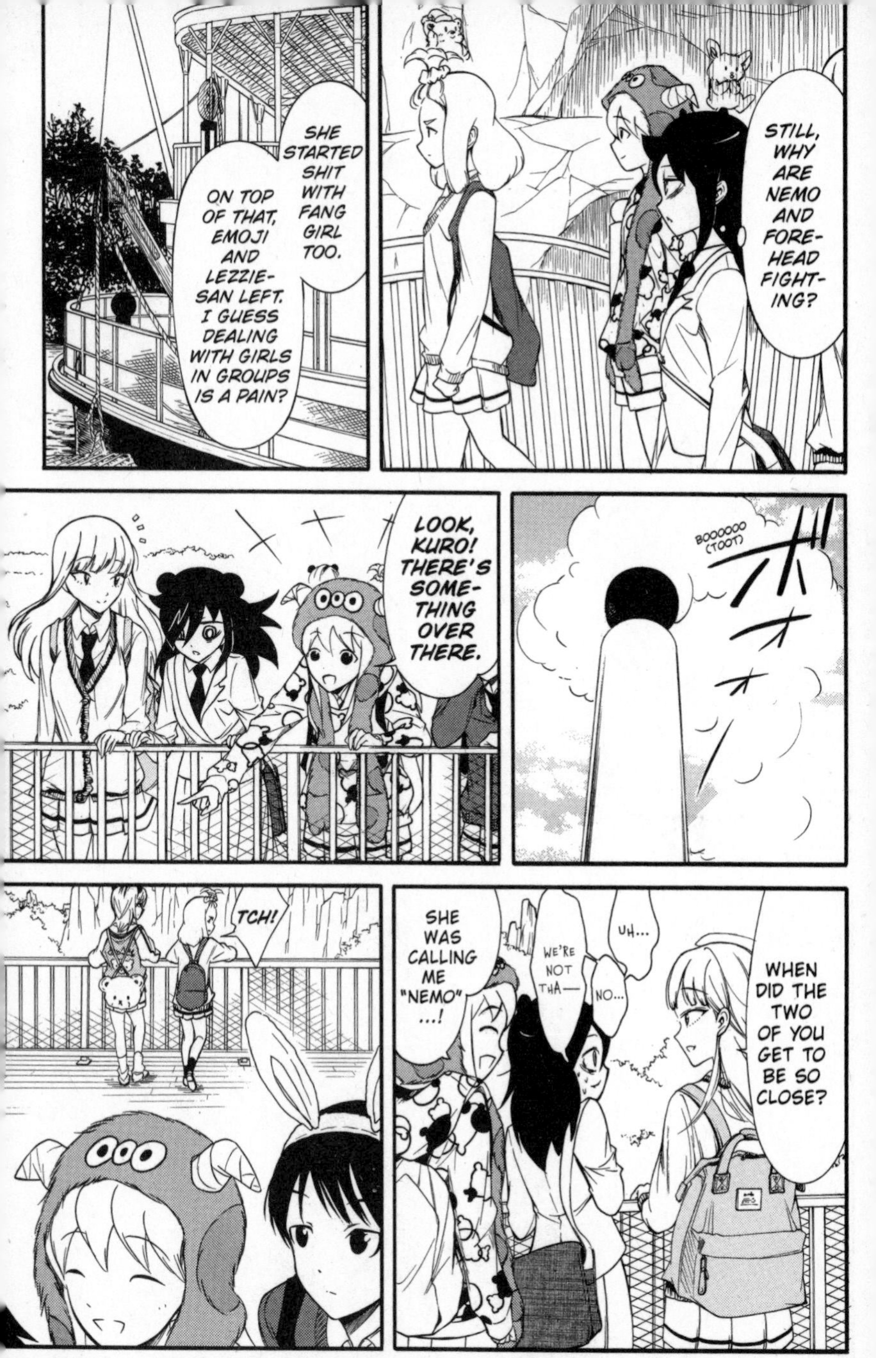
STILL, WHY ARE NEMO AND FOREHEAD FIGHTING?
SHE STARTED SHIT WITH FANG GIRL TOO.
ON TOP OF THAT, EMOJI AND LEZZIE-SAN LEFT. I GUESS DEALING WITH GIRLS IN GROUPS IS A PAIN?
BOOOOOO (TOOT)
LOOK, KURO! THERE'S SOMETHING OVER THERE.
WHEN DID THE TWO OF YOU GET TO BE SO CLOSE?
UH...
NO...
WE'RE NOT THA—
SHE WAS CALLING ME "NEMO"...!
TCH!

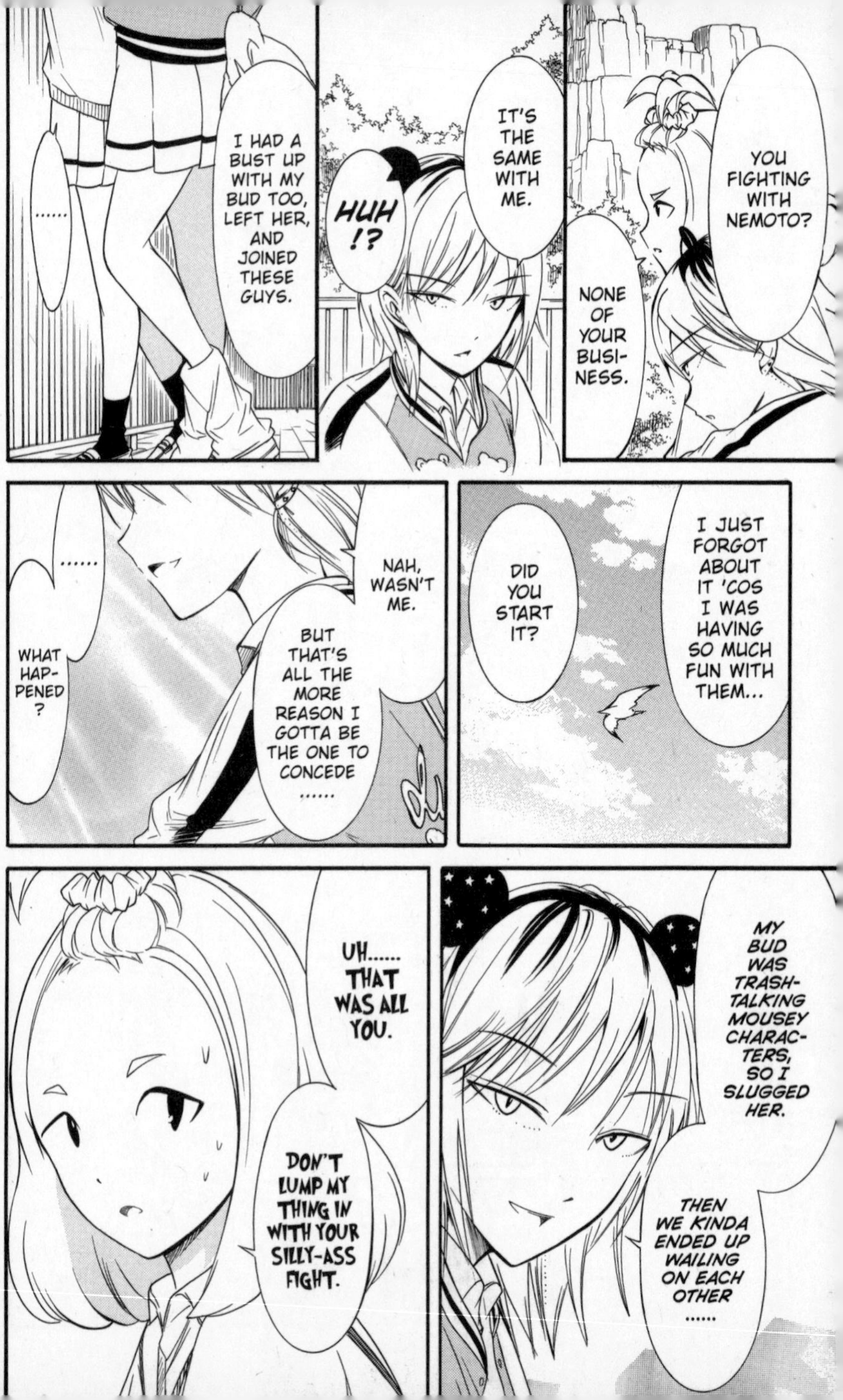
YOU FIGHTING WITH NEMOTO?
NONE OF YOUR BUSINESS.
IT'S THE SAME WITH ME.
HUH!?
I HAD A BUST UP WITH MY BUD TOO, LEFT HER, AND JOINED THESE GUYS.
......
I JUST FORGOT ABOUT IT 'COS I WAS HAVING SO MUCH FUN WITH THEM...
DID YOU START IT?
NAH, WASN'T ME.
BUT THAT'S ALL THE MORE REASON I GOTTA BE THE ONE TO CONCEDE ......
......
WHAT HAPPENED?
MY BUD WAS TRASH-TALKING MOUSEY CHARACTERS, SO I SLUGGED HER.
THEN WE KINDA ENDED UP WAILING ON EACH OTHER ......
UH...... THAT WAS ALL YOU.
DON'T LUMP MY THING IN WITH YOUR SILLY-ASS FIGHT.

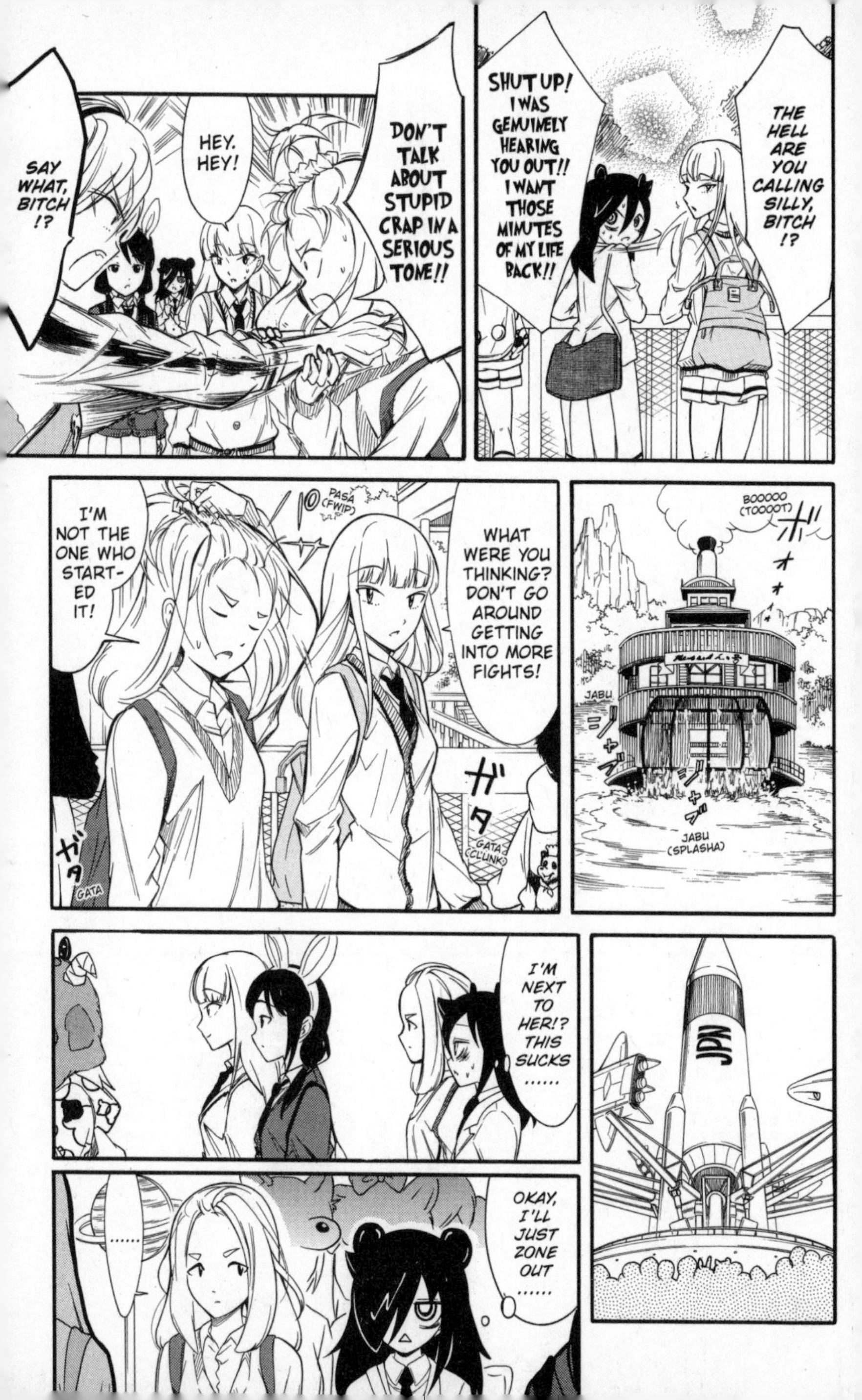
THE HELL ARE YOU CALLING SILLY, BITCH!?
SHUT UP! I WAS GENUINELY HEARING YOU OUT!! I WANT THOSE MINUTES OF MY LIFE BACK!!
DON'T TALK ABOUT STUPID CRAP IN A SERIOUS TONE!!
HEY. HEY!
SAY WHAT, BITCH!?
BOOOOO (TOOOOT)
JABU
JABU (SPLASHA)
WHAT WERE YOU THINKING? DON'T GO AROUND GETTING INTO MORE FIGHTS!
PASA (FWIP)
I'M NOT THE ONE WHO START-ED IT!
GATA (CL'UNK)
GATA
JPN
I'M NEXT TO HER!? THIS SUCKS......
OKAY, I'LL JUST ZONE OUT......
......

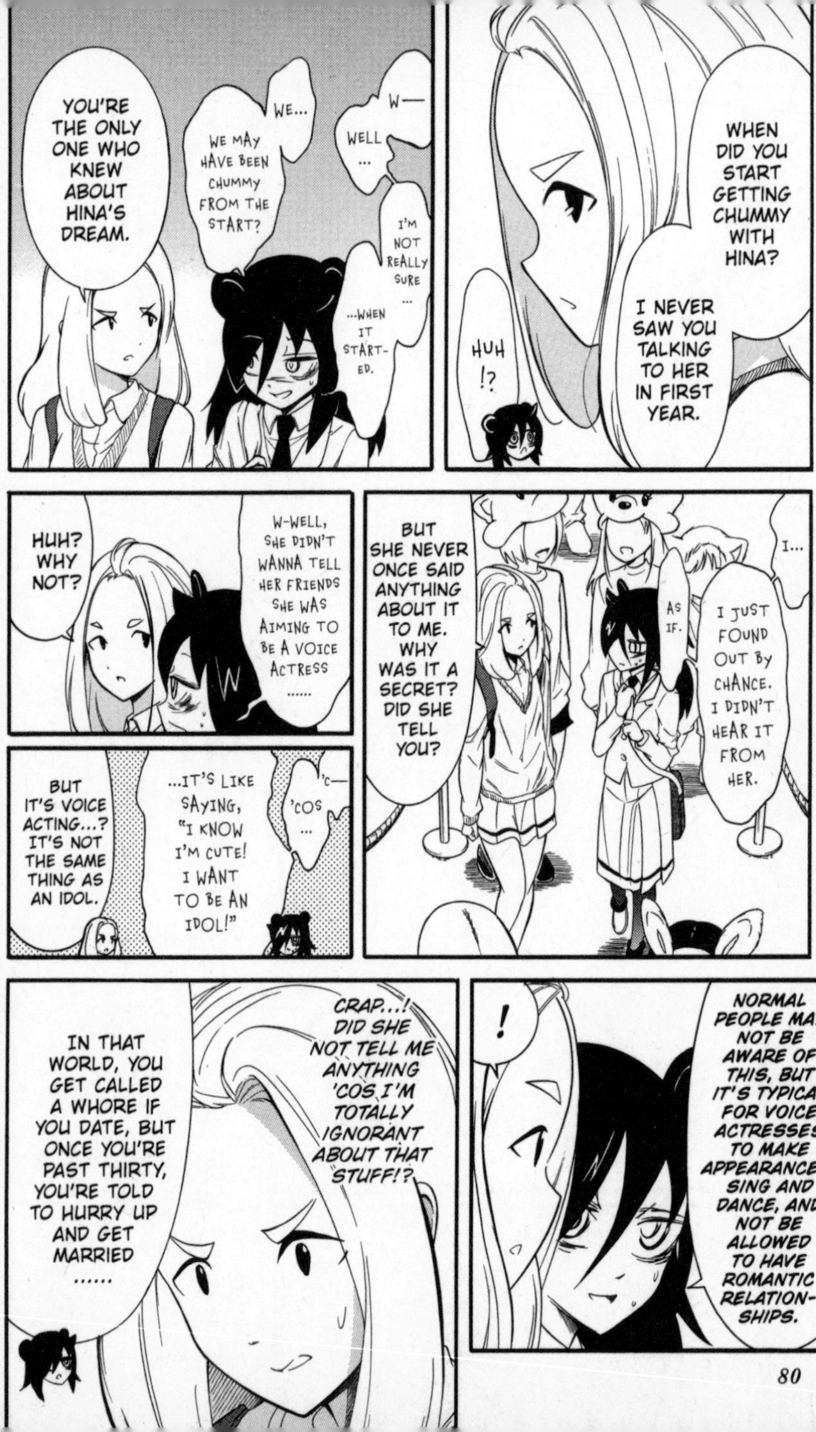
WHEN DID YOU START GETTING CHUMMY WITH HINA?
I NEVER SAW YOU TALKING TO HER IN FIRST YEAR.
HUH !?
W— WELL ...
I'M NOT REALLY SURE ... ...WHEN IT STARTED.
WE... WE MAY HAVE BEEN CHUMMY FROM THE START?
YOU'RE THE ONLY ONE WHO KNEW ABOUT HINA'S DREAM.
BUT SHE NEVER ONCE SAID ANYTHING ABOUT IT TO ME. WHY WAS IT A SECRET? DID SHE TELL YOU?
I...
I JUST FOUND OUT BY CHANCE. I DIDN'T HEAR IT FROM HER.
AS IF.
W-WELL, SHE DIDN'T WANNA TELL HER FRIENDS SHE WAS AIMING TO BE A VOICE ACTRESS ......
HUH? WHY NOT?
'C— 'COS ...
...IT'S LIKE SAYING, "I KNOW I'M CUTE! I WANT TO BE AN IDOL!"
BUT IT'S VOICE ACTING...? IT'S NOT THE SAME THING AS AN IDOL.
!
NORMAL PEOPLE MAY NOT BE AWARE OF THIS, BUT IT'S TYPICAL FOR VOICE ACTRESSES TO MAKE APPEARANCES, SING AND DANCE, AND NOT BE ALLOWED TO HAVE ROMANTIC RELATIONSHIPS.
CRAP...! DID SHE NOT TELL ME ANYTHING 'COS I'M TOTALLY IGNORANT ABOUT THAT STUFF!?
IN THAT WORLD, YOU GET CALLED A WHORE IF YOU DATE, BUT ONCE YOU'RE PAST THIRTY, YOU'RE TOLD TO HURRY UP AND GET MARRIED ......

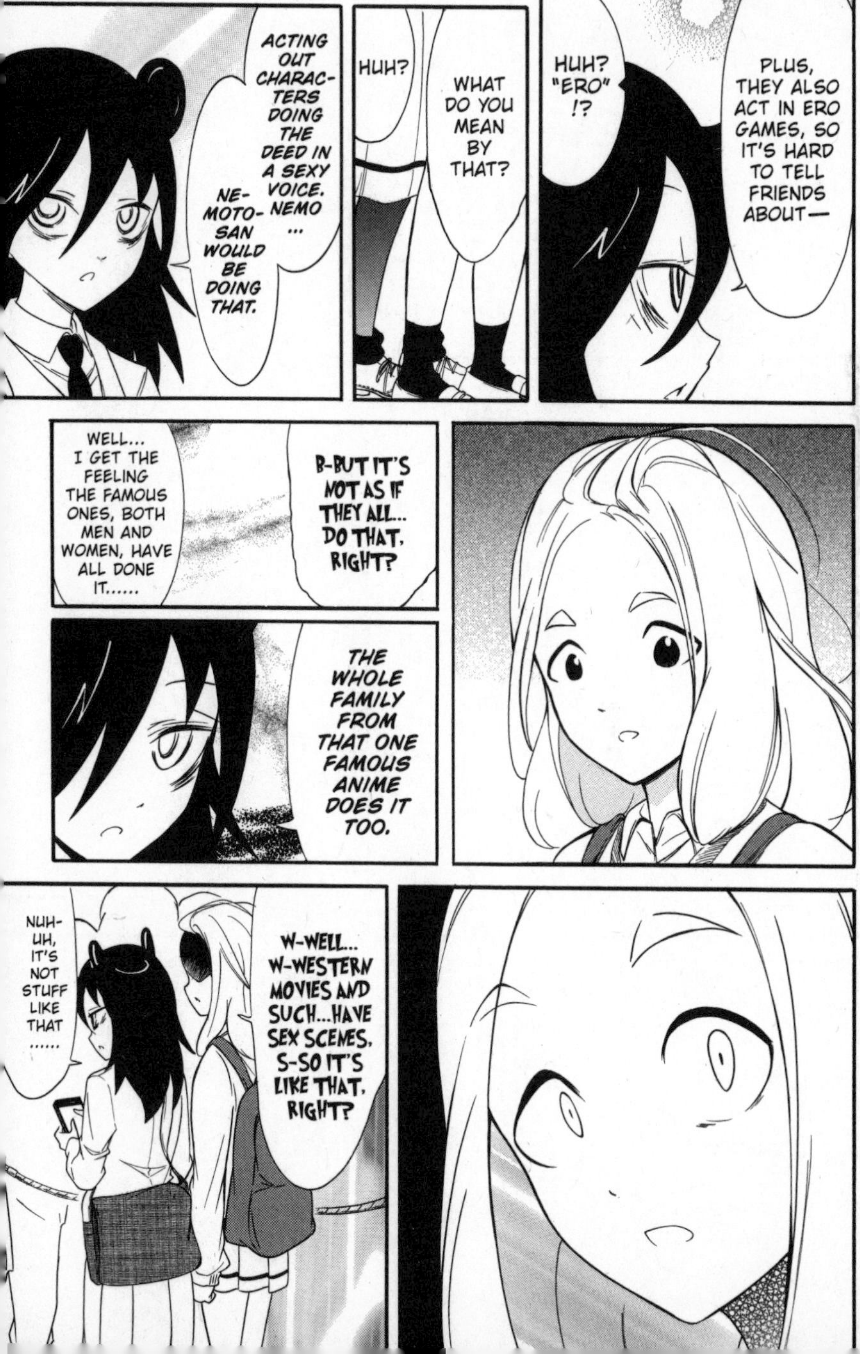
PLUS, THEY ALSO ACT IN ERO GAMES, SO IT'S HARD TO TELL FRIENDS ABOUT—
HUH? "ERO" !?
WHAT DO YOU MEAN BY THAT?
HUH?
ACTING OUT CHARACTERS DOING THE DEED IN A SEXY VOICE. NEMO ...
NE-MOTO-SAN WOULD BE DOING THAT.
B-BUT IT'S NOT AS IF THEY ALL... DO THAT, RIGHT?
WELL... I GET THE FEELING THE FAMOUS ONES, BOTH MEN AND WOMEN, HAVE ALL DONE IT......
THE WHOLE FAMILY FROM THAT ONE FAMOUS ANIME DOES IT TOO.
W-WELL... W-WESTERN MOVIES AND SUCH...HAVE SEX SCENES. S-SO IT'S LIKE THAT, RIGHT?
NUH-UH, IT'S NOT STUFF LIKE THAT ......

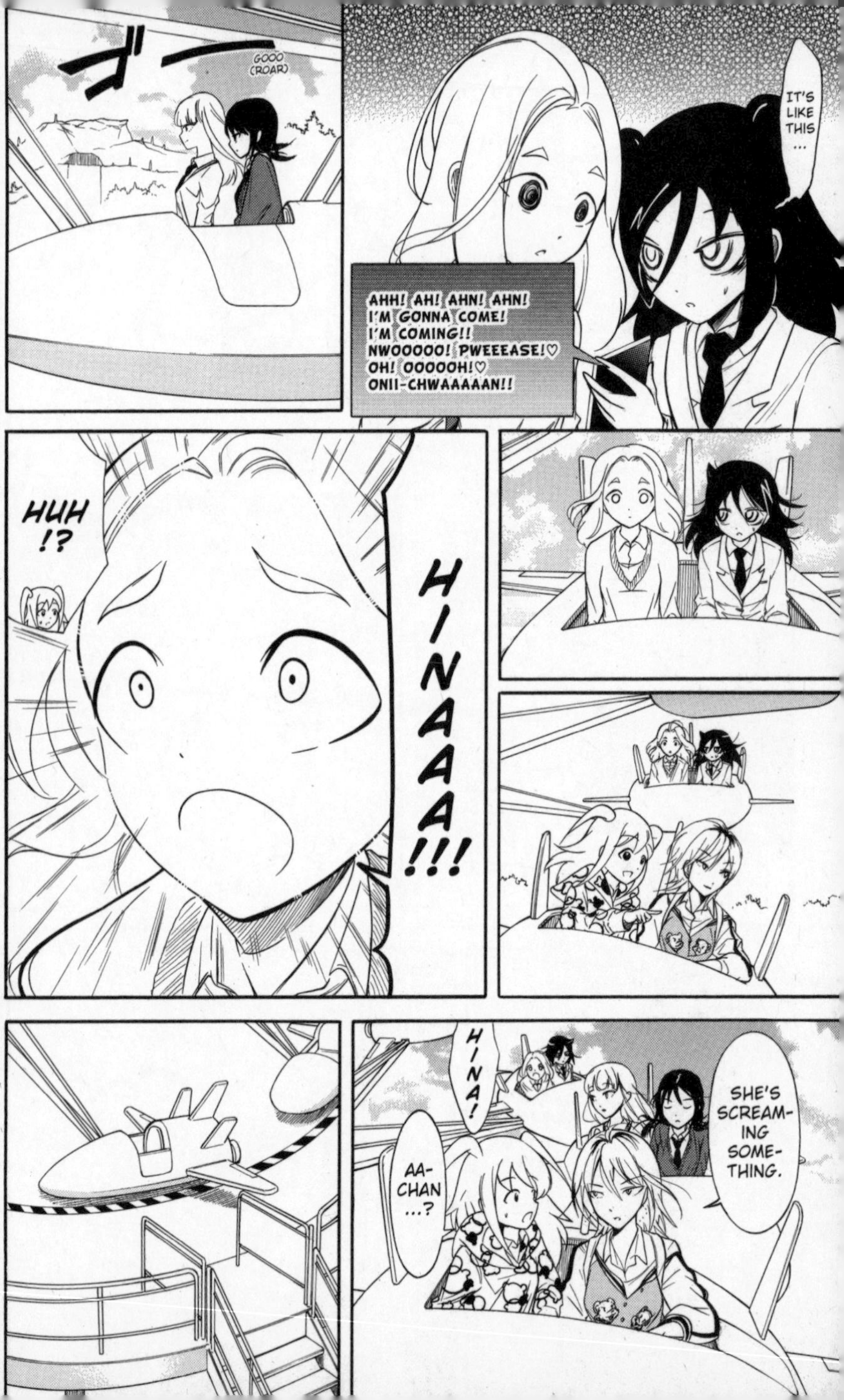
IT'S LIKE THIS ...
AHH! AH! AHN! AHN! I'M GONNA COME! I'M COMING!! NWOOOOO! PWEEEASE!♡ OH! OOOOOH!♡ ONII-CHWAAAAAN!!
GOOO (ROAR)
HINAAAA!!!
HUH !?
SHE'S SCREAMING SOMETHING.
HINA!
AA-CHAN ...?

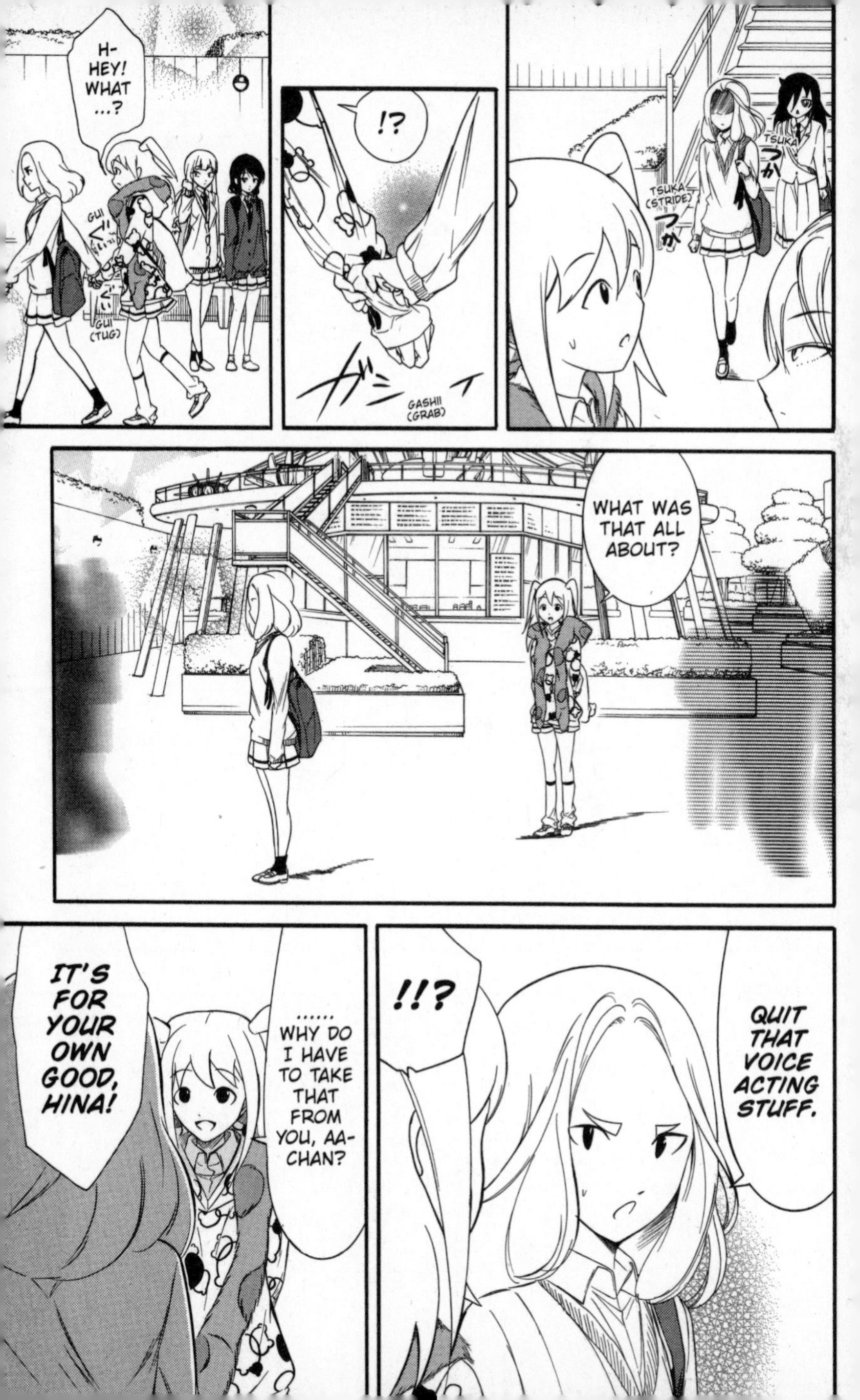
TSUKA
つか
TSUKA (STRIDE)
つか
!?
GASHII (GRAB)
H-HEY! WHAT ...?
GUI
ぐい
ぐい
GUI (TUG)
WHAT WAS THAT ALL ABOUT?
QUIT THAT VOICE ACTING STUFF.
!!?
...... WHY DO I HAVE TO TAKE THAT FROM YOU, AA-CHAN?
IT'S FOR YOUR OWN GOOD, HINA!

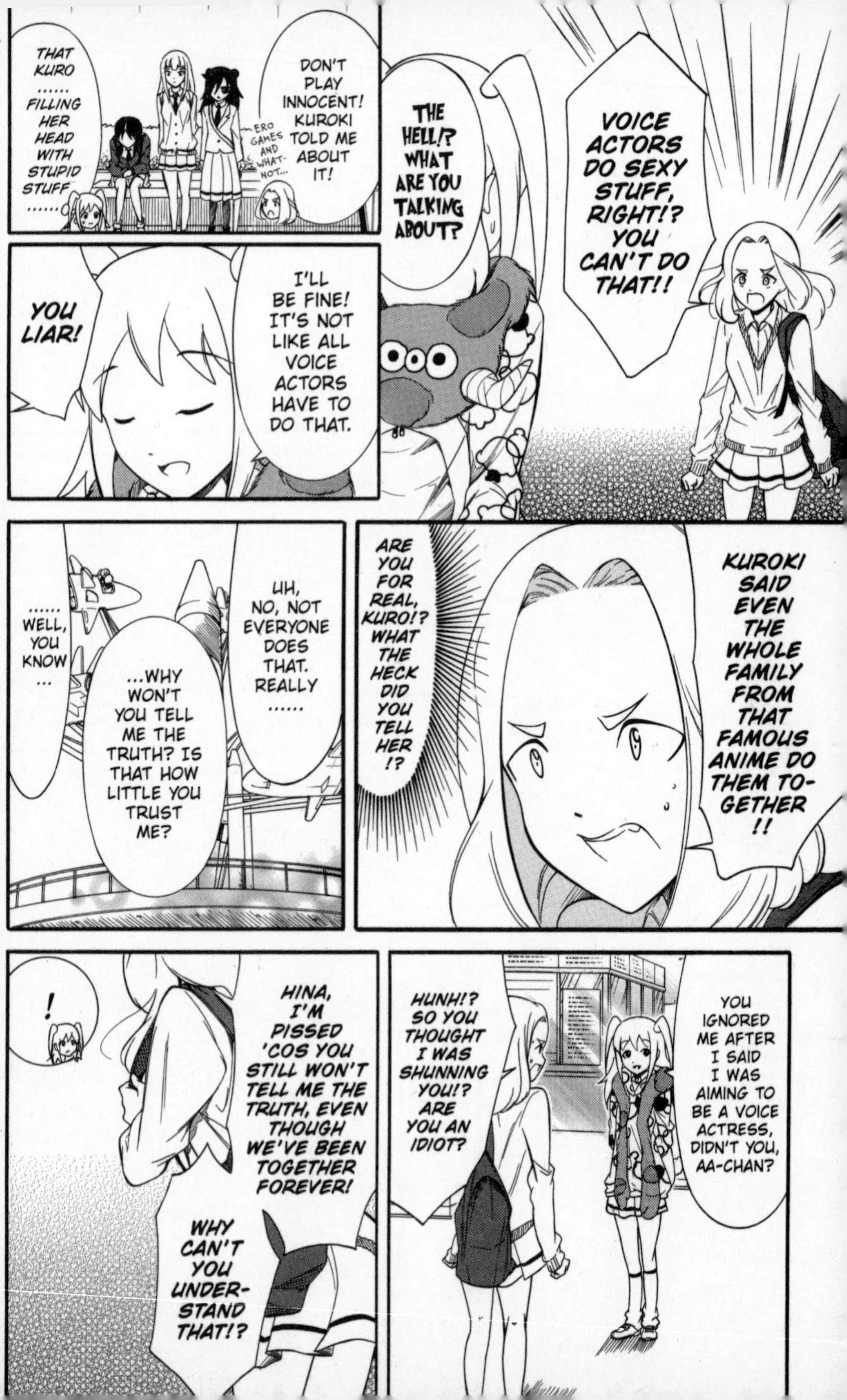
VOICE ACTORS DO SEXY STUFF, RIGHT!? YOU CAN'T DO THAT!!
THE HELL!? WHAT ARE YOU TALKING ABOUT?
DON'T PLAY INNOCENT! KUROKI TOLD ME ABOUT IT!
ERO GAMES AND WHAT-NOT...
THAT KURO...... FILLING HER HEAD WITH STUPID STUFF......
I'LL BE FINE! IT'S NOT LIKE ALL VOICE ACTORS HAVE TO DO THAT.
YOU LIAR!
KUROKI SAID EVEN THE WHOLE FAMILY FROM THAT FAMOUS ANIME DO THEM TO-GETHER!!
ARE YOU FOR REAL, KURO!? WHAT THE HECK DID YOU TELL HER!?
UH, NO, NOT EVERYONE DOES THAT. REALLY......
...WHY WON'T YOU TELL ME THE TRUTH? IS THAT HOW LITTLE YOU TRUST ME?
......WELL, YOU KNOW...
YOU IGNORED ME AFTER I SAID I WAS AIMING TO BE A VOICE ACTRESS, DIDN'T YOU, AA-CHAN?
HUNH!? SO YOU THOUGHT I WAS SHUNNING YOU!? ARE YOU AN IDIOT?
HINA, I'M PISSED 'COS YOU STILL WON'T TELL ME THE TRUTH, EVEN THOUGH WE'VE BEEN TOGETHER FOREVER!
WHY CAN'T YOU UNDER-STAND THAT!?
!

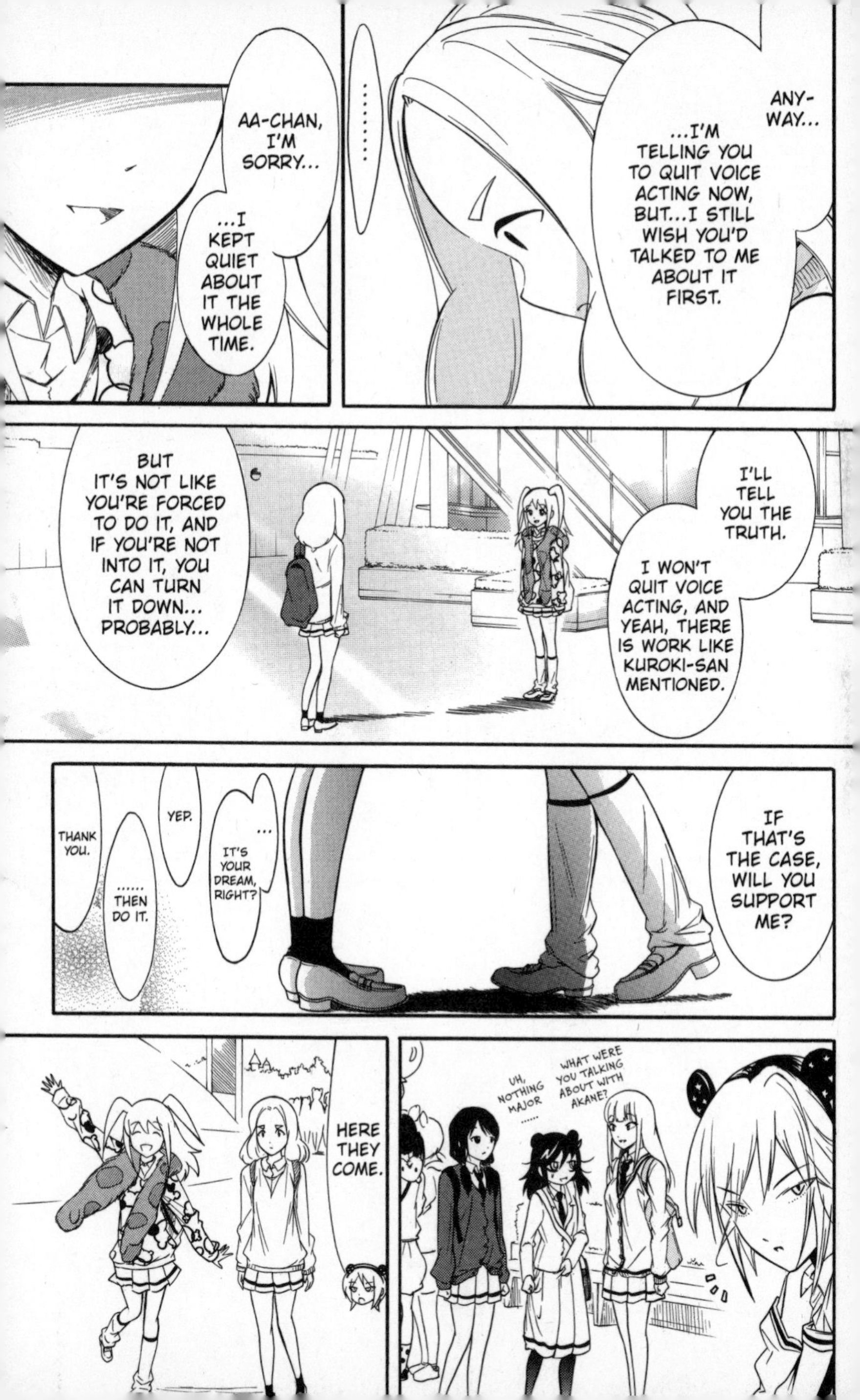
ANY-WAY...
...I'M TELLING YOU TO QUIT VOICE ACTING NOW, BUT...I STILL WISH YOU'D TALKED TO ME ABOUT IT FIRST.
......
AA-CHAN, I'M SORRY...
...I KEPT QUIET ABOUT IT THE WHOLE TIME.
I'LL TELL YOU THE TRUTH.
I WON'T QUIT VOICE ACTING, AND YEAH, THERE IS WORK LIKE KUROKI-SAN MENTIONED.
BUT IT'S NOT LIKE YOU'RE FORCED TO DO IT, AND IF YOU'RE NOT INTO IT, YOU CAN TURN IT DOWN... PROBABLY...
IF THAT'S THE CASE, WILL YOU SUPPORT ME?
...
IT'S YOUR DREAM, RIGHT?
YEP.
......THEN DO IT.
THANK YOU.
WHAT WERE YOU TALKING ABOUT WITH AKANE?
UH, NOTHING MAJOR ......
HERE THEY COME.

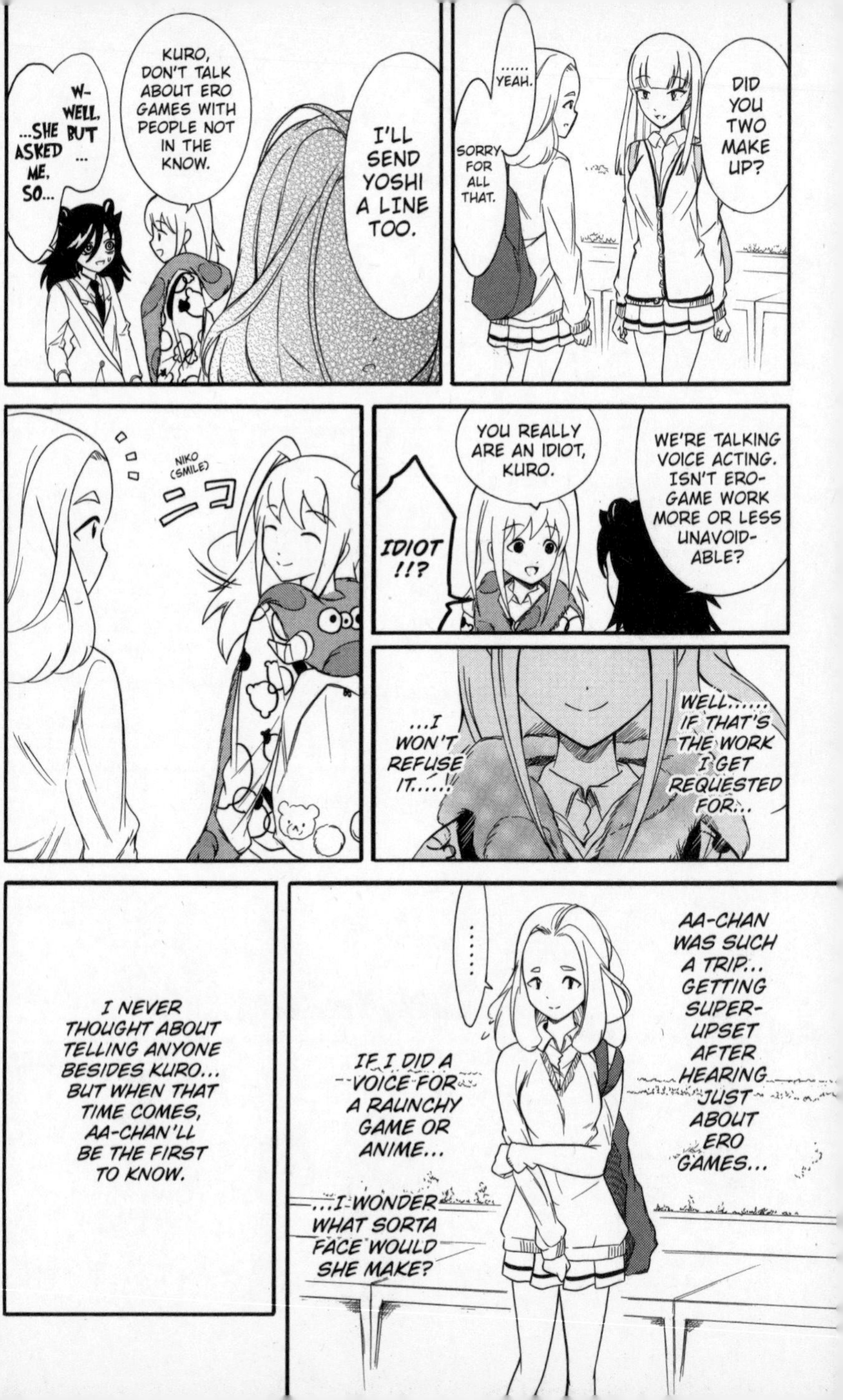
DID YOU TWO MAKE UP?
......YEAH.
SORRY FOR ALL THAT.
I'LL SEND YOSHI A LINE TOO.
KURO, DON'T TALK ABOUT ERO GAMES WITH PEOPLE NOT IN THE KNOW.
W-WELL, BUT ...
...SHE ASKED ME. SO...
WE'RE TALKING VOICE ACTING. ISN'T ERO-GAME WORK MORE OR LESS UNAVOID-ABLE?
YOU REALLY ARE AN IDIOT, KURO.
IDIOT !!?
WELL..... IF THAT'S THE WORK I GET REQUESTED FOR...
...I WON'T REFUSE IT.....!
NIKO (SMILE)
ニコ
AA-CHAN WAS SUCH A TRIP... GETTING SUPER-UPSET AFTER HEARING JUST ABOUT ERO GAMES...
......
IF I DID A VOICE FOR A RAUNCHY GAME OR ANIME...
...I WONDER WHAT SORTA FACE WOULD SHE MAKE?
I NEVER THOUGHT ABOUT TELLING ANYONE BESIDES KURO... BUT WHEN THAT TIME COMES, AA-CHAN'LL BE THE FIRST TO KNOW.

No Matter How I Look at It, It's You Guys' Fault I'm Not Popular!

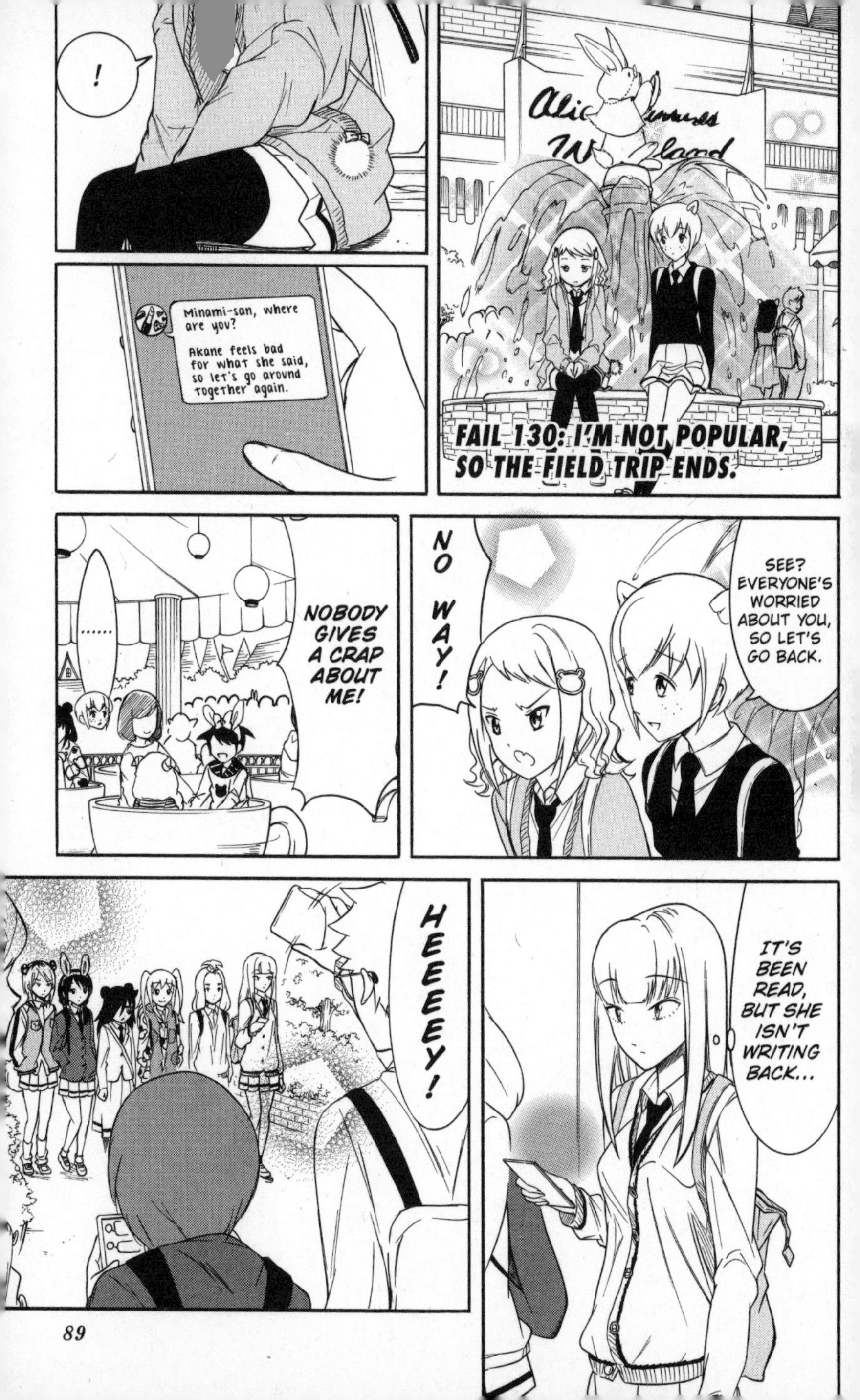
FAIL 130: I'M NOT POPULAR, SO THE FIELD TRIP ENDS.
!
Minami-san, where are you?
Akane feels bad for what she said, so let's go around together again.
SEE? EVERYONE'S WORRIED ABOUT YOU, SO LET'S GO BACK.
NO WAY!
NOBODY GIVES A CRAP ABOUT ME!
......
IT'S BEEN READ, BUT SHE ISN'T WRITING BACK...
HEEEEEY!

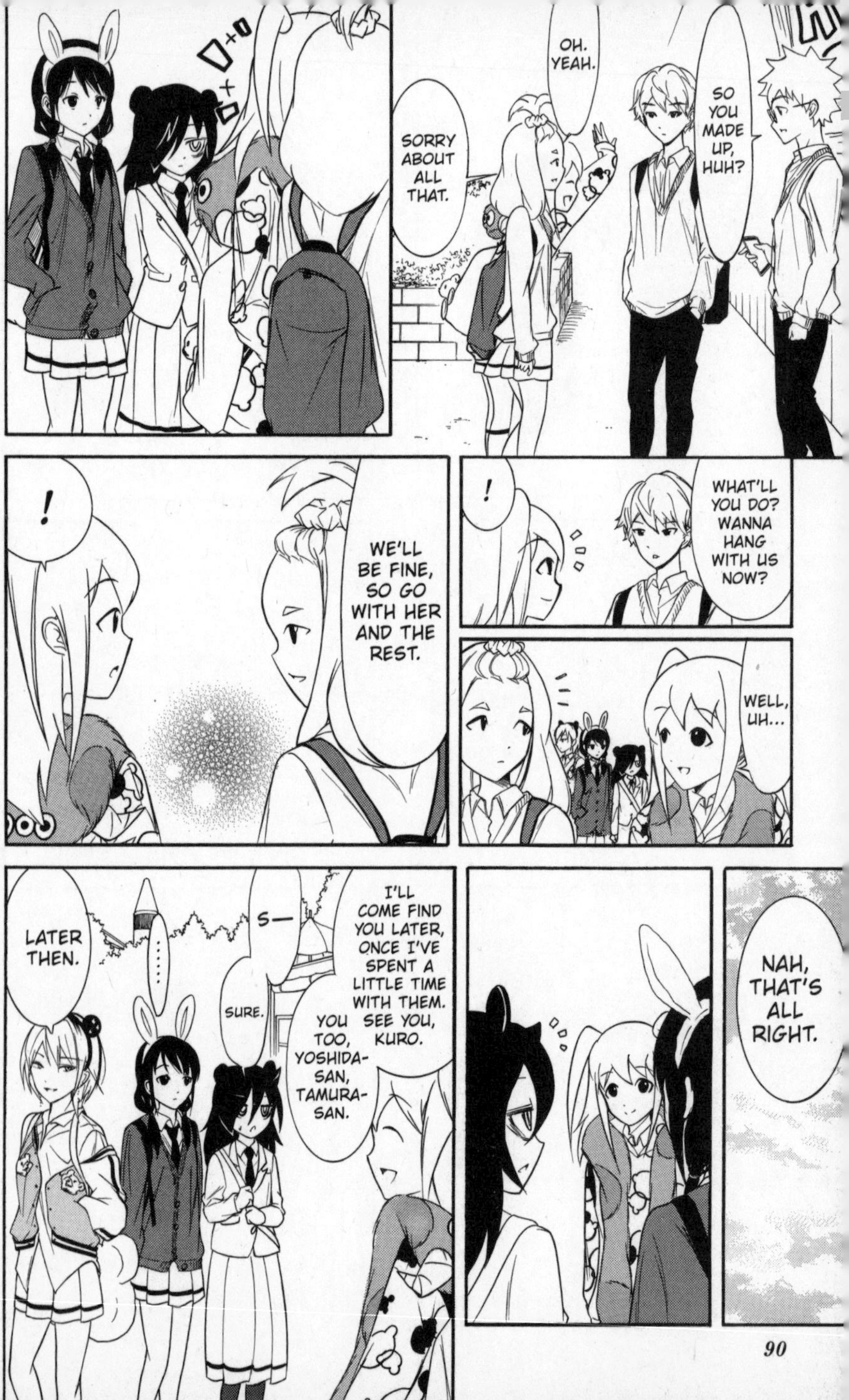
SO YOU MADE UP, HUH?
OH. YEAH.
SORRY ABOUT ALL THAT.
WHAT'LL YOU DO? WANNA HANG WITH US NOW?
!
WELL, UH...
WE'LL BE FINE, SO GO WITH HER AND THE REST.
!
NAH, THAT'S ALL RIGHT.
I'LL COME FIND YOU LATER, ONCE I'VE SPENT A LITTLE TIME WITH THEM. SEE YOU, KURO.
YOU TOO, YOSHIDA-SAN, TAMURA-SAN.
S—
SURE.
......
LATER THEN.

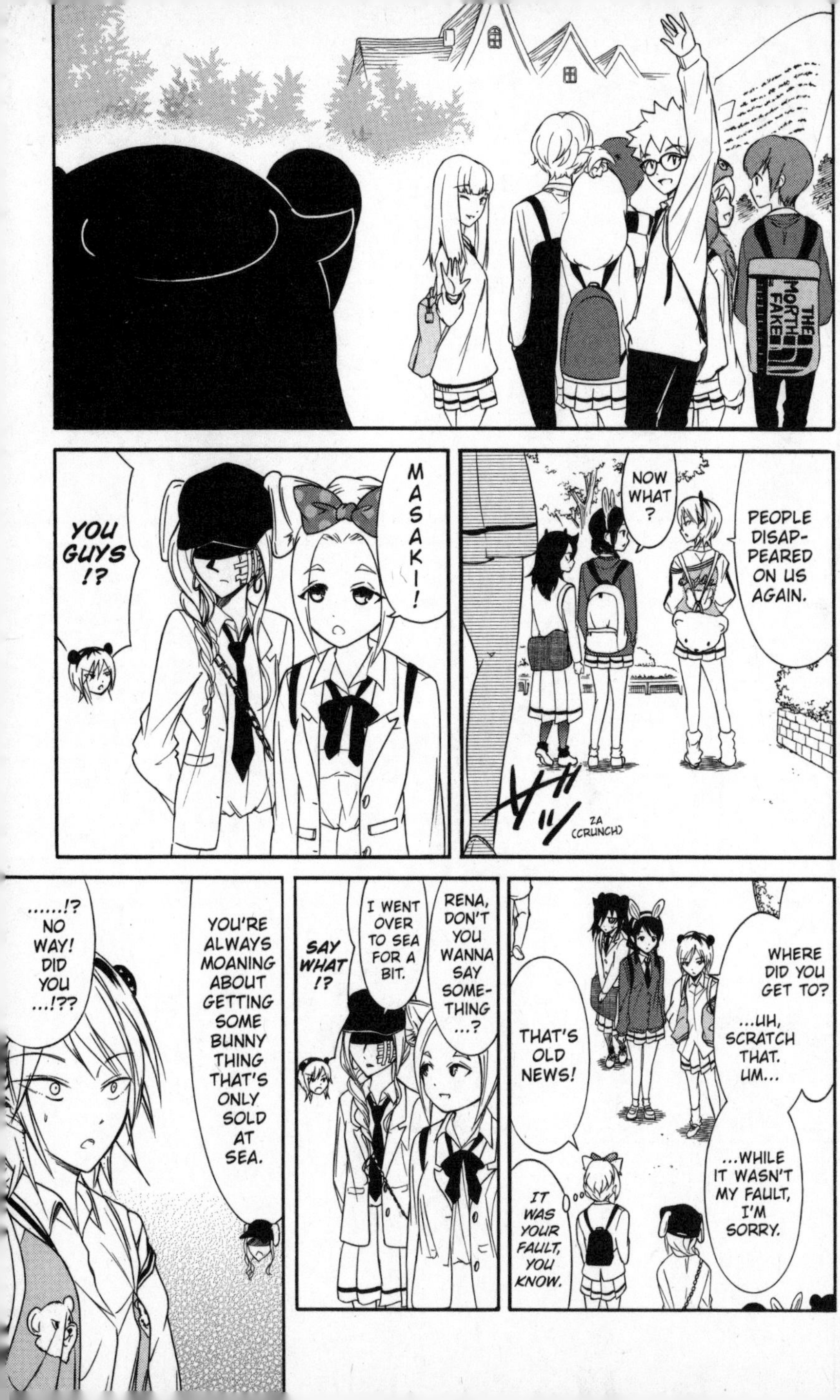
THE NORTH FAKE
PEOPLE DISAPPEARED ON US AGAIN.
NOW WHAT?
ZA (CRUNCH)
MASAKI!
YOU GUYS!?
WHERE DID YOU GET TO?
...UH, SCRATCH THAT. UM...
...WHILE IT WASN'T MY FAULT, I'M SORRY.
THAT'S OLD NEWS!
IT WAS YOUR FAULT, YOU KNOW.
RENA, DON'T YOU WANNA SAY SOMETHING...?
I WENT OVER TO SEA FOR A BIT.
SAY WHAT!?
YOU'RE ALWAYS MOANING ABOUT GETTING SOME BUNNY THING THAT'S ONLY SOLD AT SEA.
......!? NO WAY! DID YOU ...!??

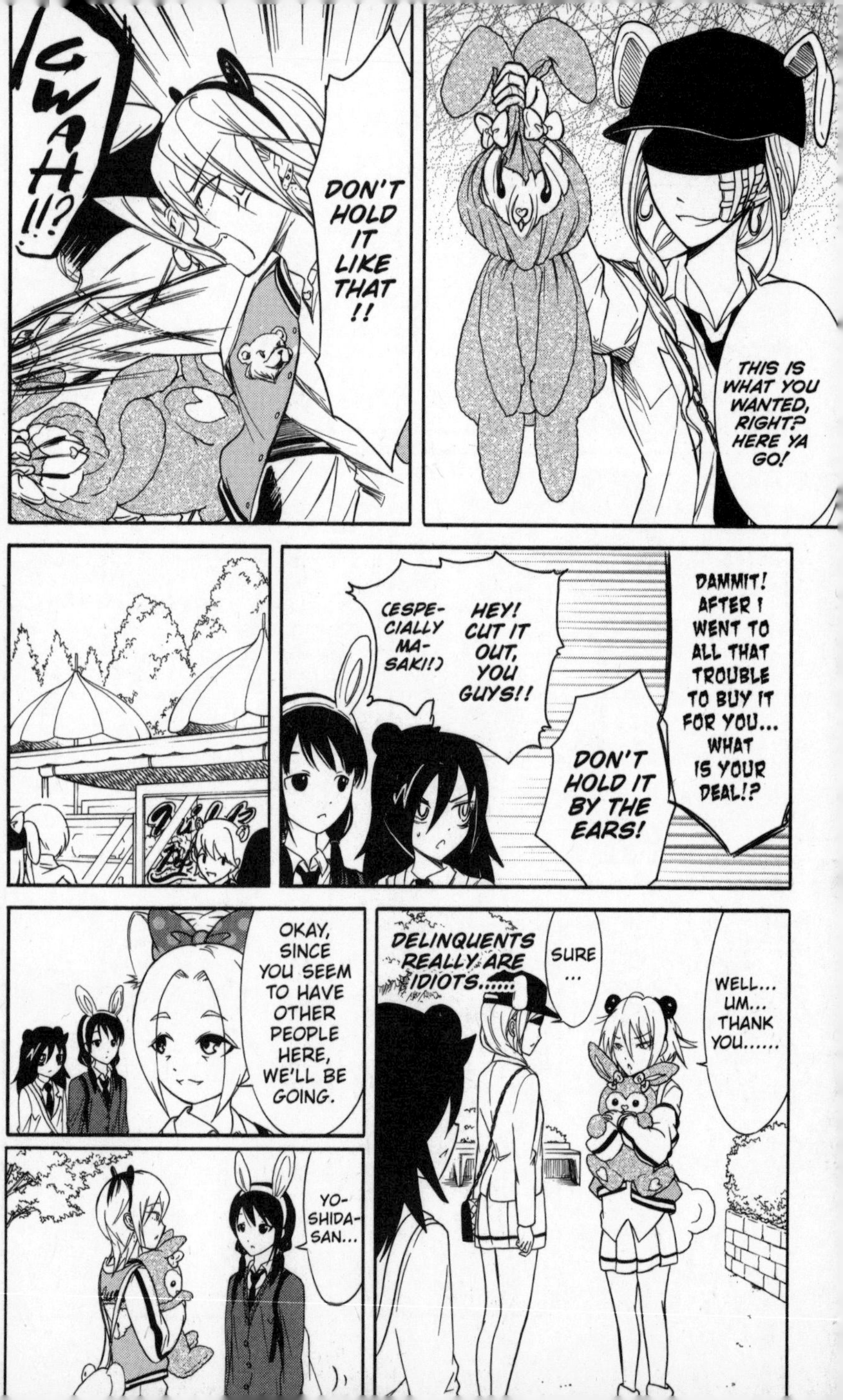
THIS IS WHAT YOU WANTED, RIGHT? HERE YA GO!
DON'T HOLD IT LIKE THAT!!
GWAH!!?
DAMMIT! AFTER I WENT TO ALL THAT TROUBLE TO BUY IT FOR YOU... WHAT IS YOUR DEAL!?
DON'T HOLD IT BY THE EARS!
HEY! CUT IT OUT, YOU GUYS!!
(ESPECIALLY MASAKI!)
WELL... UM... THANK YOU......
SURE ...
DELINQUENTS REALLY ARE IDIOTS......
OKAY, SINCE YOU SEEM TO HAVE OTHER PEOPLE HERE, WE'LL BE GOING.
YOSHIDA-SAN...

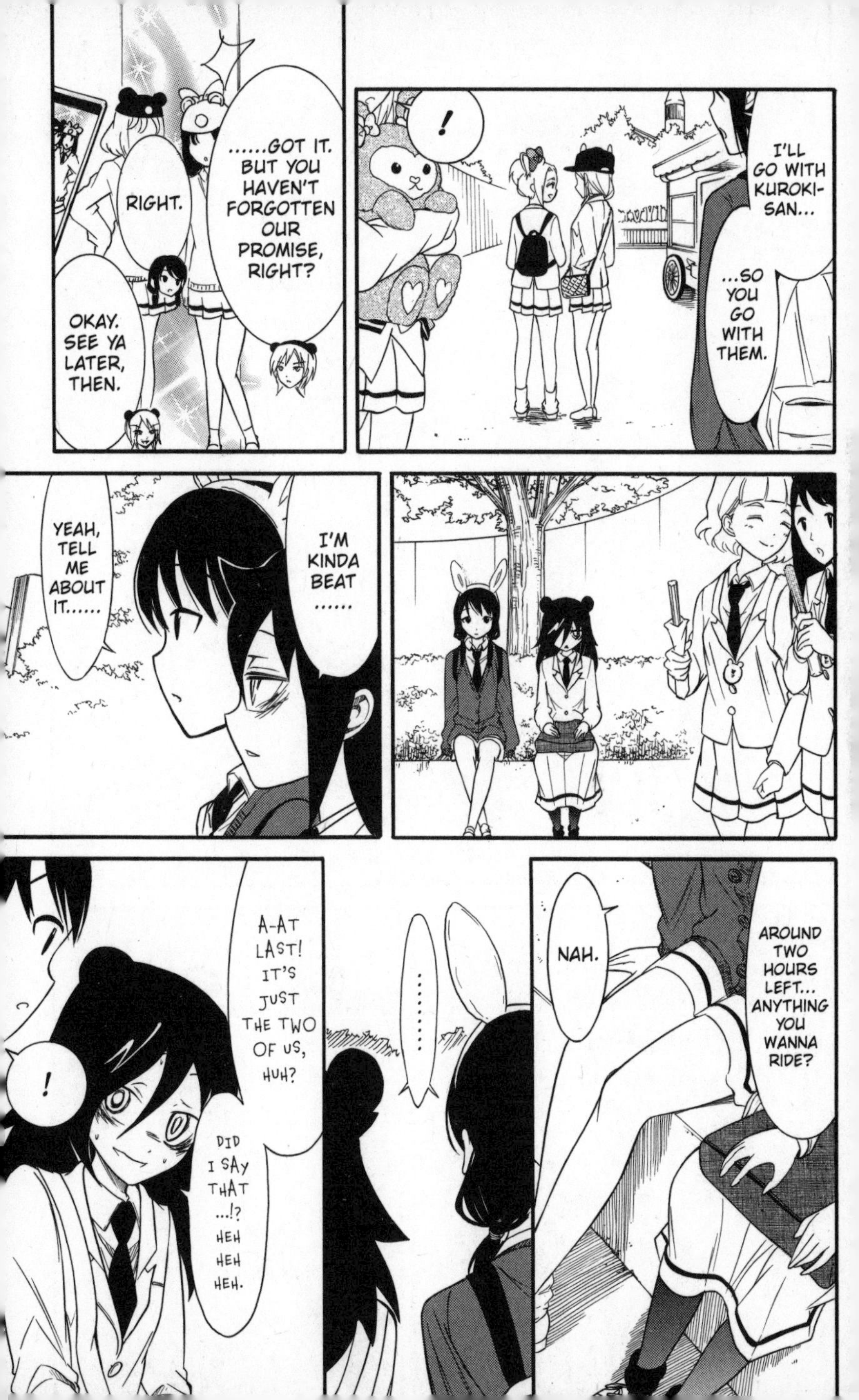
I'LL GO WITH KUROKI-SAN...
...SO YOU GO WITH THEM.
!
......GOT IT. BUT YOU HAVEN'T FORGOTTEN OUR PROMISE, RIGHT?
RIGHT.
OKAY. SEE YA LATER, THEN.
I'M KINDA BEAT......
YEAH, TELL ME ABOUT IT......
AROUND TWO HOURS LEFT... ANYTHING YOU WANNA RIDE?
NAH.
....
A-AT LAST! IT'S JUST THE TWO OF US, HUH?
!
DID I SAY THAT...!? HEH HEH HEH.

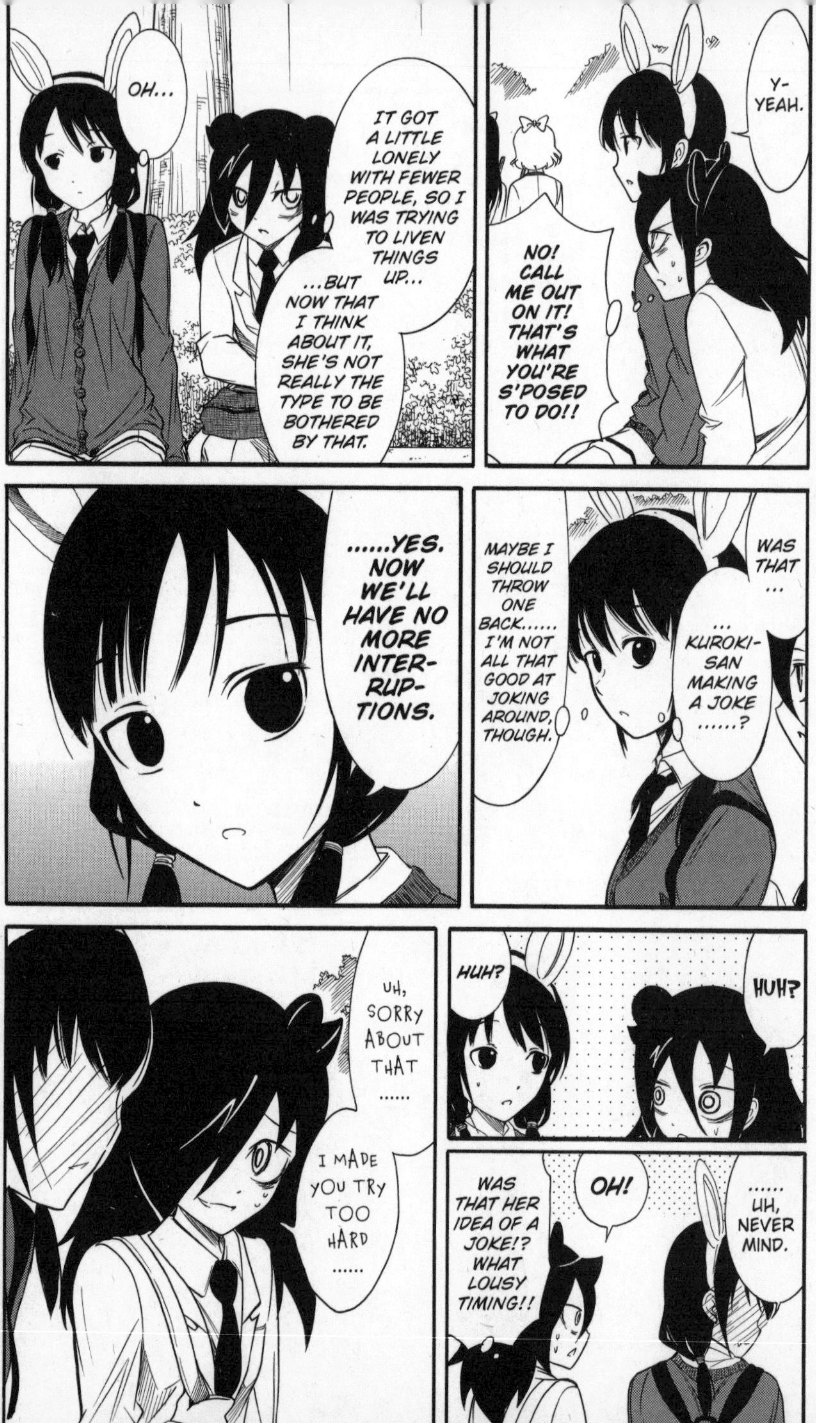
Y-YEAH.
NO! CALL ME OUT ON IT! THAT'S WHAT YOU'RE S'POSED TO DO!!
IT GOT A LITTLE LONELY WITH FEWER PEOPLE, SO I WAS TRYING TO LIVEN THINGS UP...
...BUT NOW THAT I THINK ABOUT IT, SHE'S NOT REALLY THE TYPE TO BE BOTHERED BY THAT.
OH...
WAS THAT ...
...KUROKI-SAN MAKING A JOKE ......?
MAYBE I SHOULD THROW ONE BACK...... I'M NOT ALL THAT GOOD AT JOKING AROUND, THOUGH.
......YES. NOW WE'LL HAVE NO MORE INTER-RUP-TIONS.
HUH?
HUH?
......UH, NEVER MIND.
OH!
WAS THAT HER IDEA OF A JOKE!? WHAT LOUSY TIMING!!
UH, SORRY ABOUT THAT ......
I MADE YOU TRY TOO HARD ......

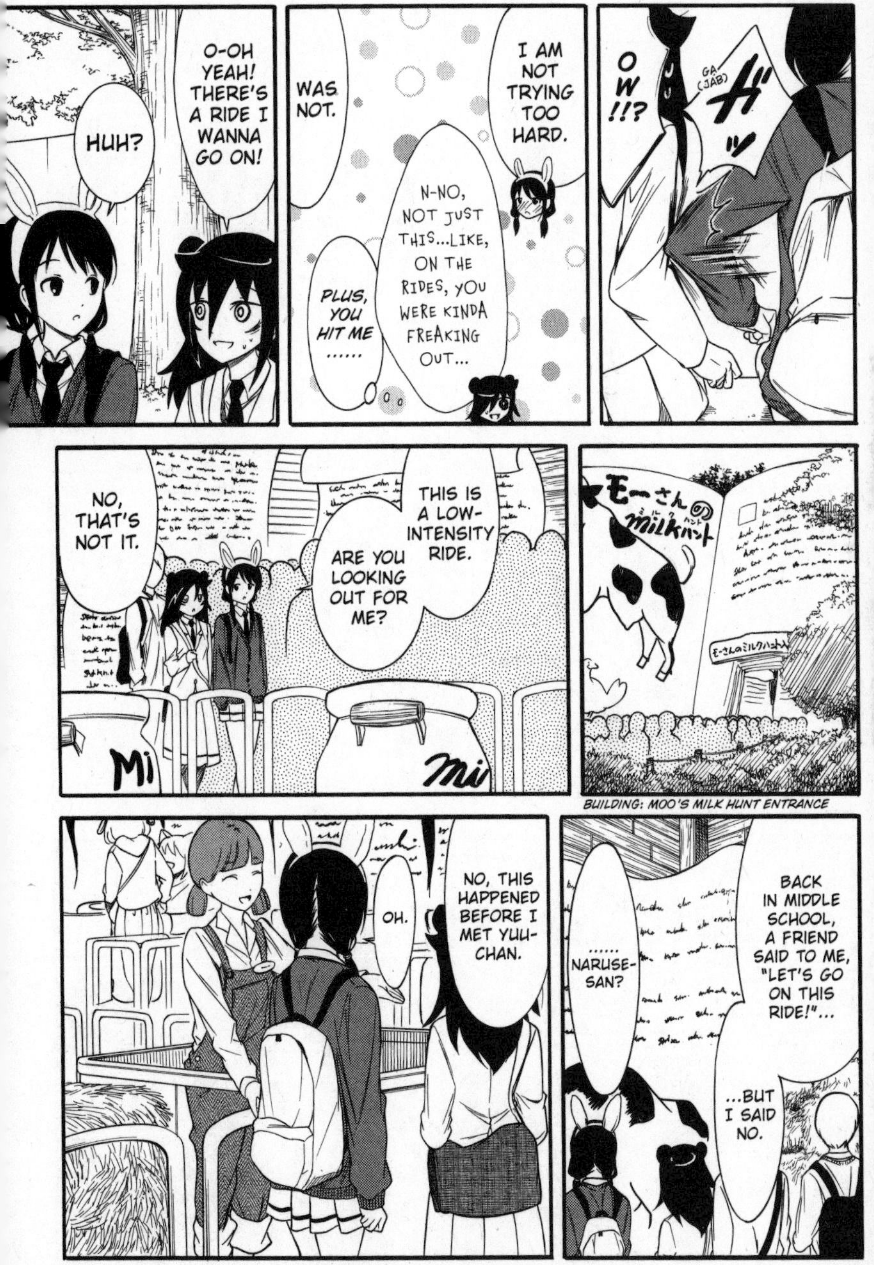
OW!!?
GA (JAB)
ガッ
I AM NOT TRYING TOO HARD.
WAS NOT.
N-NO, NOT JUST THIS...LIKE, ON THE RIDES, YOU WERE KINDA FREAKING OUT...
PLUS, YOU HIT ME ......
O-OH YEAH! THERE'S A RIDE I WANNA GO ON!
HUH?
モーさんのmilkハント
BUILDING: MOO'S MILK HUNT ENTRANCE
THIS IS A LOW-INTENSITY RIDE.
ARE YOU LOOKING OUT FOR ME?
NO, THAT'S NOT IT.
Mi
Mi
BACK IN MIDDLE SCHOOL, A FRIEND SAID TO ME, "LET'S GO ON THIS RIDE!"...
...BUT I SAID NO.
...... NARUSE-SAN?
NO, THIS HAPPENED BEFORE I MET YUU-CHAN.
OH.

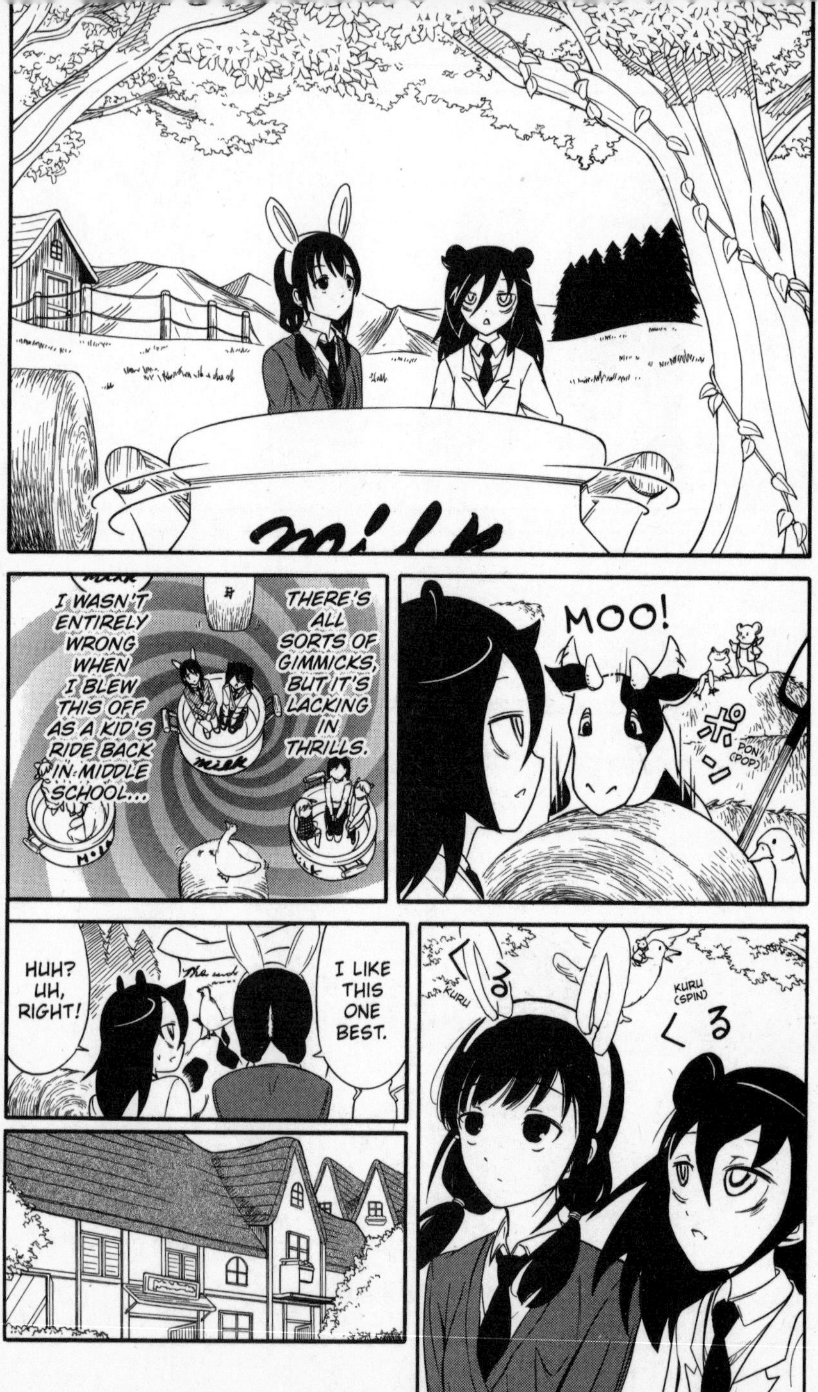
MOO!
ポン
PON (POP)
THERE'S ALL SORTS OF GIMMICKS, BUT IT'S LACKING IN THRILLS.
I WASN'T ENTIRELY WRONG WHEN I BLEW THIS OFF AS A KID'S RIDE BACK IN MIDDLE SCHOOL...
くる
KURU
くる
KURU (SPIN)
I LIKE THIS ONE BEST.
HUH? UH, RIGHT!

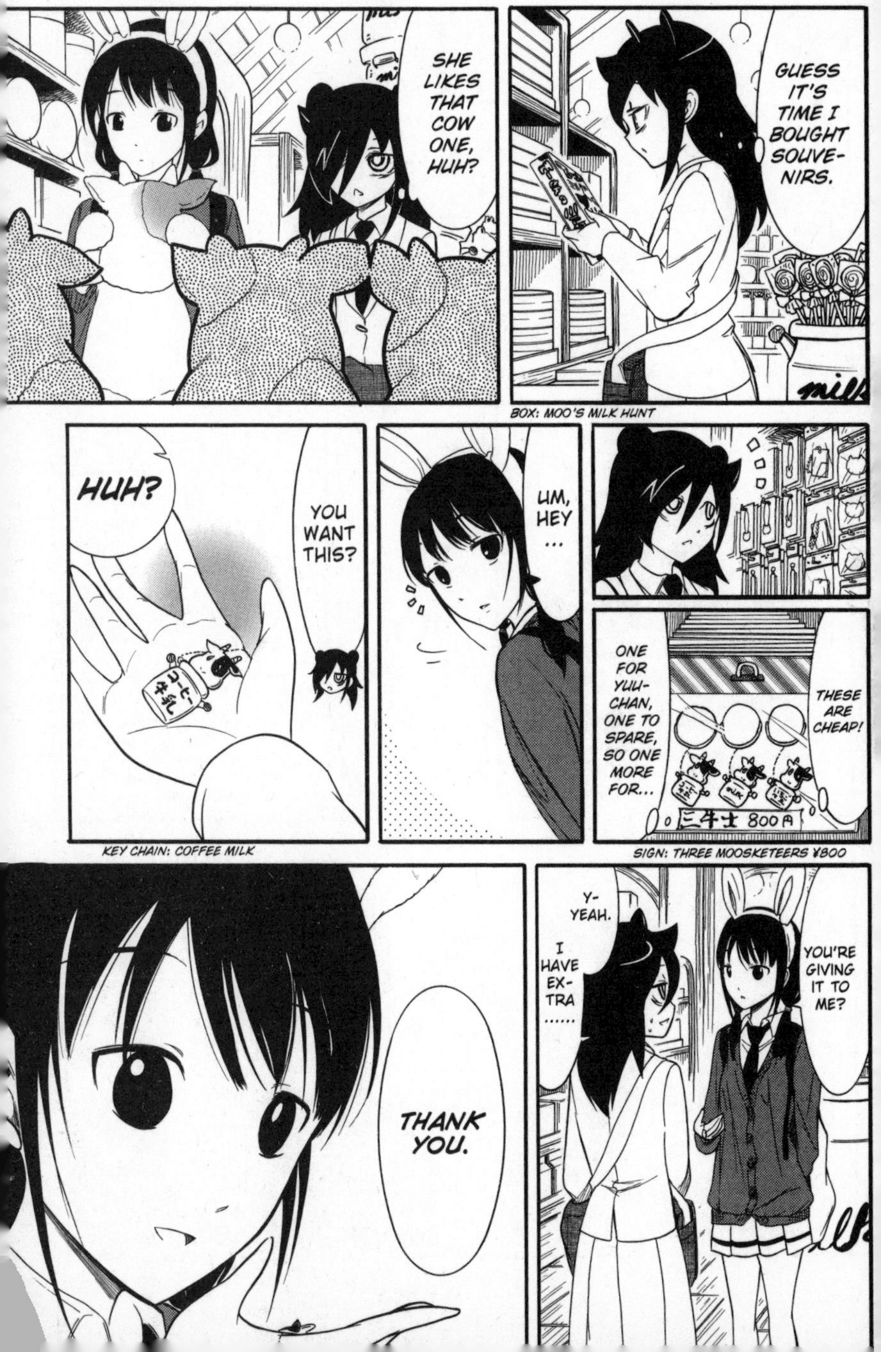
GUESS IT'S TIME I BOUGHT SOUVENIRS.
BOX: MOO'S MILK HUNT
SHE LIKES THAT COW ONE, HUH?
THESE ARE CHEAP!
ONE FOR YUU-CHAN, ONE TO SPARE, SO ONE MORE FOR...
三牛士 800円
SIGN: THREE MOOSKETEERS ¥800
UM, HEY ...
YOU WANT THIS?
HUH?
KEY CHAIN: COFFEE MILK
YOU'RE GIVING IT TO ME?
Y-YEAH.
I HAVE EXTRA ......
THANK YOU.

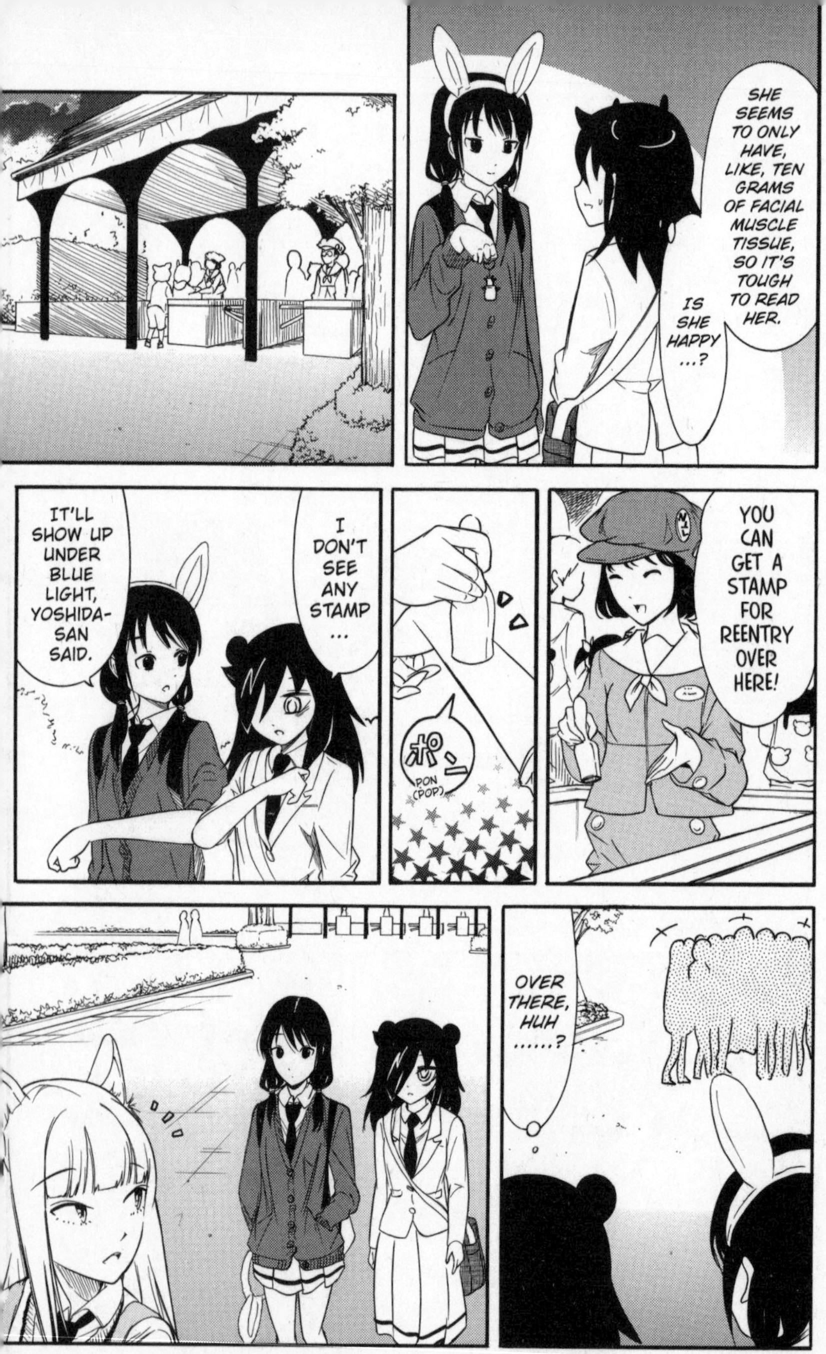
SHE SEEMS TO ONLY HAVE, LIKE, TEN GRAMS OF FACIAL MUSCLE TISSUE, SO IT'S TOUGH TO READ HER.
IS SHE HAPPY ...?
YOU CAN GET A STAMP FOR REENTRY OVER HERE!
ポン
PON (POP)
I DON'T SEE ANY STAMP ...
IT'LL SHOW UP UNDER BLUE LIGHT, YOSHIDA-SAN SAID.
OVER THERE, HUH ......?

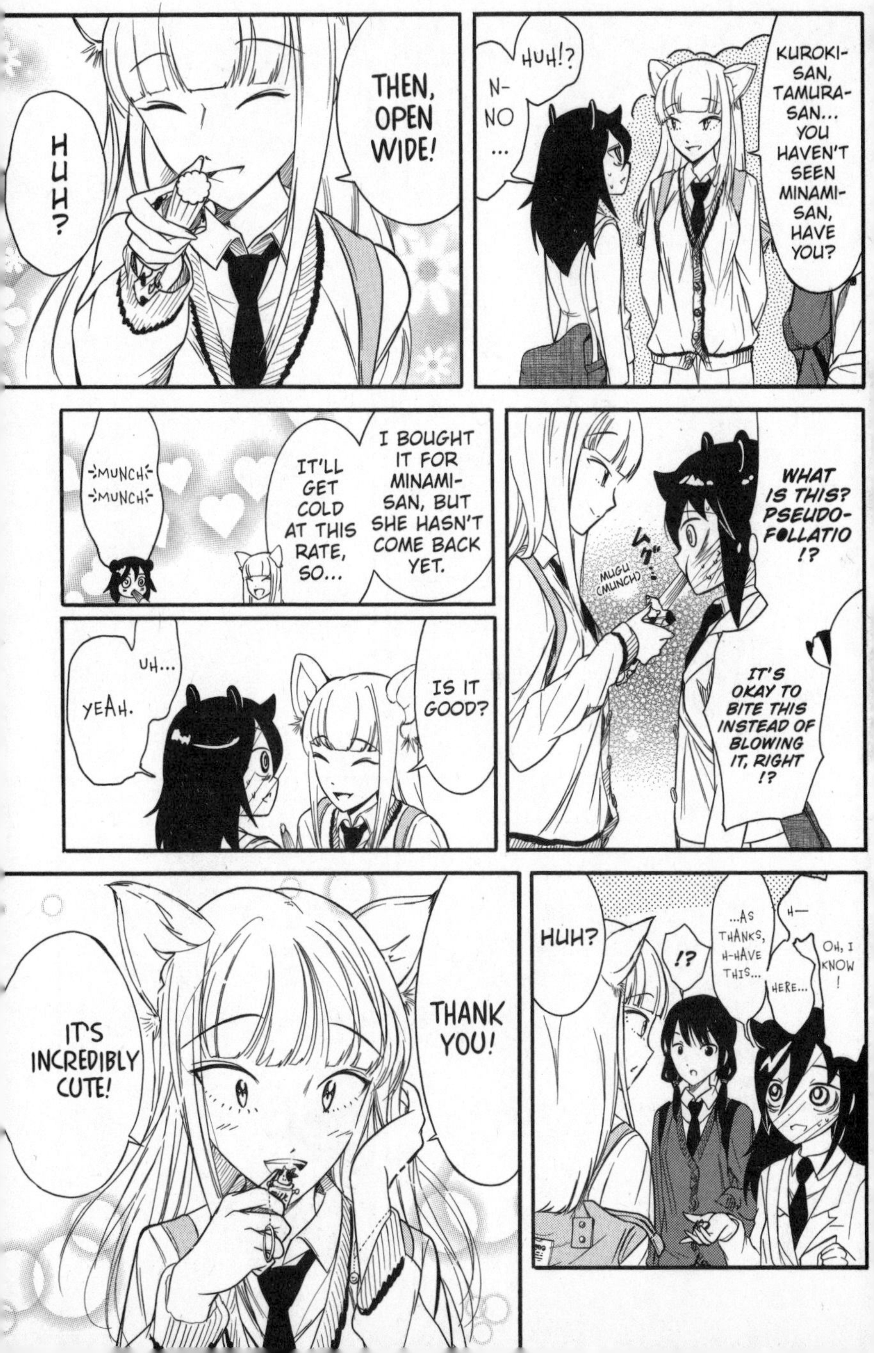
KUROKI-SAN, TAMURA-SAN... YOU HAVEN'T SEEN MINAMI-SAN, HAVE YOU?
HUH!?
N-NO ...
THEN, OPEN WIDE!
HUH?
WHAT IS THIS? PSEUDO-FOLLATIO !?
ムグ
MUGU (MUNCH)
IT'S OKAY TO BITE THIS INSTEAD OF BLOWING IT, RIGHT !?
I BOUGHT IT FOR MINAMI-SAN, BUT SHE HASN'T COME BACK YET.
IT'LL GET COLD AT THIS RATE, SO...
MUNCH MUNCH
IS IT GOOD?
UH...
YEAH.
H—
OH, I KNOW!
HERE...
...AS THANKS, H-HAVE THIS...
!?
HUH?
THANK YOU!
IT'S INCREDIBLY CUTE!

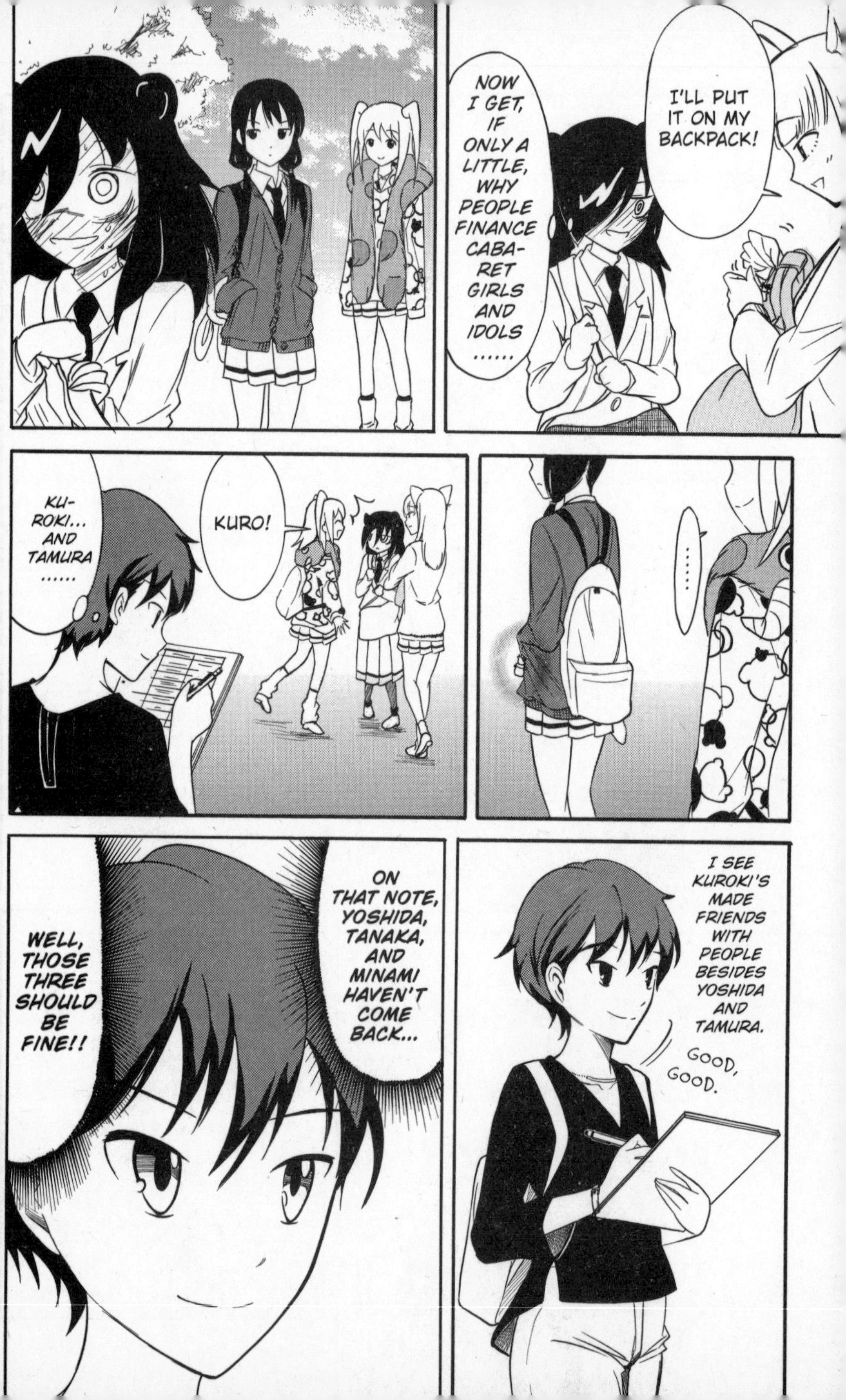
I'LL PUT IT ON MY BACKPACK!
NOW I GET, IF ONLY A LITTLE, WHY PEOPLE FINANCE CABA-RET GIRLS AND IDOLS ......
......
KURO!
KU-ROKI... AND TAMURA ......
I SEE KUROKI'S MADE FRIENDS WITH PEOPLE BESIDES YOSHIDA AND TAMURA.
GOOD, GOOD.
ON THAT NOTE, YOSHIDA, TANAKA, AND MINAMI HAVEN'T COME BACK...
WELL, THOSE THREE SHOULD BE FINE!!

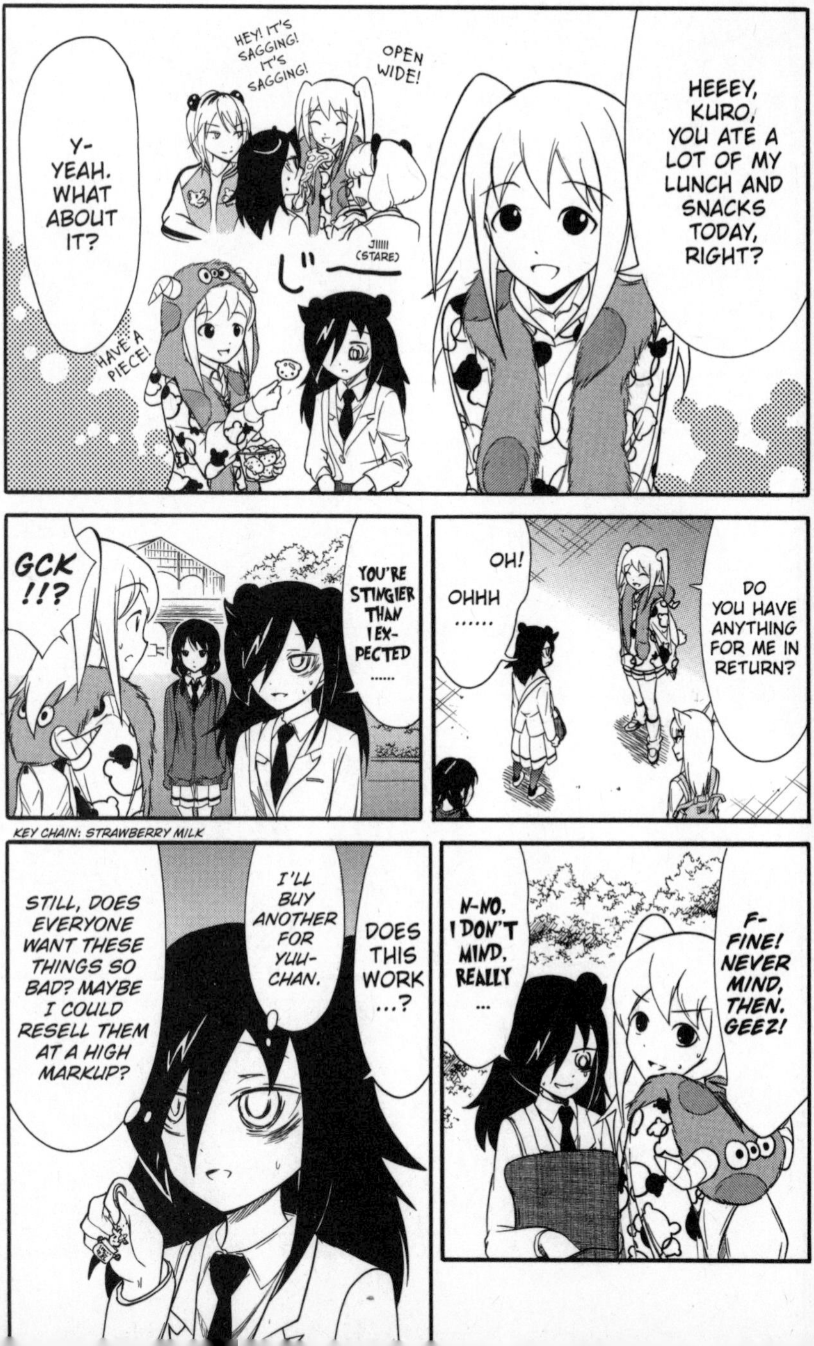
HEEEY, KURO, YOU ATE A LOT OF MY LUNCH AND SNACKS TODAY, RIGHT?
OPEN WIDE!
HEY! IT'S SAGGING! IT'S SAGGING!
Y-YEAH. WHAT ABOUT IT?
JIIIII (STARE)
HAVE A PIECE!
DO YOU HAVE ANYTHING FOR ME IN RETURN?
OH!
OHHH ......
YOU'RE STINGIER THAN I EXPECTED ......
GCK !!?
KEY CHAIN: STRAWBERRY MILK
F-FINE! NEVER MIND, THEN. GEEZ!
N-NO. I DON'T MIND, REALLY ...
DOES THIS WORK ...?
I'LL BUY ANOTHER FOR YUU-CHAN.
STILL, DOES EVERYONE WANT THESE THINGS SO BAD? MAYBE I COULD RESELL THEM AT A HIGH MARKUP?

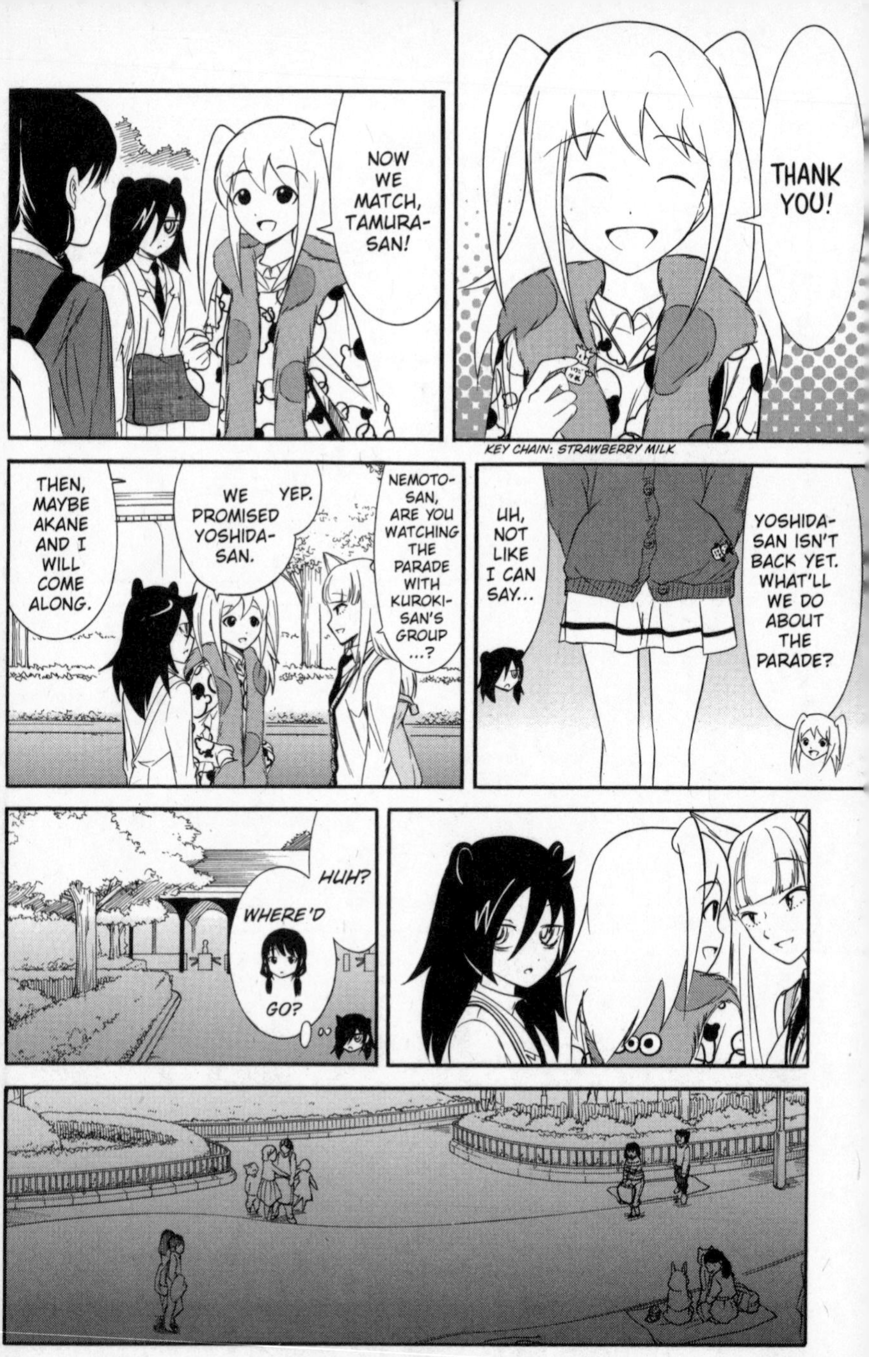
THANK YOU!
KEY CHAIN: STRAWBERRY MILK
NOW WE MATCH, TAMURA-SAN!
YOSHIDA-SAN ISN'T BACK YET. WHAT'LL WE DO ABOUT THE PARADE?
UH, NOT LIKE I CAN SAY...
NEMOTO-SAN, ARE YOU WATCHING THE PARADE WITH KUROKI-SAN'S GROUP ...?
YEP.
WE PROMISED YOSHIDA-SAN.
THEN, MAYBE AKANE AND I WILL COME ALONG.
HUH?
WHERE'D
GO?

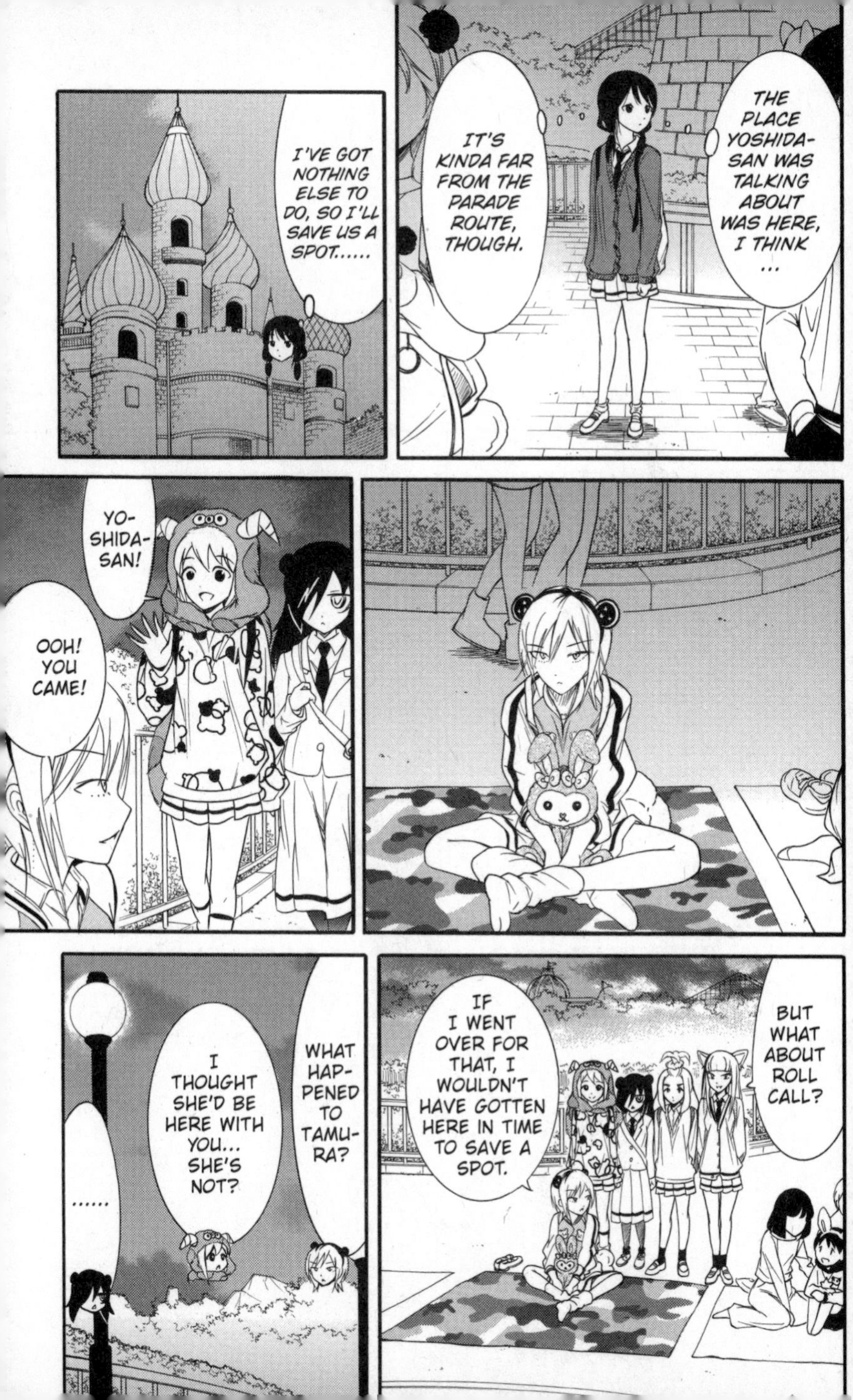
THE PLACE YOSHIDA-SAN WAS TALKING ABOUT WAS HERE, I THINK...
IT'S KINDA FAR FROM THE PARADE ROUTE, THOUGH.
I'VE GOT NOTHING ELSE TO DO, SO I'LL SAVE US A SPOT......
YO-SHIDA-SAN!
OOH! YOU CAME!
...
BUT WHAT ABOUT ROLL CALL?
IF I WENT OVER FOR THAT, I WOULDN'T HAVE GOTTEN HERE IN TIME TO SAVE A SPOT.
WHAT HAP-PENED TO TAMU-RA?
I THOUGHT SHE'D BE HERE WITH YOU... SHE'S NOT?
......

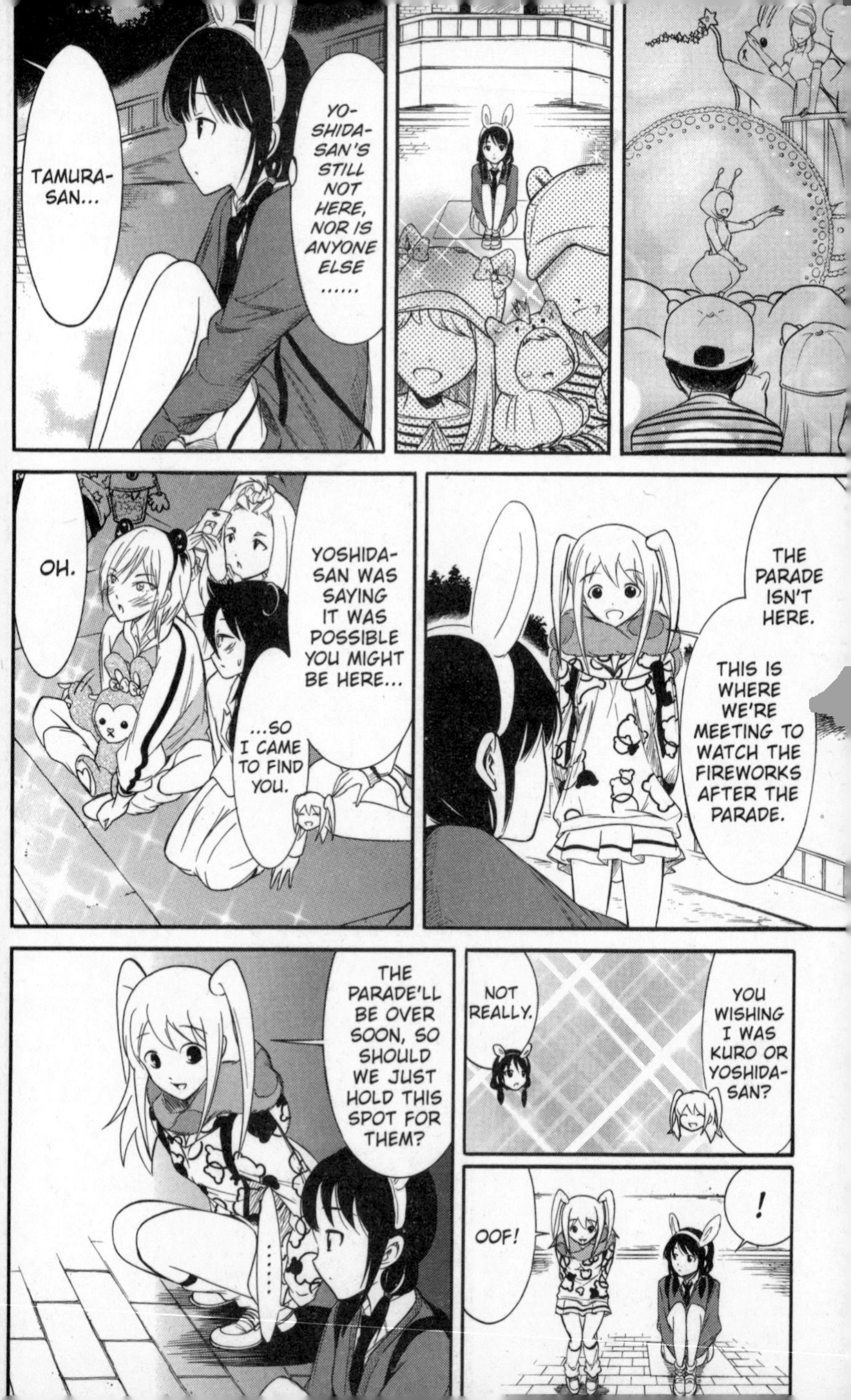
YO-SHIDA-SAN'S STILL NOT HERE, NOR IS ANYONE ELSE ......
TAMURA-SAN...
THE PARADE ISN'T HERE.
THIS IS WHERE WE'RE MEETING TO WATCH THE FIREWORKS AFTER THE PARADE.
YOSHIDA-SAN WAS SAYING IT WAS POSSIBLE YOU MIGHT BE HERE...
...SO I CAME TO FIND YOU.
OH.
YOU WISHING I WAS KURO OR YOSHIDA-SAN?
NOT REALLY.
!
OOF!
THE PARADE'LL BE OVER SOON, SO SHOULD WE JUST HOLD THIS SPOT FOR THEM?
......

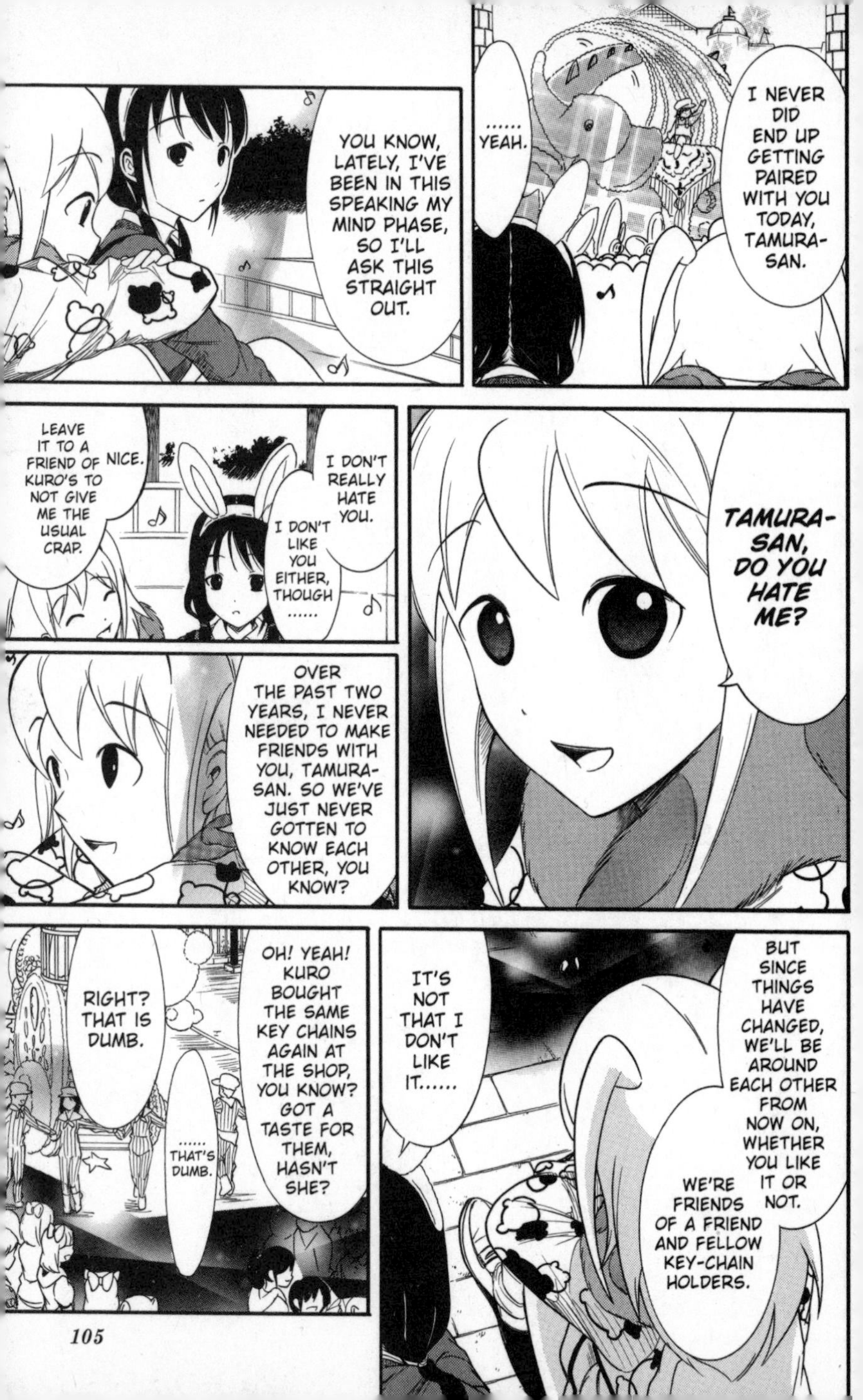
I NEVER DID END UP GETTING PAIRED WITH YOU TODAY, TAMURA-SAN.
......YEAH.
YOU KNOW, LATELY, I'VE BEEN IN THIS SPEAKING MY MIND PHASE, SO I'LL ASK THIS STRAIGHT OUT.
TAMURA-SAN, DO YOU HATE ME?
I DON'T REALLY HATE YOU.
I DON'T LIKE YOU EITHER, THOUGH......
NICE.
LEAVE IT TO A FRIEND OF KURO'S TO NOT GIVE ME THE USUAL CRAP.
OVER THE PAST TWO YEARS, I NEVER NEEDED TO MAKE FRIENDS WITH YOU, TAMURA-SAN. SO WE'VE JUST NEVER GOTTEN TO KNOW EACH OTHER, YOU KNOW?
BUT SINCE THINGS HAVE CHANGED, WE'LL BE AROUND EACH OTHER FROM NOW ON, WHETHER YOU LIKE IT OR NOT.
WE'RE FRIENDS OF A FRIEND AND FELLOW KEY-CHAIN HOLDERS.
IT'S NOT THAT I DON'T LIKE IT......
OH! YEAH! KURO BOUGHT THE SAME KEY CHAINS AGAIN AT THE SHOP, YOU KNOW? GOT A TASTE FOR THEM, HASN'T SHE?
......THAT'S DUMB.
RIGHT? THAT IS DUMB.

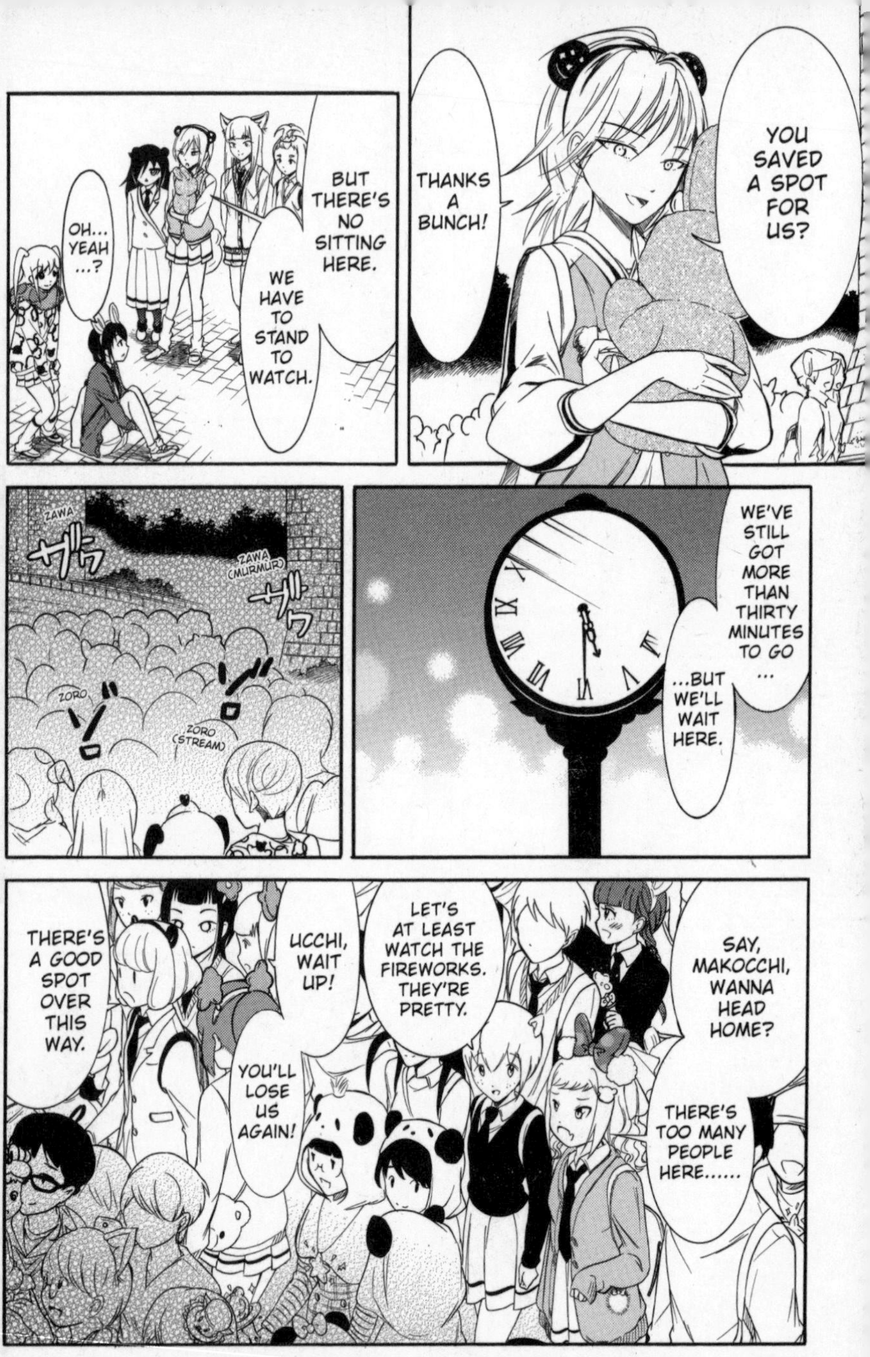
YOU SAVED A SPOT FOR US?
THANKS A BUNCH!
BUT THERE'S NO SITTING HERE.
WE HAVE TO STAND TO WATCH.
OH... YEAH ...?
WE'VE STILL GOT MORE THAN THIRTY MINUTES TO GO ...
...BUT WE'LL WAIT HERE.
ZAWA
ZAWA (MURMUR)
ZORO
ZORO (STREAM)
SAY, MAKOCCHI, WANNA HEAD HOME?
THERE'S TOO MANY PEOPLE HERE......
LET'S AT LEAST WATCH THE FIREWORKS. THEY'RE PRETTY.
UCCHI, WAIT UP!
YOU'LL LOSE US AGAIN!
THERE'S A GOOD SPOT OVER THIS WAY.

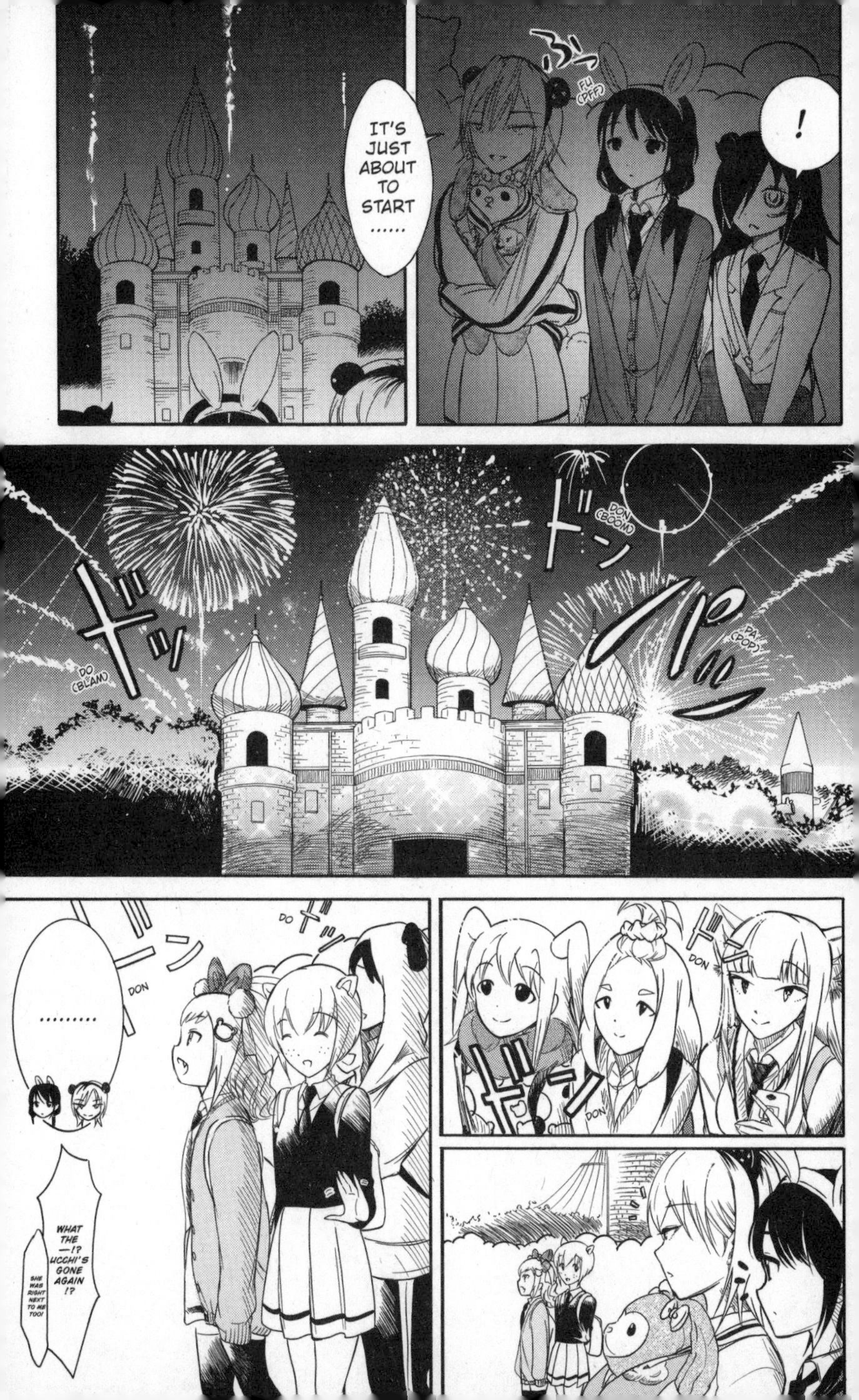
FU (PFF)
!
IT'S JUST ABOUT TO START ......
DON (BOOM)
PA (POP)
DO (BLAM)
DON
DON
DO
DON
....
WHAT THE—!? UCCHI'S GONE AGAIN !?
SHE WAS RIGHT NEXT TO ME TOO!

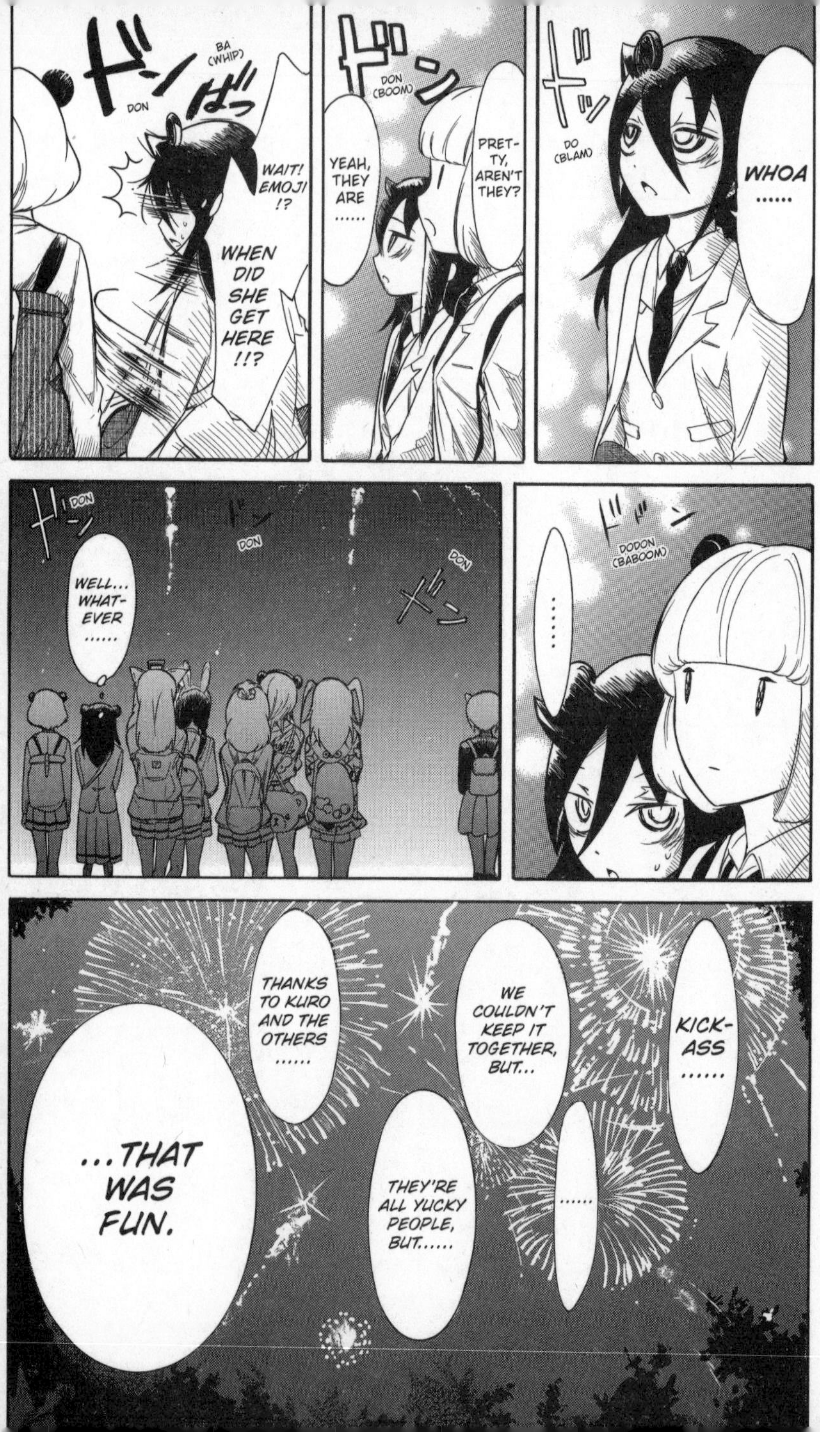
DO (BLAM)
WHOA ......
DON (BOOM)
PRET-TY, AREN'T THEY?
YEAH, THEY ARE ......
DON
BA (WHIP)
WAIT! EMOJI!?
WHEN DID SHE GET HERE!!?
DODON (BABOOM)
......
DON
DON
DON
WELL... WHATEVER ......
KICK-ASS ......
WE COULDN'T KEEP IT TOGETHER, BUT...
......
THANKS TO KURO AND THE OTHERS ......
THEY'RE ALL YUCKY PEOPLE, BUT......
...THAT WAS FUN.

No Matter How I
Look at It, It's You
Guys' Fault I'm Not
Popular!

CROWD, SUB, AND MAIN CHARACTERS

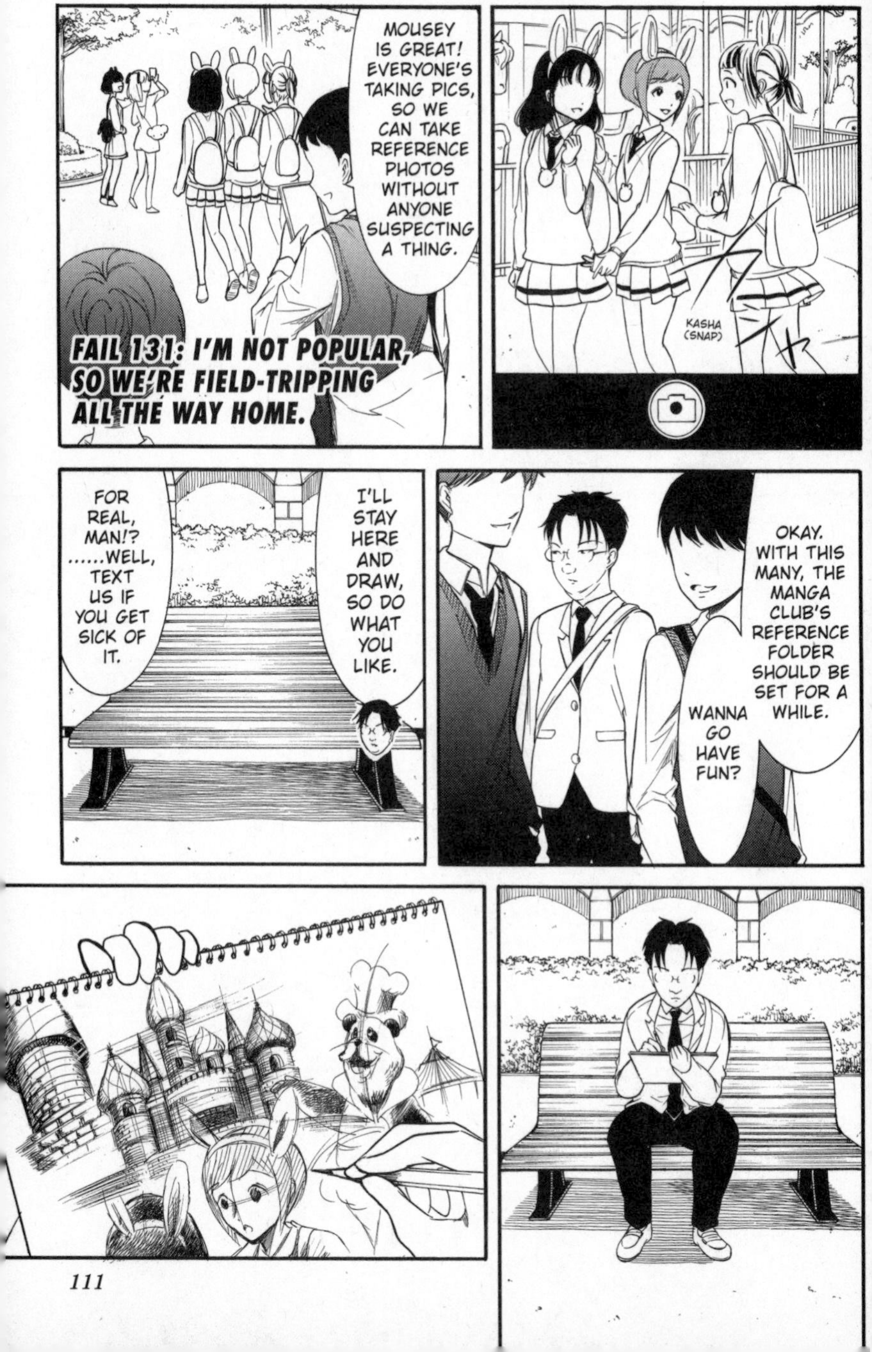
KASHA (SNAP)
MOUSEY IS GREAT! EVERYONE'S TAKING PICS, SO WE CAN TAKE REFERENCE PHOTOS WITHOUT ANYONE SUSPECTING A THING.
FAIL 131: I'M NOT POPULAR, SO WE'RE FIELD-TRIPPING ALL THE WAY HOME.
OKAY. WITH THIS MANY, THE MANGA CLUB'S REFERENCE FOLDER SHOULD BE SET FOR A WHILE.
WANNA GO HAVE FUN?
I'LL STAY HERE AND DRAW, SO DO WHAT YOU LIKE.
FOR REAL, MAN!? ......WELL, TEXT US IF YOU GET SICK OF IT.

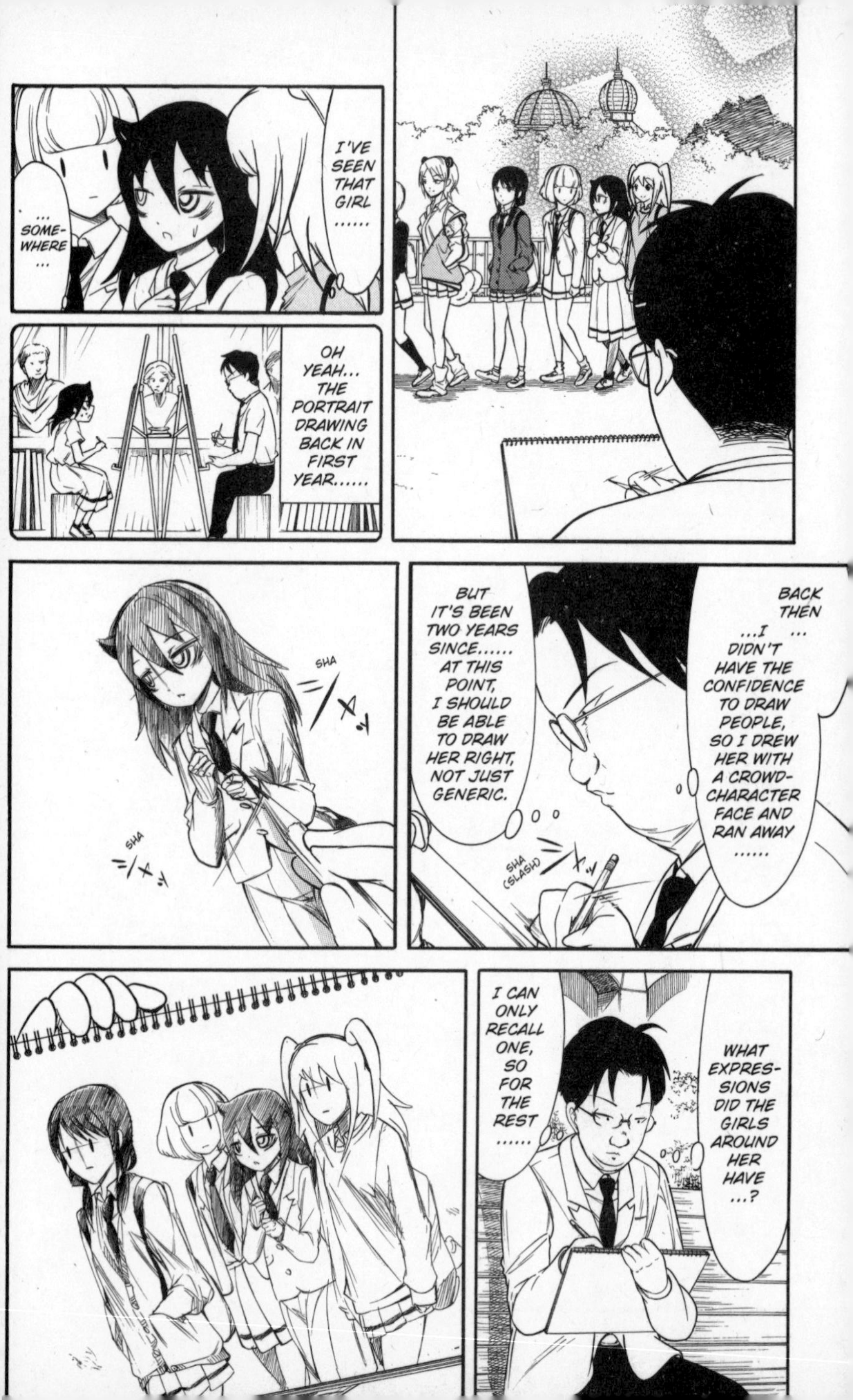
I'VE SEEN THAT GIRL......
...SOMEWHERE...
OH YEAH... THE PORTRAIT DRAWING BACK IN FIRST YEAR......
BACK THEN... ...I DIDN'T HAVE THE CONFIDENCE TO DRAW PEOPLE, SO I DREW HER WITH A CROWD-CHARACTER FACE AND RAN AWAY......
BUT IT'S BEEN TWO YEARS SINCE...... AT THIS POINT, I SHOULD BE ABLE TO DRAW HER RIGHT, NOT JUST GENERIC.
SHA (SLASH)
SHA
SHA
WHAT EXPRESSIONS DID THE GIRLS AROUND HER HAVE...?
I CAN ONLY RECALL ONE, SO FOR THE REST......

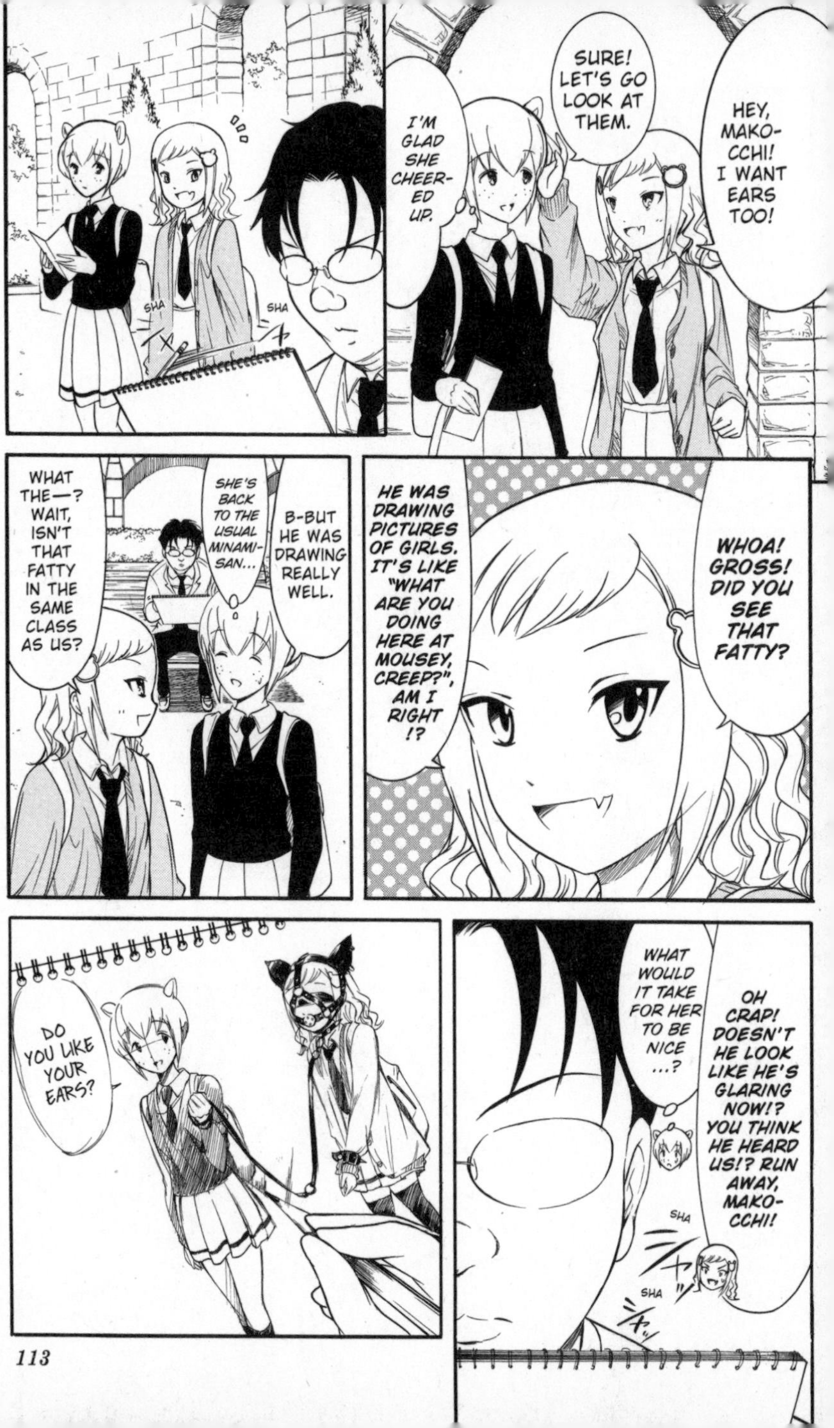
HEY, MAKO-CCHI! I WANT EARS TOO!
SURE! LET'S GO LOOK AT THEM.
I'M GLAD SHE CHEER-ED UP.
SHA
SHA
WHOA! GROSS! DID YOU SEE THAT FATTY?
HE WAS DRAWING PICTURES OF GIRLS. IT'S LIKE "WHAT ARE YOU DOING HERE AT MOUSEY, CREEP?", AM I RIGHT!?
B-BUT HE WAS DRAWING REALLY WELL.
SHE'S BACK TO THE USUAL MINAMI-SAN...
WHAT THE—? WAIT, ISN'T THAT FATTY IN THE SAME CLASS AS US?
OH CRAP! DOESN'T HE LOOK LIKE HE'S GLARING NOW!? YOU THINK HE HEARD US!? RUN AWAY, MAKO-CCHI!
WHAT WOULD IT TAKE FOR HER TO BE NICE ...?
SHA
SHA
DO YOU LIKE YOUR EARS?

THE LINK

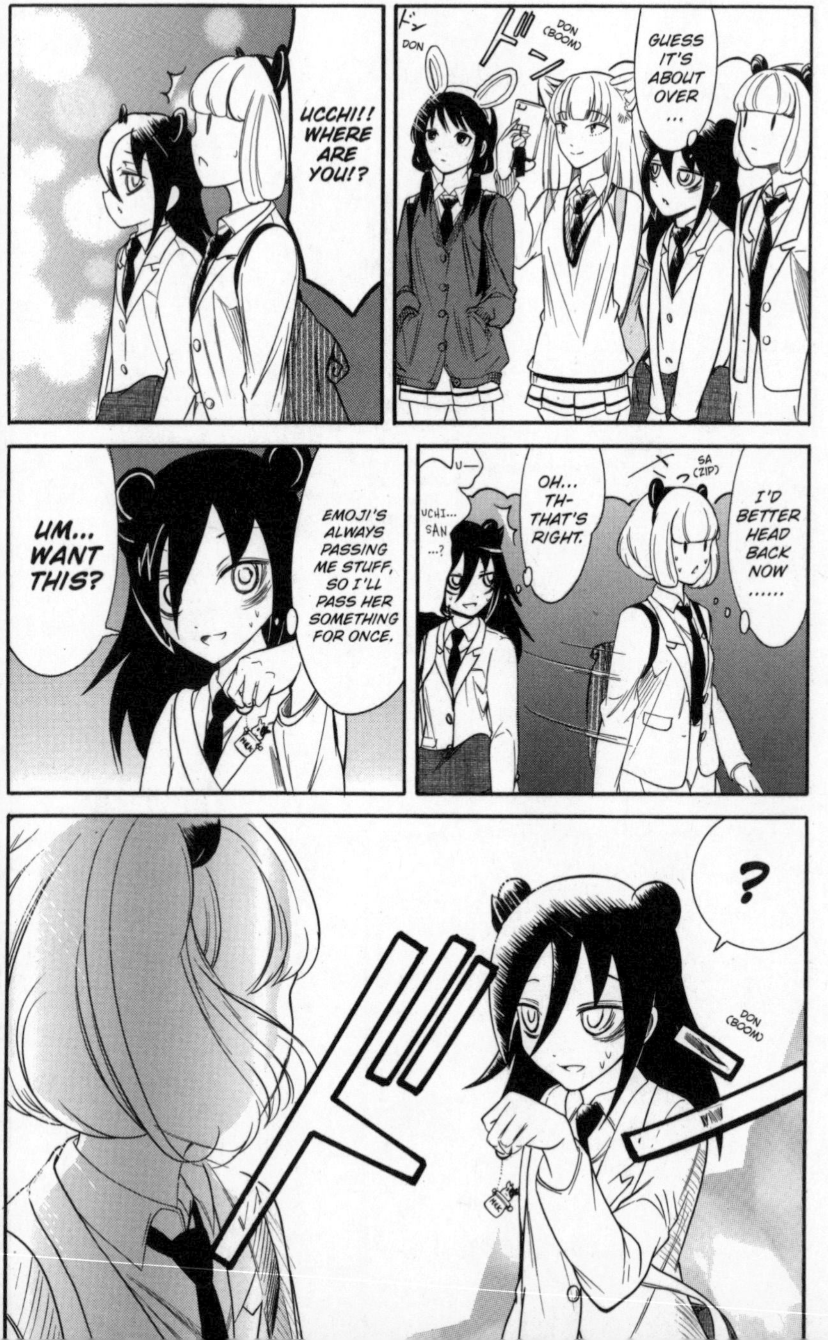
GUESS IT'S ABOUT OVER ...
DON (BOOM)
ドン
DON
UCCHI!! WHERE ARE YOU!?
I'D BETTER HEAD BACK NOW ......
SA (ZIP)
OH... TH-THAT'S RIGHT.
U—
UCHI... SAN ...?
EMOJI'S ALWAYS PASSING ME STUFF, SO I'LL PASS HER SOMETHING FOR ONCE.
UM... WANT THIS?
?
DON (BOOM)

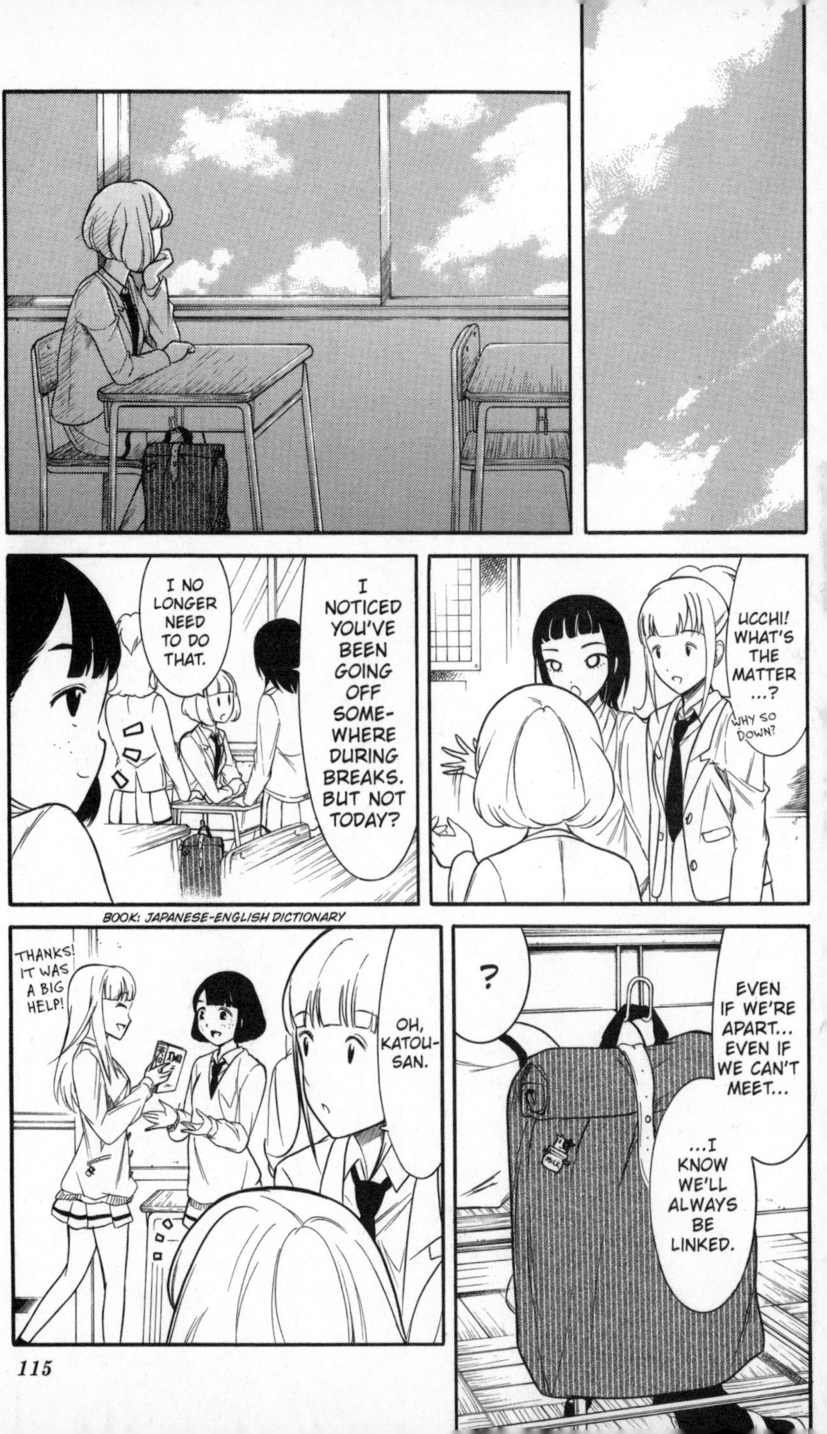
UCCHI! WHAT'S THE MATTER ...?
WHY SO DOWN?
I NOTICED YOU'VE BEEN GOING OFF SOME-WHERE DURING BREAKS. BUT NOT TODAY?
I NO LONGER NEED TO DO THAT.
BOOK: JAPANESE-ENGLISH DICTIONARY
?
EVEN IF WE'RE APART... EVEN IF WE CAN'T MEET...
...I KNOW WE'LL ALWAYS BE LINKED.
OH, KATOU-SAN.
THANKS! IT WAS A BIG HELP!

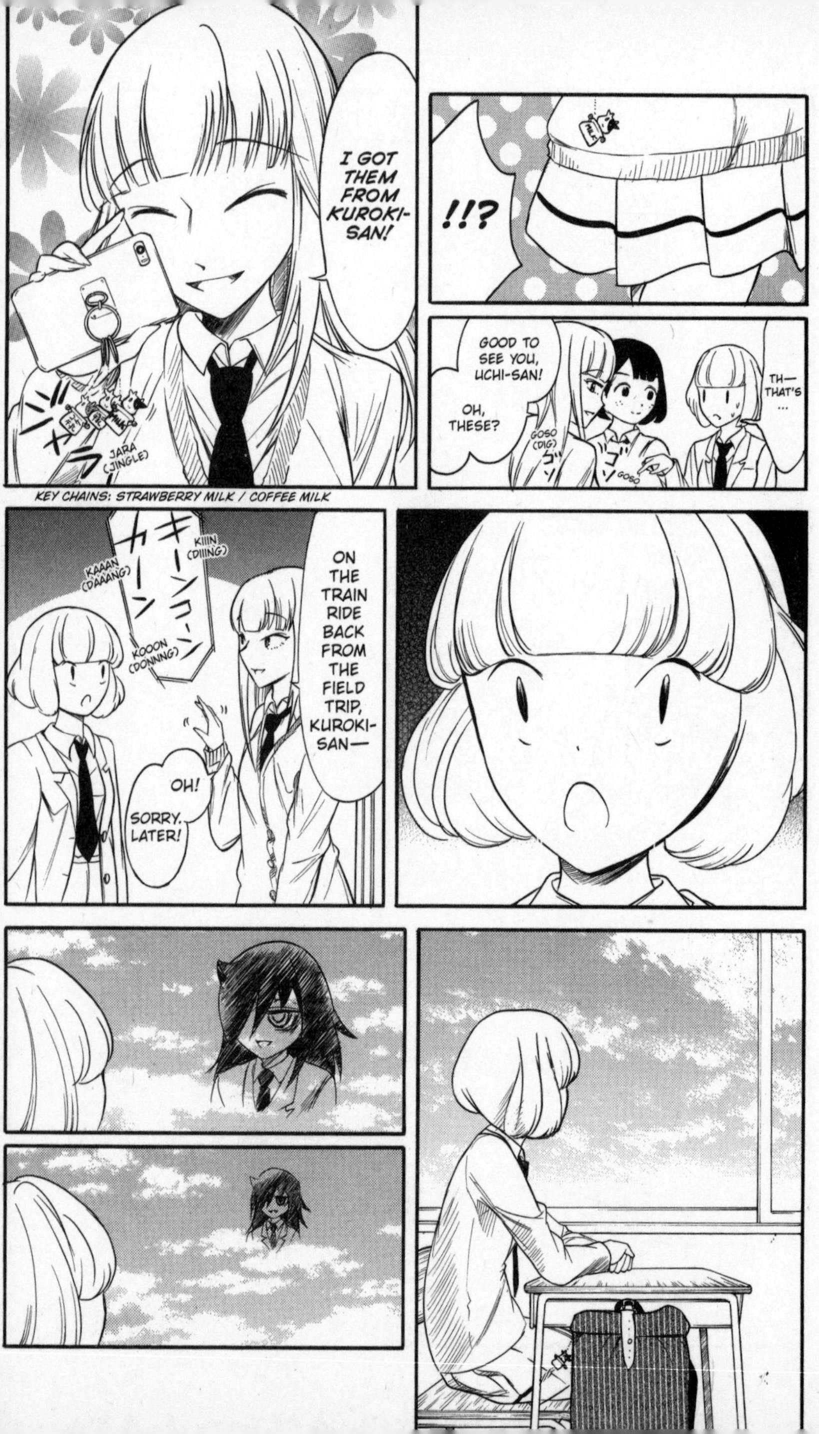
!!?
TH— THAT'S ...
GOOD TO SEE YOU, UCHI-SAN!
OH, THESE?
GOSO (DIG)
GOSO
I GOT THEM FROM KUROKI-SAN!
JARA (JINGLE)
KEY CHAINS: STRAWBERRY MILK / COFFEE MILK
ON THE TRAIN RIDE BACK FROM THE FIELD TRIP, KUROKI-SAN—
KIIIN (DIIING)
KAAAN (DAAANG)
KOOON (DONNING)
OH!
SORRY. LATER!

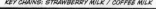

HEAD OVER HEELS

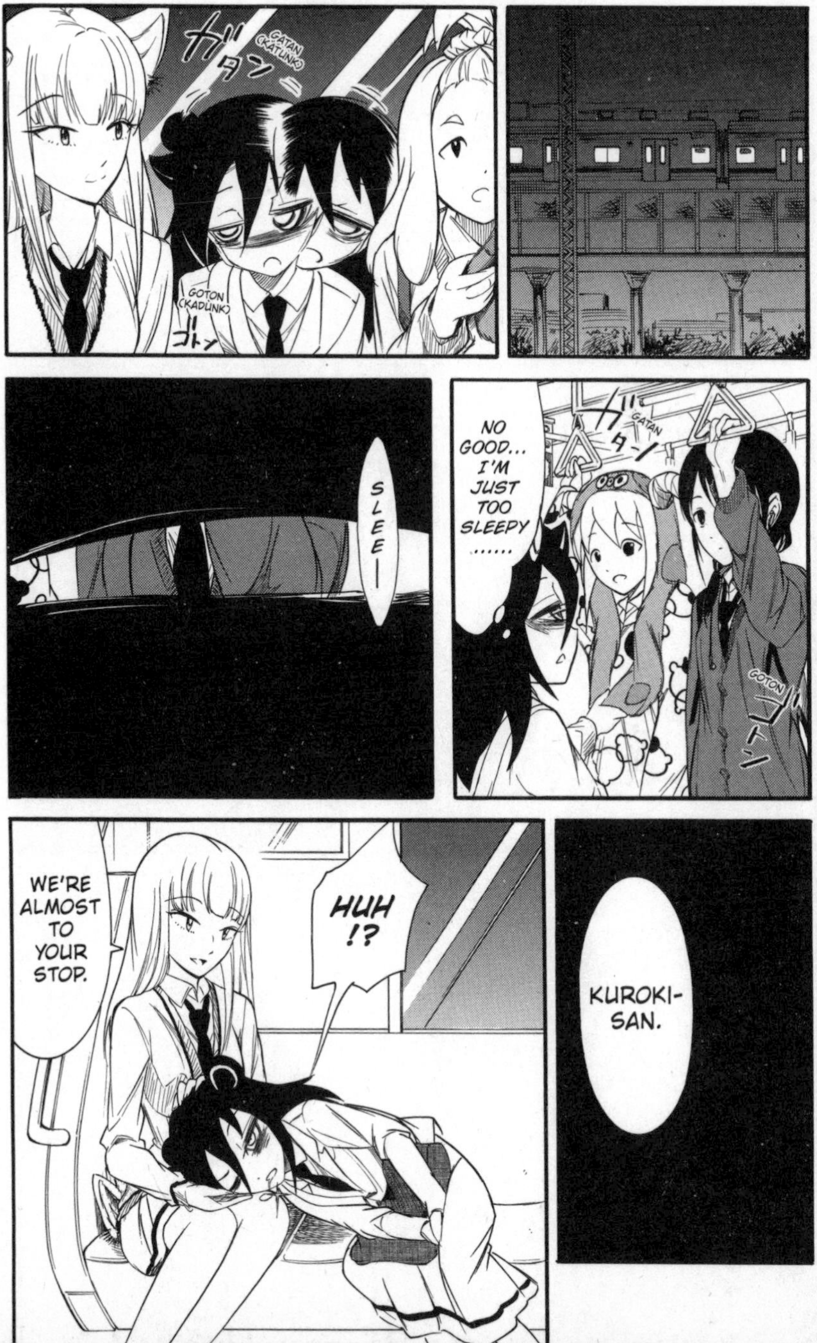

GATAN (KATUNK)
GOTON (KADUNK)
NO GOOD... I'M JUST TOO SLEEPY.......
GATAN
GOTON
SLEE—
KUROKI-SAN.
WE'RE ALMOST TO YOUR STOP.
HUH !?

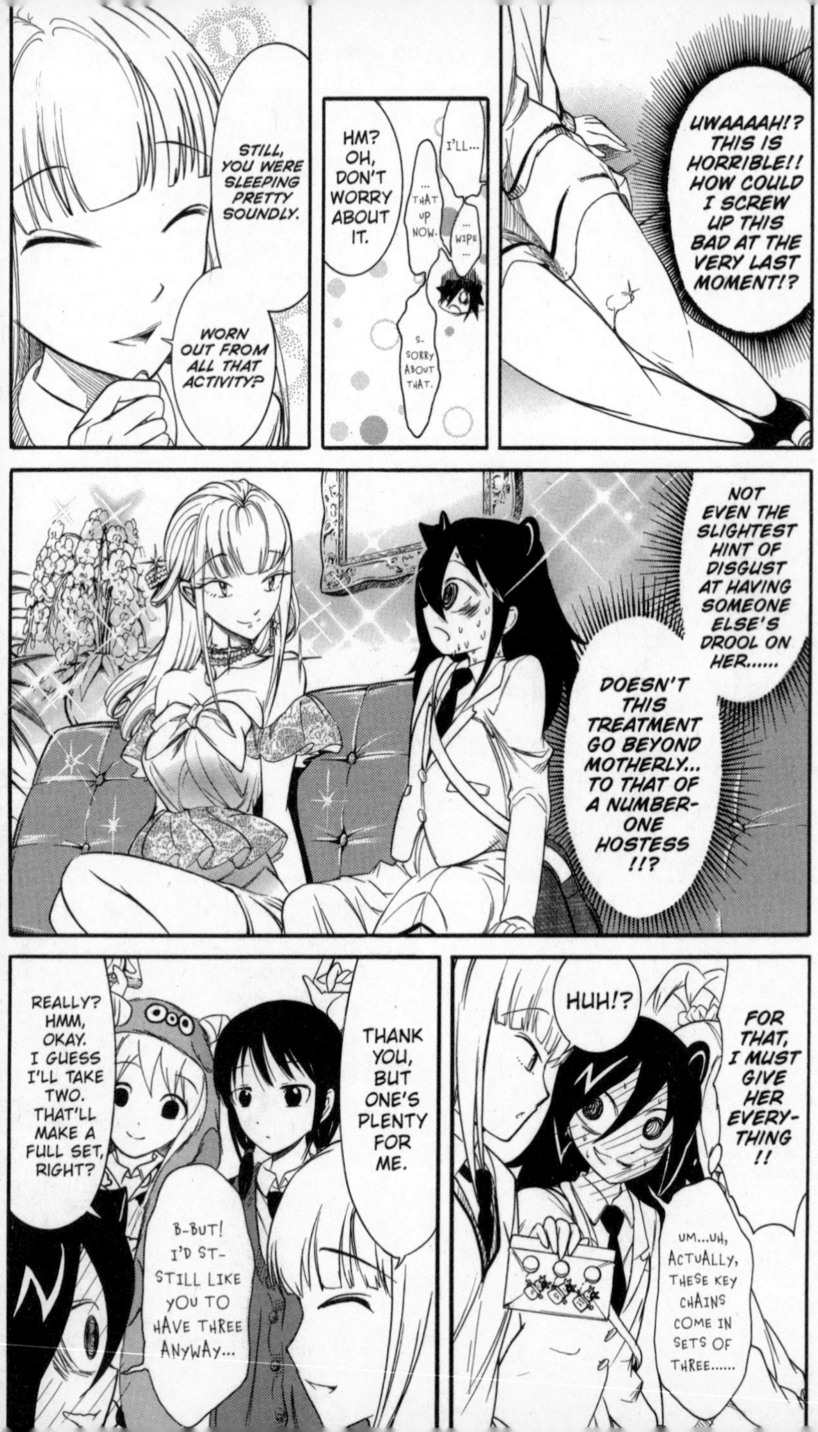
UWAAAAH!? THIS IS HORRIBLE!! HOW COULD I SCREW UP THIS BAD AT THE VERY LAST MOMENT!?
I'LL...
...WIPE...
...THAT UP NOW.
HM? OH, DON'T WORRY ABOUT IT.
S-SORRY ABOUT THAT.
STILL, YOU WERE SLEEPING PRETTY SOUNDLY.
WORN OUT FROM ALL THAT ACTIVITY?
NOT EVEN THE SLIGHTEST HINT OF DISGUST AT HAVING SOMEONE ELSE'S DROOL ON HER......
DOESN'T THIS TREATMENT GO BEYOND MOTHERLY... TO THAT OF A NUMBER-ONE HOSTESS!!?
FOR THAT, I MUST GIVE HER EVERYTHING!!
HUH!?
UM...UH, ACTUALLY, THESE KEY CHAINS COME IN SETS OF THREE......
THANK YOU, BUT ONE'S PLENTY FOR ME.
REALLY? HMM, OKAY. I GUESS I'LL TAKE TWO. THAT'LL MAKE A FULL SET, RIGHT?
B-BUT! I'D ST-STILL LIKE YOU TO HAVE THREE ANYWAY...

NoMatter **How** I **Look** at It, **It's** You **Guys' Fault** I'm **Not** **Popular!**

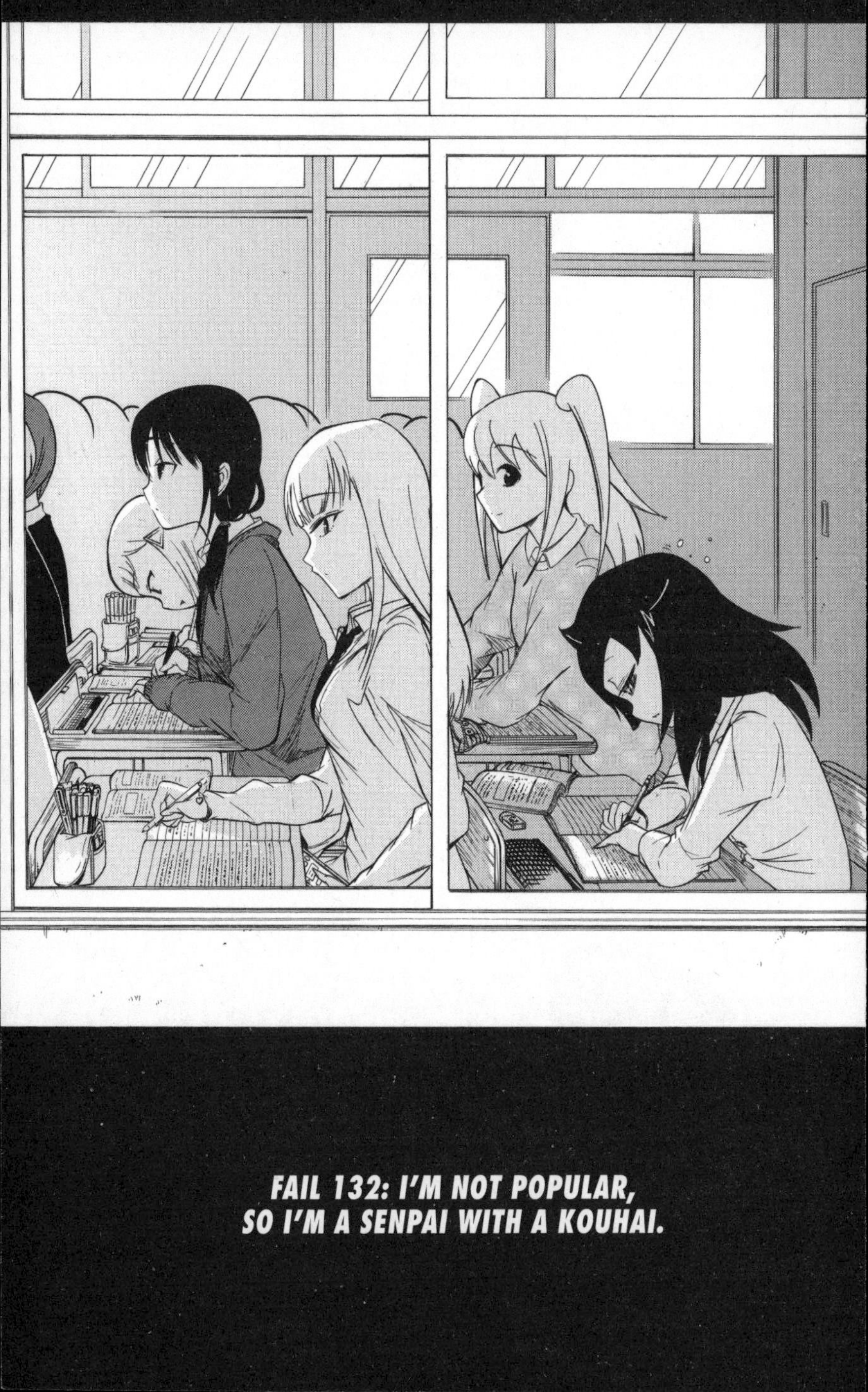

FAIL 132: I'M NOT POPULAR, SO I'M A SENPAI WITH A KOUHAI.

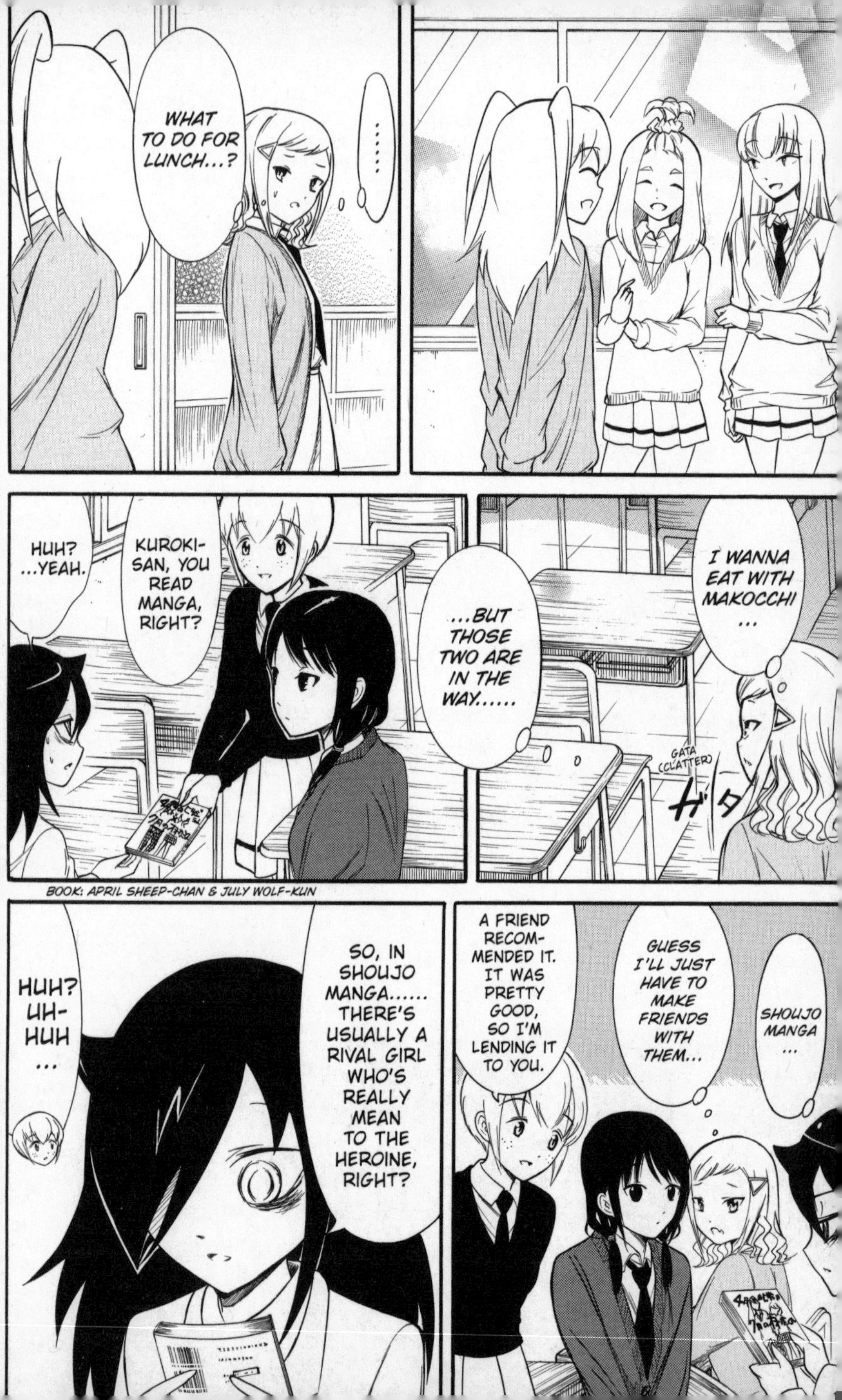
......
WHAT TO DO FOR LUNCH...?
I WANNA EAT WITH MAKOCCHI...
...BUT THOSE TWO ARE IN THE WAY......
GATA (CLATTER)
KUROKI-SAN, YOU READ MANGA, RIGHT?
HUH? ...YEAH.
BOOK: APRIL SHEEP-CHAN & JULY WOLF-KUN
SHOUJO MANGA...
GUESS I'LL JUST HAVE TO MAKE FRIENDS WITH THEM...
A FRIEND RECOMMENDED IT. IT WAS PRETTY GOOD, SO I'M LENDING IT TO YOU.
SO, IN SHOUJO MANGA...... THERE'S USUALLY A RIVAL GIRL WHO'S REALLY MEAN TO THE HEROINE, RIGHT?
HUH? UH-HUH...

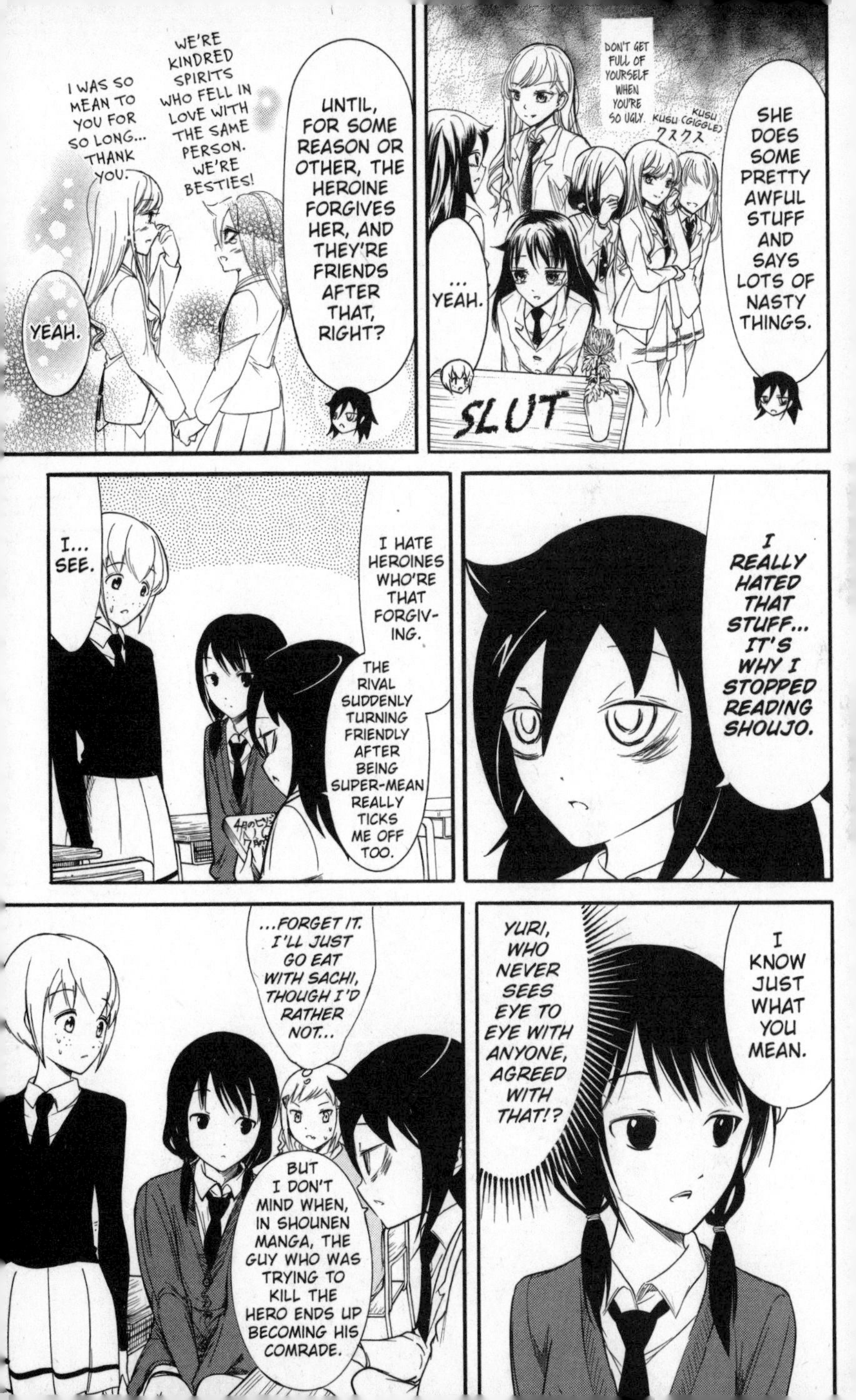
SHE DOES SOME PRETTY AWFUL STUFF AND SAYS LOTS OF NASTY THINGS.
DON'T GET FULL OF YOURSELF WHEN YOU'RE SO UGLY.
KUSU KUSU (GIGGLE) クスクス
... YEAH.
SLUT
UNTIL, FOR SOME REASON OR OTHER, THE HEROINE FORGIVES HER, AND THEY'RE FRIENDS AFTER THAT, RIGHT?
WE'RE KINDRED SPIRITS WHO FELL IN LOVE WITH THE SAME PERSON. WE'RE BESTIES!
I WAS SO MEAN TO YOU FOR SO LONG... THANK YOU.
YEAH.
I REALLY HATED THAT STUFF... IT'S WHY I STOPPED READING SHOUJO.
I HATE HEROINES WHO'RE THAT FORGIVING.
THE RIVAL SUDDENLY TURNING FRIENDLY AFTER BEING SUPER-MEAN REALLY TICKS ME OFF TOO.
I... SEE.
I KNOW JUST WHAT YOU MEAN.
YURI, WHO NEVER SEES EYE TO EYE WITH ANYONE, AGREED WITH THAT!?
...FORGET IT. I'LL JUST GO EAT WITH SACHI, THOUGH I'D RATHER NOT...
BUT I DON'T MIND WHEN, IN SHOUNEN MANGA, THE GUY WHO WAS TRYING TO KILL THE HERO ENDS UP BECOMING HIS COMRADE.

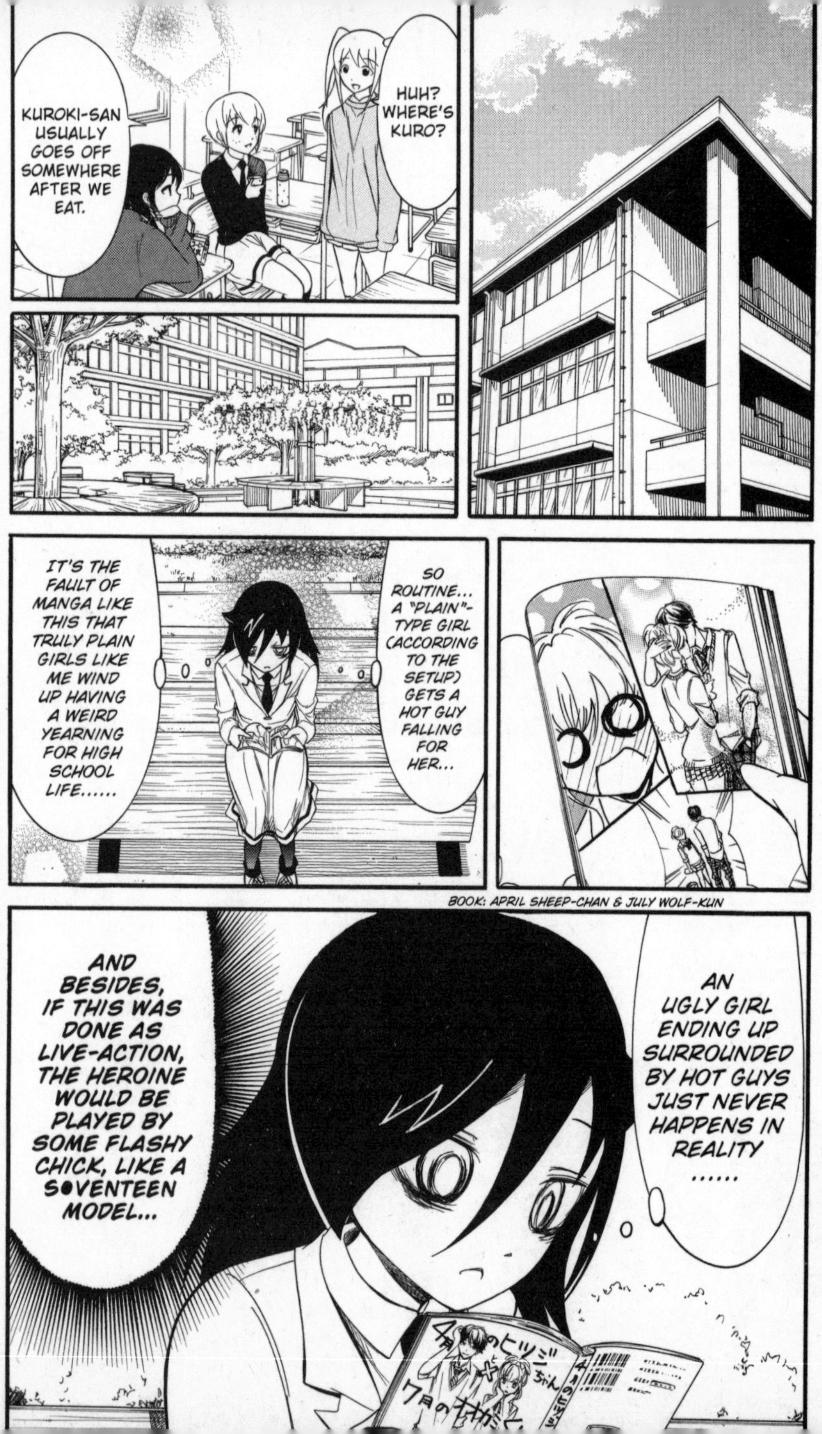
HUH? WHERE'S KURO?
KUROKI-SAN USUALLY GOES OFF SOMEWHERE AFTER WE EAT.
BOOK: APRIL SHEEP-CHAN & JULY WOLF-KUN
SO ROUTINE... A "PLAIN"-TYPE GIRL (ACCORDING TO THE SETUP) GETS A HOT GUY FALLING FOR HER...
IT'S THE FAULT OF MANGA LIKE THIS THAT TRULY PLAIN GIRLS LIKE ME WIND UP HAVING A WEIRD YEARNING FOR HIGH SCHOOL LIFE......
AN UGLY GIRL ENDING UP SURROUNDED BY HOT GUYS JUST NEVER HAPPENS IN REALITY ......
AND BESIDES, IF THIS WAS DONE AS LIVE-ACTION, THE HEROINE WOULD BE PLAYED BY SOME FLASHY CHICK, LIKE A S●VENTEEN MODEL...

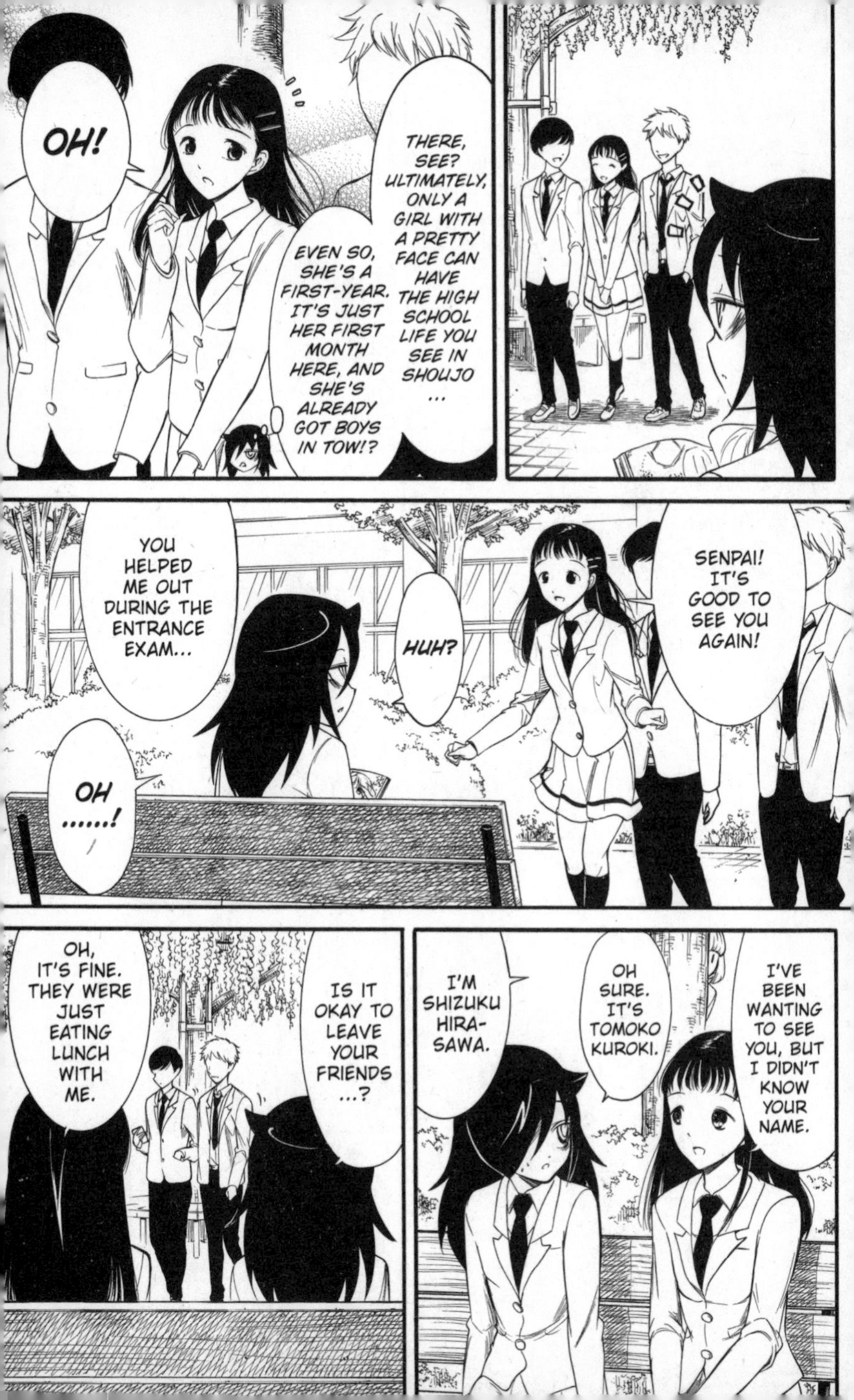

THERE, SEE? ULTIMATELY, ONLY A GIRL WITH A PRETTY FACE CAN HAVE THE HIGH SCHOOL LIFE YOU SEE IN SHOUJO...
EVEN SO, SHE'S A FIRST-YEAR. IT'S JUST HER FIRST MONTH HERE, AND SHE'S ALREADY GOT BOYS IN TOW!?
OH!
SENPAI! IT'S GOOD TO SEE YOU AGAIN!
HUH?
YOU HELPED ME OUT DURING THE ENTRANCE EXAM...
OH ......!
I'VE BEEN WANTING TO SEE YOU, BUT I DIDN'T KNOW YOUR NAME.
OH SURE. IT'S TOMOKO KUROKI.
I'M SHIZUKU HIRA-SAWA.
IS IT OKAY TO LEAVE YOUR FRIENDS...?
OH, IT'S FINE. THEY WERE JUST EATING LUNCH WITH ME.

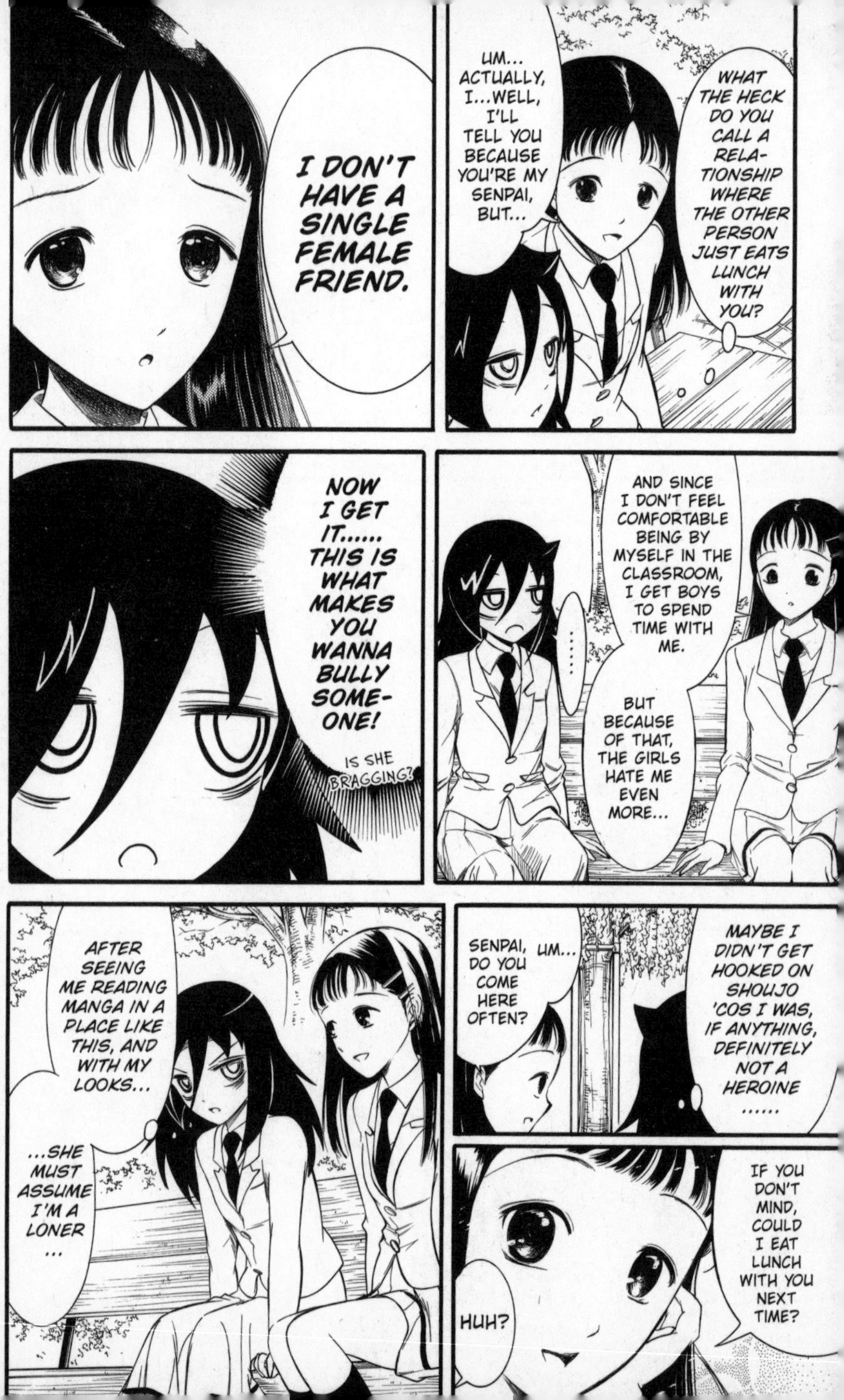
WHAT THE HECK DO YOU CALL A RELATIONSHIP WHERE THE OTHER PERSON JUST EATS LUNCH WITH YOU?
UM... ACTUALLY, I...WELL, I'LL TELL YOU BECAUSE YOU'RE MY SENPAI, BUT...
I DON'T HAVE A SINGLE FEMALE FRIEND.
AND SINCE I DON'T FEEL COMFORTABLE BEING BY MYSELF IN THE CLASSROOM, I GET BOYS TO SPEND TIME WITH ME.
BUT BECAUSE OF THAT, THE GIRLS HATE ME EVEN MORE...
......
NOW I GET IT...... THIS IS WHAT MAKES YOU WANNA BULLY SOME-ONE!
IS SHE BRAGGING?
MAYBE I DIDN'T GET HOOKED ON SHOUJO 'COS I WAS, IF ANYTHING, DEFINITELY NOT A HEROINE ......
UM...
SENPAI, DO YOU COME HERE OFTEN?
IF YOU DON'T MIND, COULD I EAT LUNCH WITH YOU NEXT TIME?
HUH?
AFTER SEEING ME READING MANGA IN A PLACE LIKE THIS, AND WITH MY LOOKS...
...SHE MUST ASSUME I'M A LONER ...

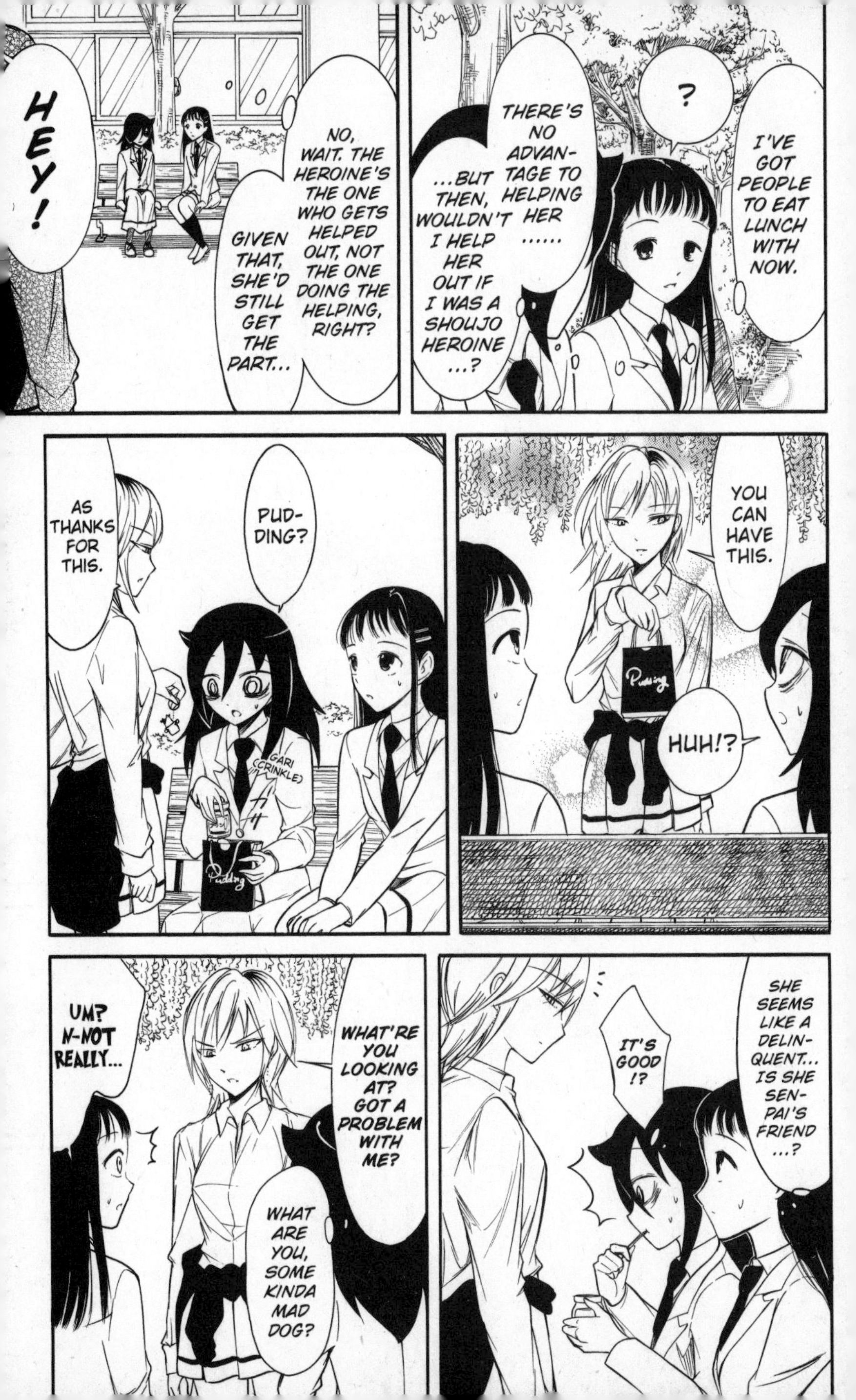
?
I'VE GOT PEOPLE TO EAT LUNCH WITH NOW.
THERE'S NO ADVANTAGE TO HELPING HER......
...BUT THEN, WOULDN'T I HELP HER OUT IF I WAS A SHOUJO HEROINE...?
NO, WAIT. THE HEROINE'S THE ONE WHO GETS HELPED OUT, NOT THE ONE DOING THE HELPING, RIGHT?
GIVEN THAT, SHE'D STILL GET THE PART...
HEY!
YOU CAN HAVE THIS.
Pudding
HUH!?
PUD-DING?
AS THANKS FOR THIS.
GARI (CRINKLE)
Pudding
SHE SEEMS LIKE A DELINQUENT... IS SHE SEN-PAI'S FRIEND...?
IT'S GOOD!?
WHAT'RE YOU LOOKING AT? GOT A PROBLEM WITH ME?
UM? N-NOT REALLY...
WHAT ARE YOU, SOME KINDA MAD DOG?

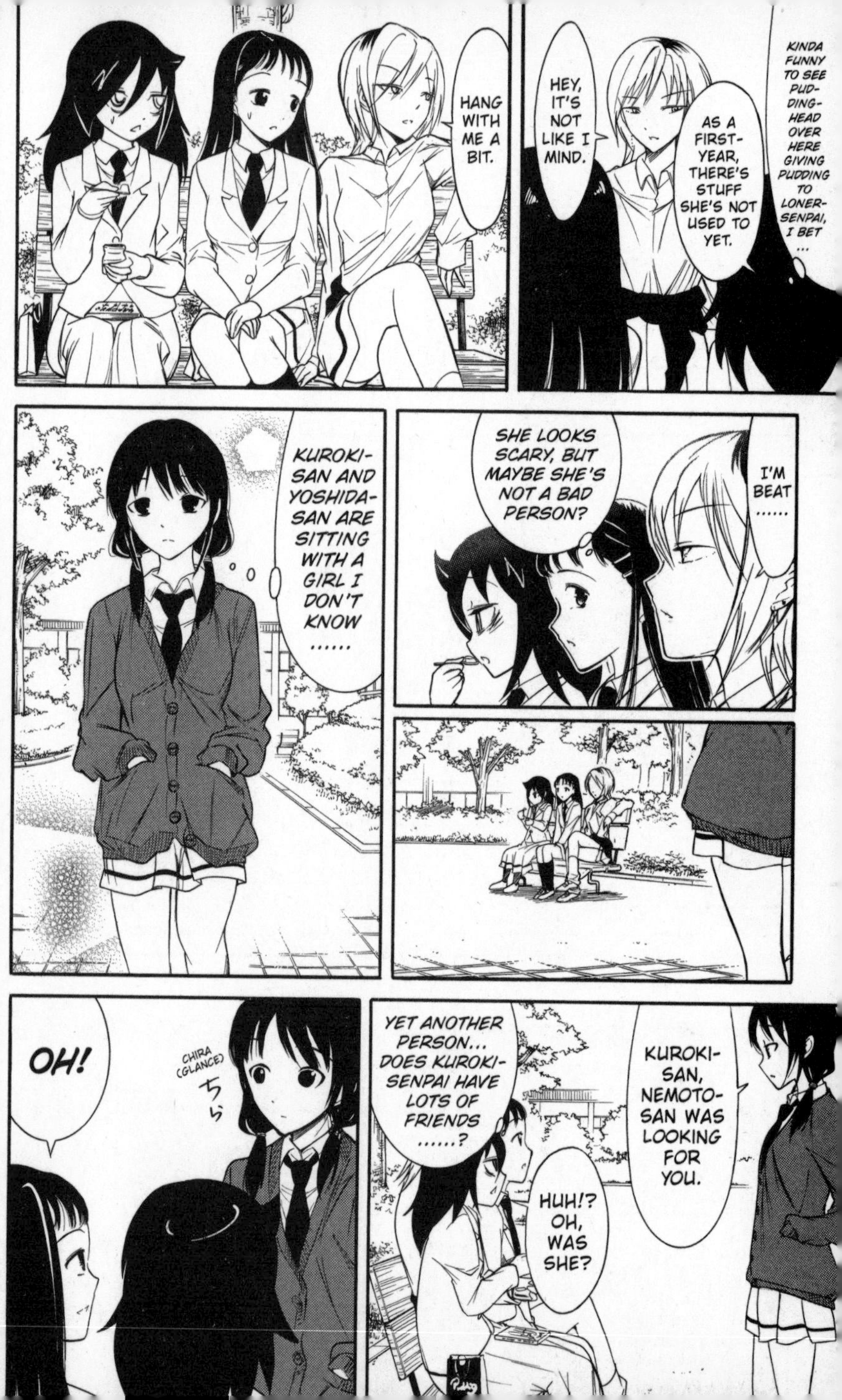
KINDA FUNNY TO SEE PUDDING-HEAD OVER HERE GIVING PUDDING TO LONER-SENPAI, I BET ...
AS A FIRST-YEAR, THERE'S STUFF SHE'S NOT USED TO YET.
HEY, IT'S NOT LIKE I MIND.
HANG WITH ME A BIT.
I'M BEAT ......
SHE LOOKS SCARY, BUT MAYBE SHE'S NOT A BAD PERSON?
KUROKI-SAN AND YOSHIDA-SAN ARE SITTING WITH A GIRL I DON'T KNOW ......
KUROKI-SAN, NEMOTO-SAN WAS LOOKING FOR YOU.
HUH!? OH, WAS SHE?
YET ANOTHER PERSON... DOES KUROKI-SENPAI HAVE LOTS OF FRIENDS ......?
CHIRA (GLANCE)
ちら
OH!

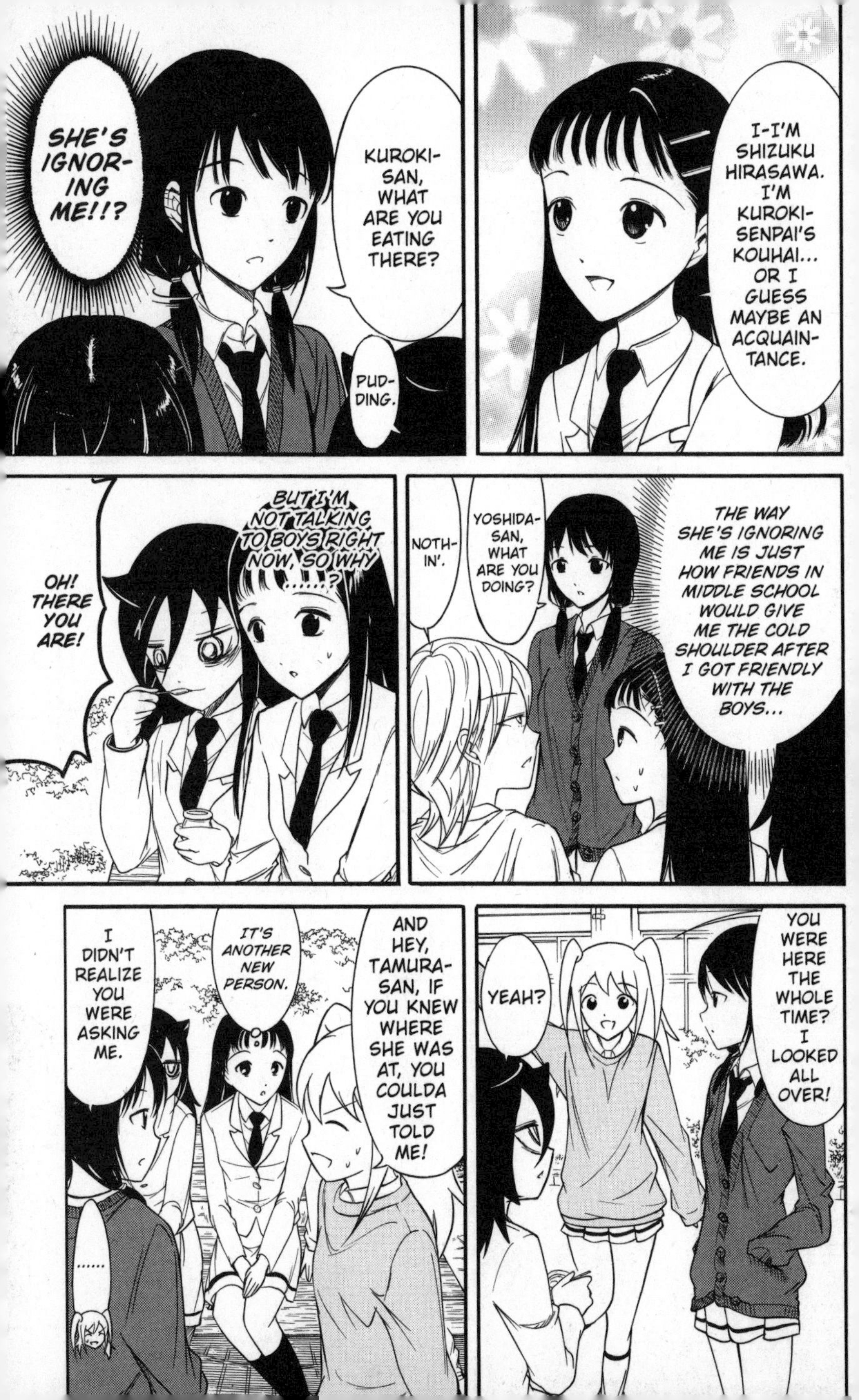
I-I'M SHIZUKU HIRASAWA. I'M KUROKI-SENPAI'S KOUHAI... OR I GUESS MAYBE AN ACQUAINTANCE.
KUROKI-SAN, WHAT ARE YOU EATING THERE?
PUDDING.
SHE'S IGNORING ME!!?
THE WAY SHE'S IGNORING ME IS JUST HOW FRIENDS IN MIDDLE SCHOOL WOULD GIVE ME THE COLD SHOULDER AFTER I GOT FRIENDLY WITH THE BOYS...
YOSHIDA-SAN, WHAT ARE YOU DOING?
NOTHIN'.
BUT I'M NOT TALKING TO BOYS RIGHT NOW, SO WHY ......?
OH! THERE YOU ARE!
YOU WERE HERE THE WHOLE TIME? I LOOKED ALL OVER!
YEAH?
AND HEY, TAMURA-SAN, IF YOU KNEW WHERE SHE WAS AT, YOU COULDA JUST TOLD ME!
IT'S ANOTHER NEW PERSON.
I DIDN'T REALIZE YOU WERE ASKING ME.
......

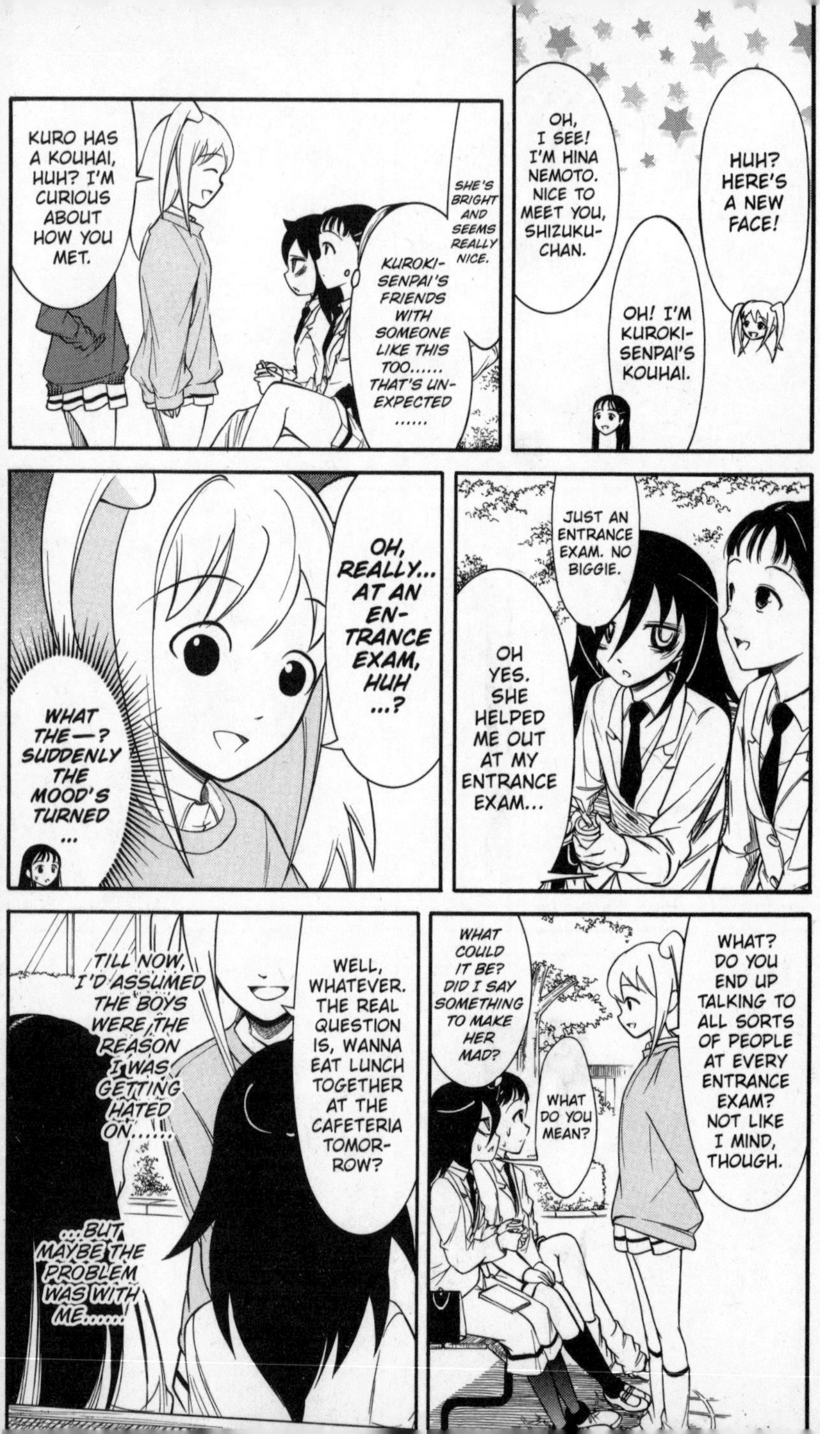
HUH? HERE'S A NEW FACE!
OH! I'M KUROKI-SENPAI'S KOUHAI.
OH, I SEE! I'M HINA NEMOTO. NICE TO MEET YOU, SHIZUKU-CHAN.
KURO HAS A KOUHAI, HUH? I'M CURIOUS ABOUT HOW YOU MET.
SHE'S BRIGHT AND SEEMS REALLY NICE.
KUROKI-SENPAI'S FRIENDS WITH SOMEONE LIKE THIS TOO...... THAT'S UNEXPECTED ......
JUST AN ENTRANCE EXAM. NO BIGGIE.
OH YES. SHE HELPED ME OUT AT MY ENTRANCE EXAM...
OH, REALLY... AT AN ENTRANCE EXAM, HUH ...?
WHAT THE—? SUDDENLY THE MOOD'S TURNED ...
WHAT? DO YOU END UP TALKING TO ALL SORTS OF PEOPLE AT EVERY ENTRANCE EXAM? NOT LIKE I MIND, THOUGH.
WHAT COULD IT BE? DID I SAY SOMETHING TO MAKE HER MAD?
WHAT DO YOU MEAN?
WELL, WHATEVER. THE REAL QUESTION IS, WANNA EAT LUNCH TOGETHER AT THE CAFETERIA TOMORROW?
TILL NOW, I'D ASSUMED THE BOYS WERE THE REASON I WAS GETTING HATED ON......
...BUT MAYBE THE PROBLEM WAS WITH ME......

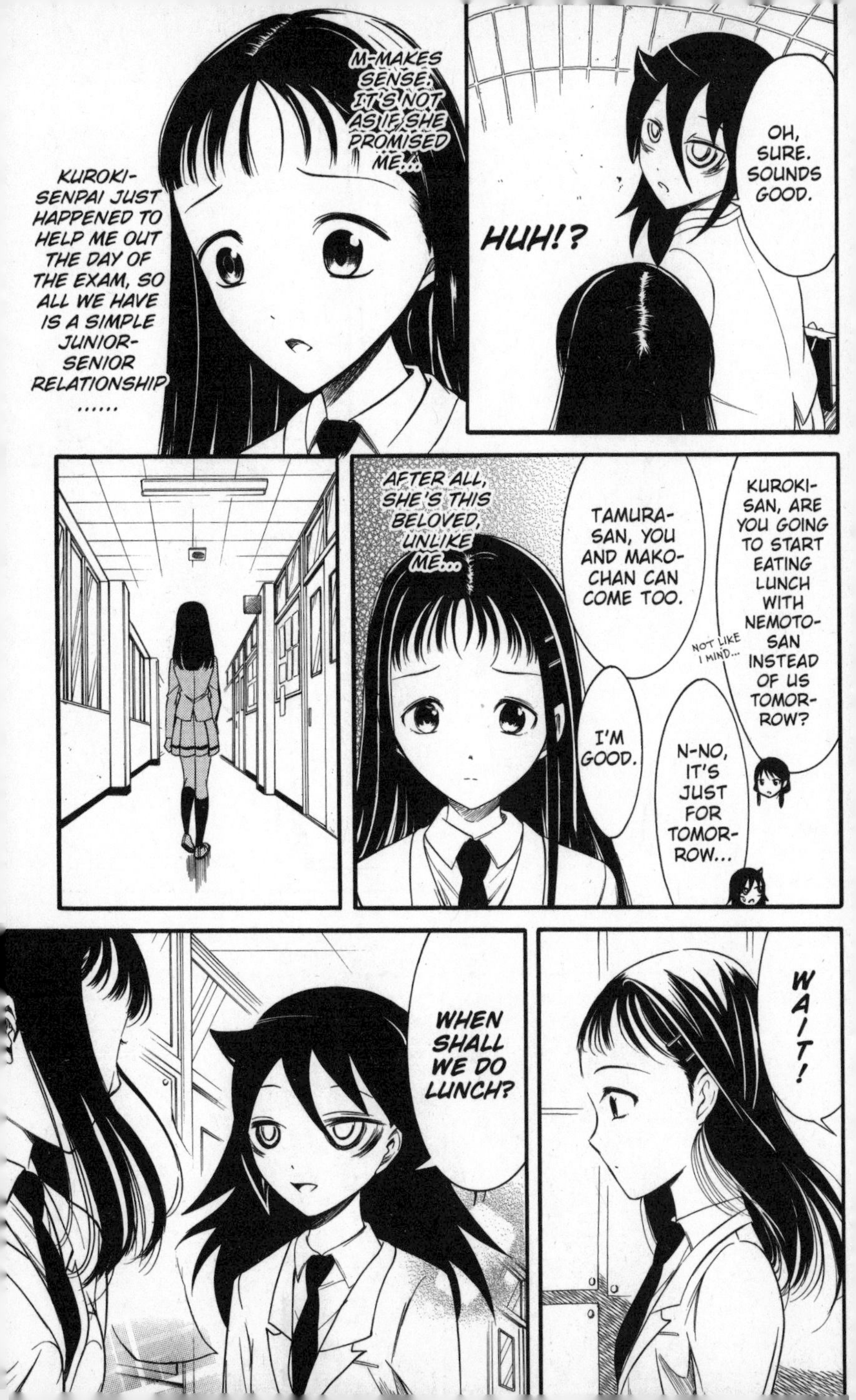
OH, SURE. SOUNDS GOOD.
HUH!?
M-MAKES SENSE. IT'S NOT AS IF SHE PROMISED ME...
KUROKI-SENPAI JUST HAPPENED TO HELP ME OUT THE DAY OF THE EXAM, SO ALL WE HAVE IS A SIMPLE JUNIOR-SENIOR RELATIONSHIP ......
KUROKI-SAN, ARE YOU GOING TO START EATING LUNCH WITH NEMOTO-SAN INSTEAD OF US TOMORROW?
TAMURA-SAN, YOU AND MAKO-CHAN CAN COME TOO.
NOT LIKE I MIND...
N-NO, IT'S JUST FOR TOMORROW...
I'M GOOD.
AFTER ALL, SHE'S THIS BELOVED, UNLIKE ME...
WAIT!
WHEN SHALL WE DO LUNCH?

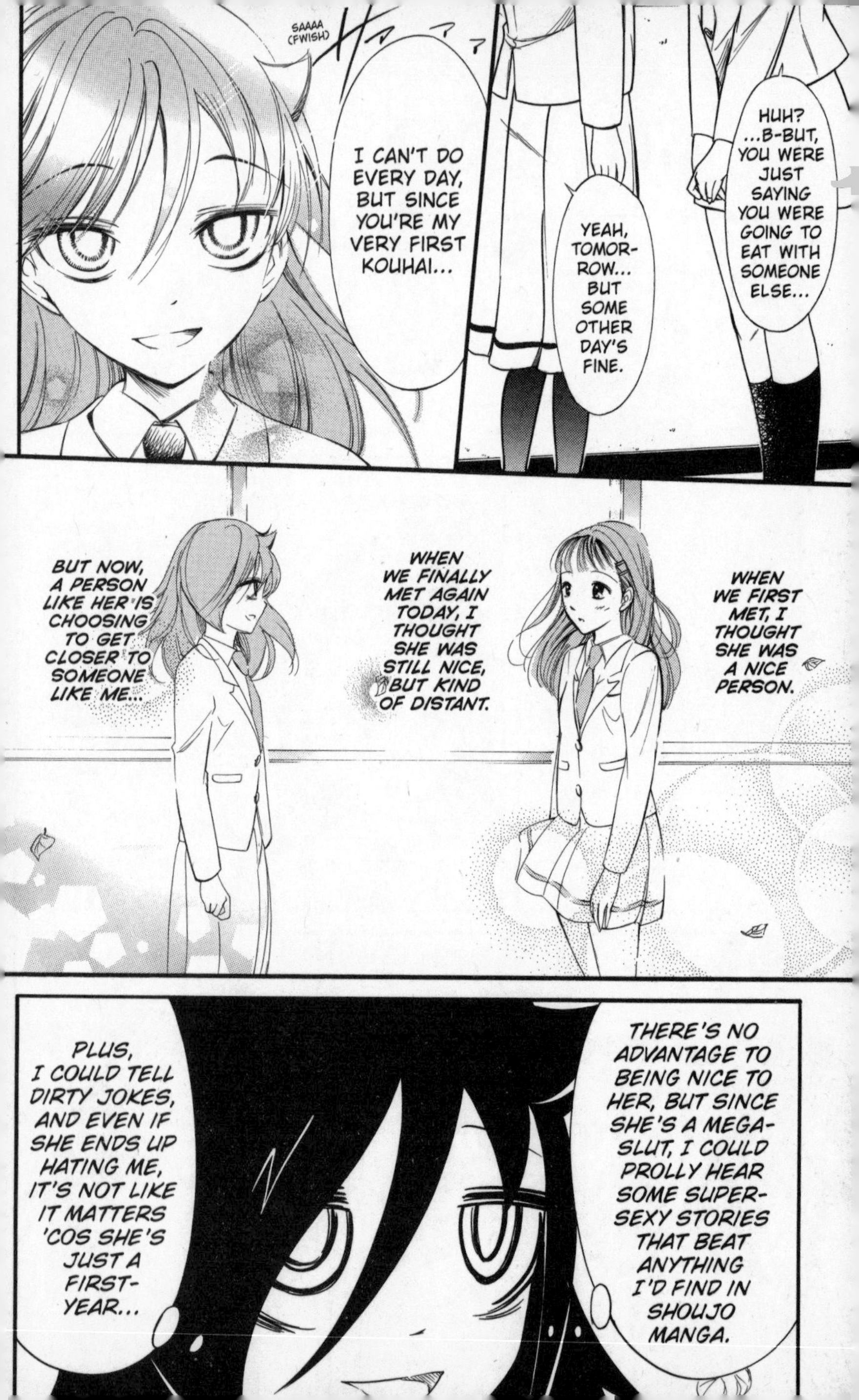
HUH? ...B-BUT, YOU WERE JUST SAYING YOU WERE GOING TO EAT WITH SOMEONE ELSE...
YEAH, TOMORROW... BUT SOME OTHER DAY'S FINE.
SAAAA (FWISH)
I CAN'T DO EVERY DAY, BUT SINCE YOU'RE MY VERY FIRST KOUHAI...
WHEN WE FIRST MET, I THOUGHT SHE WAS A NICE PERSON.
WHEN WE FINALLY MET AGAIN TODAY, I THOUGHT SHE WAS STILL NICE, BUT KIND OF DISTANT.
BUT NOW, A PERSON LIKE HER IS CHOOSING TO GET CLOSER TO SOMEONE LIKE ME...
THERE'S NO ADVANTAGE TO BEING NICE TO HER, BUT SINCE SHE'S A MEGA-SLUT, I COULD PROLLY HEAR SOME SUPER-SEXY STORIES THAT BEAT ANYTHING I'D FIND IN SHOUJO MANGA.
PLUS, I COULD TELL DIRTY JOKES, AND EVEN IF SHE ENDS UP HATING ME, IT'S NOT LIKE IT MATTERS 'COS SHE'S JUST A FIRST-YEAR...

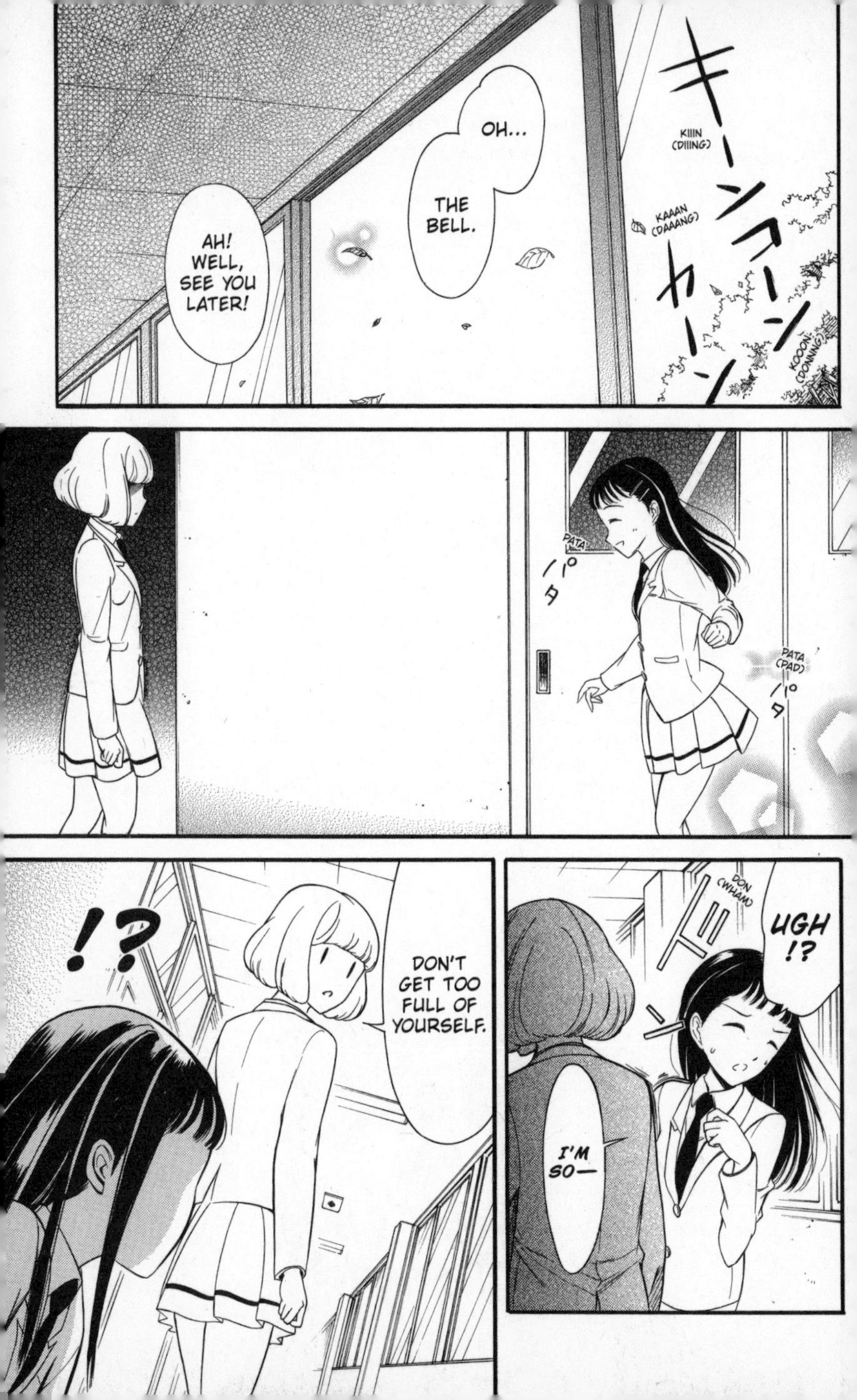
KIIIN (DIIING)
KAAAN (DAAANG)
KOOON (DONNNG)
OH... THE BELL.
AH! WELL, SEE YOU LATER!
PATA (PAD)
PATA
DON (WHAM)
UGH!?
I'M SO—
DON'T GET TOO FULL OF YOURSELF.
!?

No Matter How I Look at It, It's You Guys' Fault I'm Not Popular!

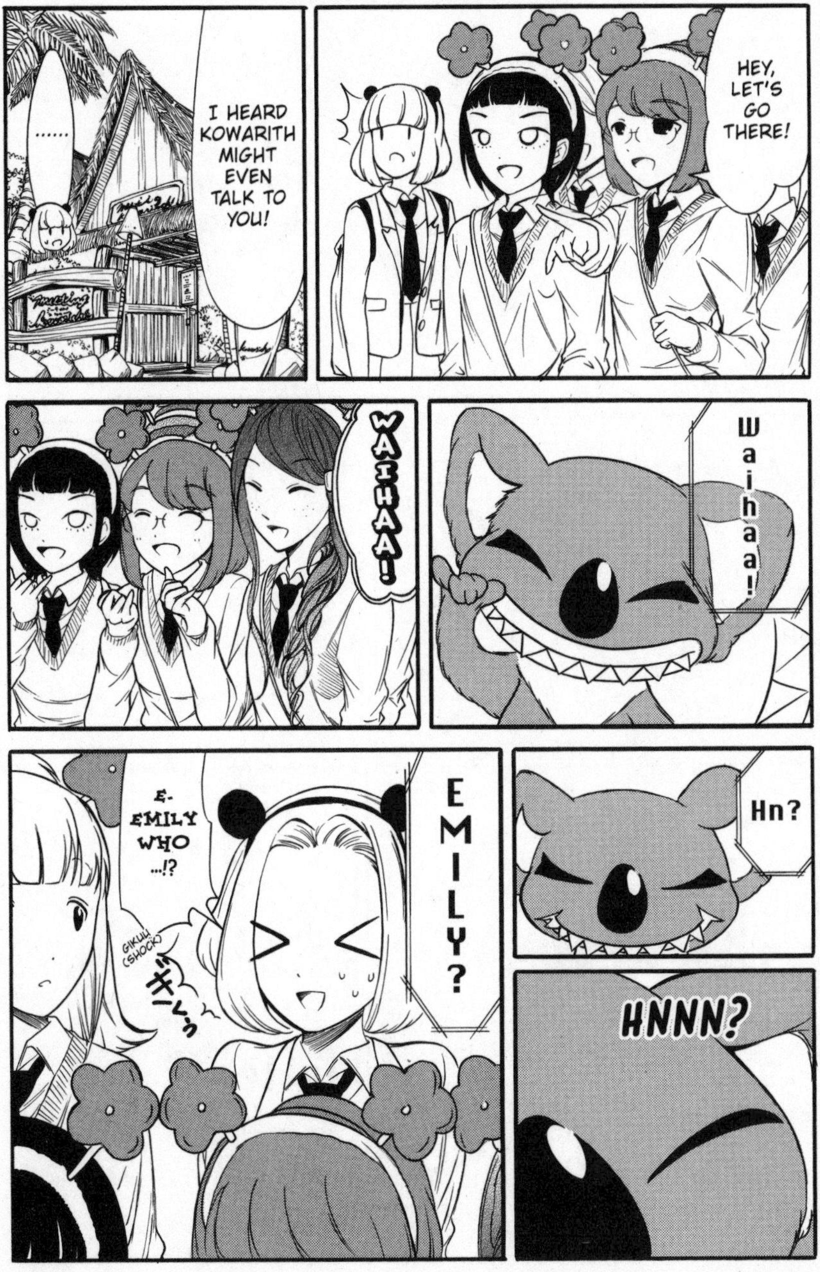
HEY, LET'S GO THERE!
I HEARD KOWARITH MIGHT EVEN TALK TO YOU!
......
Waihaaa!
WAIHAA!
Hn?
HNNN?
EMILY?
E- EMILY WHO ...!?
GIKUU (SHOCK)
ギーくっ

AFTER FAIL 130...

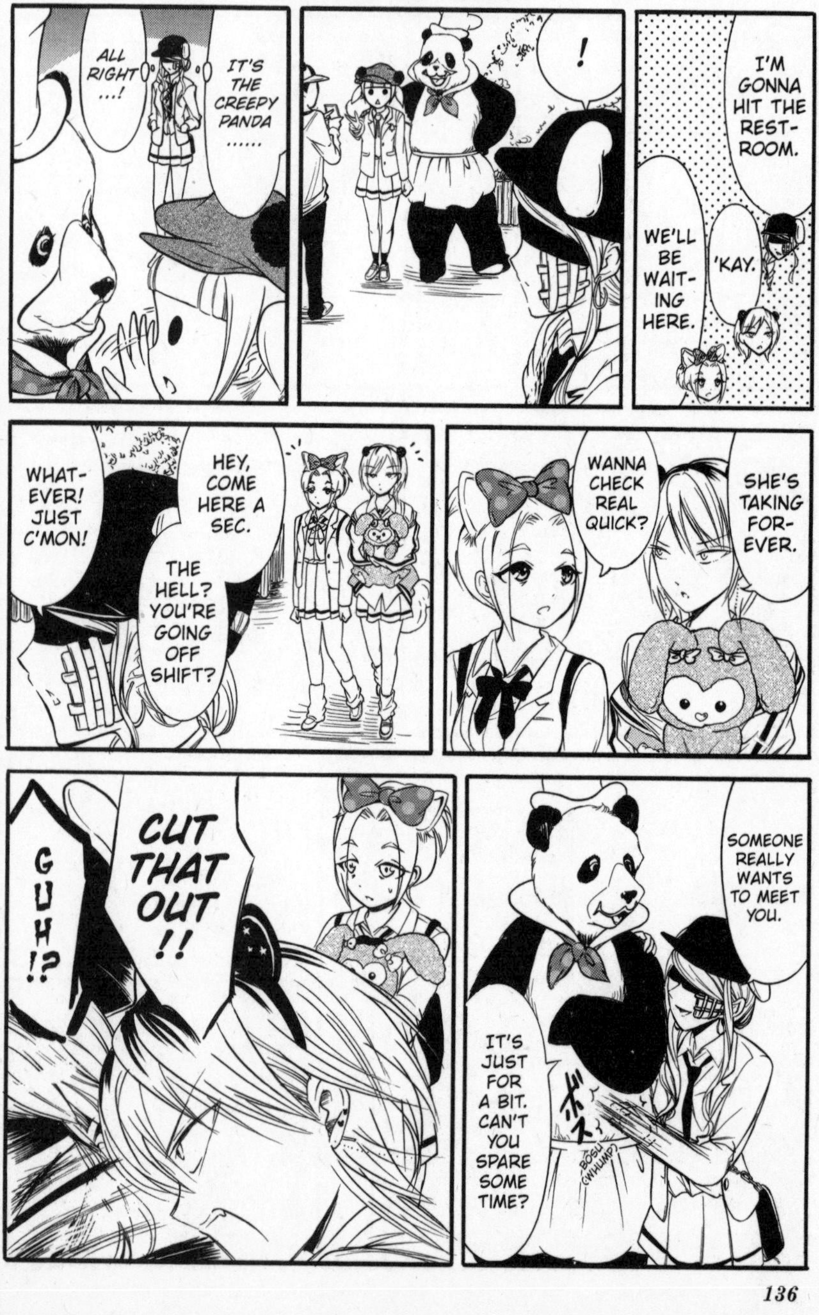

I'M GONNA HIT THE REST-ROOM.
'KAY.
WE'LL BE WAIT-ING HERE.
!
IT'S THE CREEPY PANDA......
ALL RIGHT...!
SHE'S TAKING FOR-EVER.
WANNA CHECK REAL QUICK?
HEY, COME HERE A SEC.
THE HELL? YOU'RE GOING OFF SHIFT?
WHAT-EVER! JUST C'MON!
SOMEONE REALLY WANTS TO MEET YOU.
IT'S JUST FOR A BIT. CAN'T YOU SPARE SOME TIME?
ボス
BOSU (WHUMP)
CUT THAT OUT!!
GUH!?

AFTERWORD 1: HOW WE GOT MENTALLY EXHAUSTED

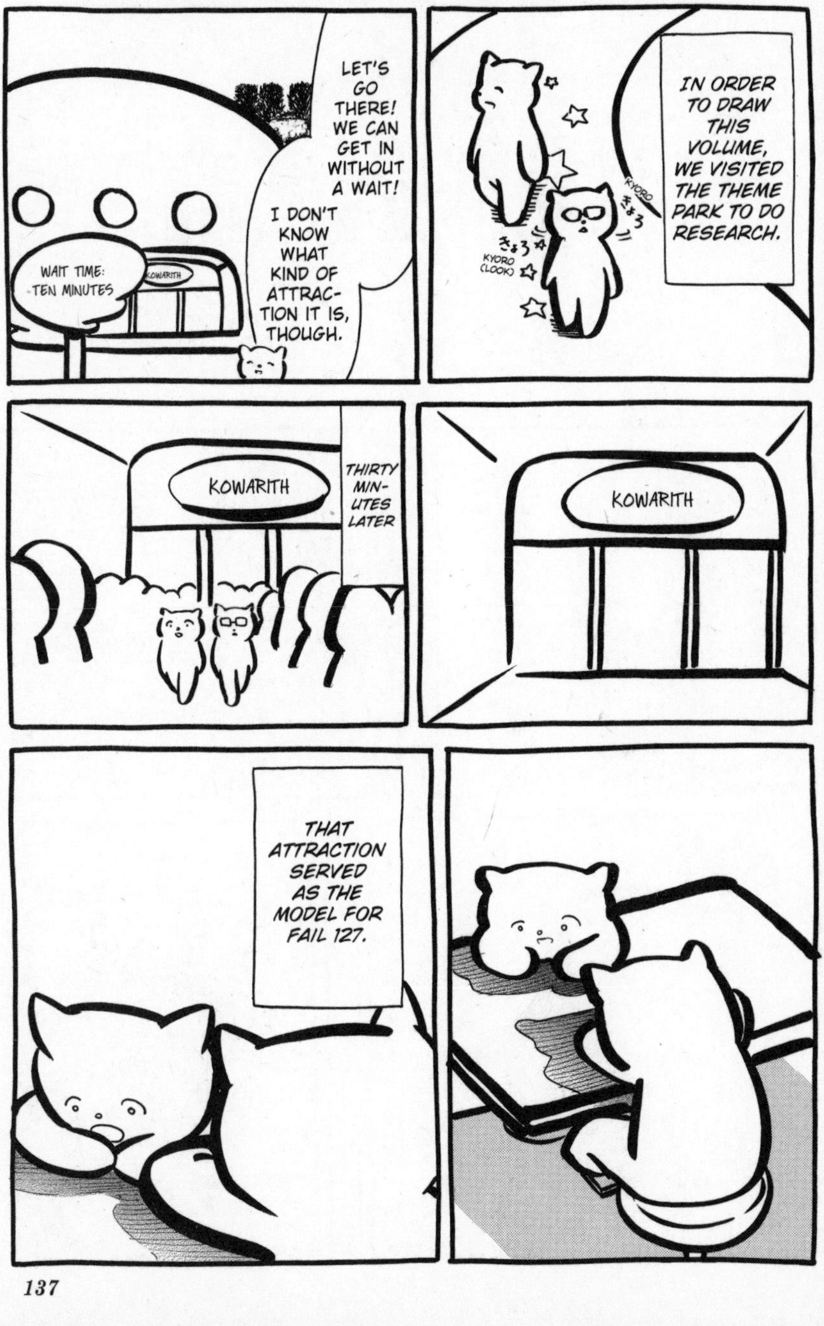
IN ORDER TO DRAW THIS VOLUME, WE VISITED THE THEME PARK TO DO RESEARCH.
きょろ
KYORO
きょろ
KYORO (LOOK)
LET'S GO THERE! WE CAN GET IN WITHOUT A WAIT!
I DON'T KNOW WHAT KIND OF ATTRACTION IT IS, THOUGH.
WAIT TIME: TEN MINUTES
KOWARITH
KOWARITH
THIRTY MINUTES LATER
KOWARITH
THAT ATTRACTION SERVED AS THE MODEL FOR FAIL 127.

AFTERWORD 2: HOW I BROKE A BONE

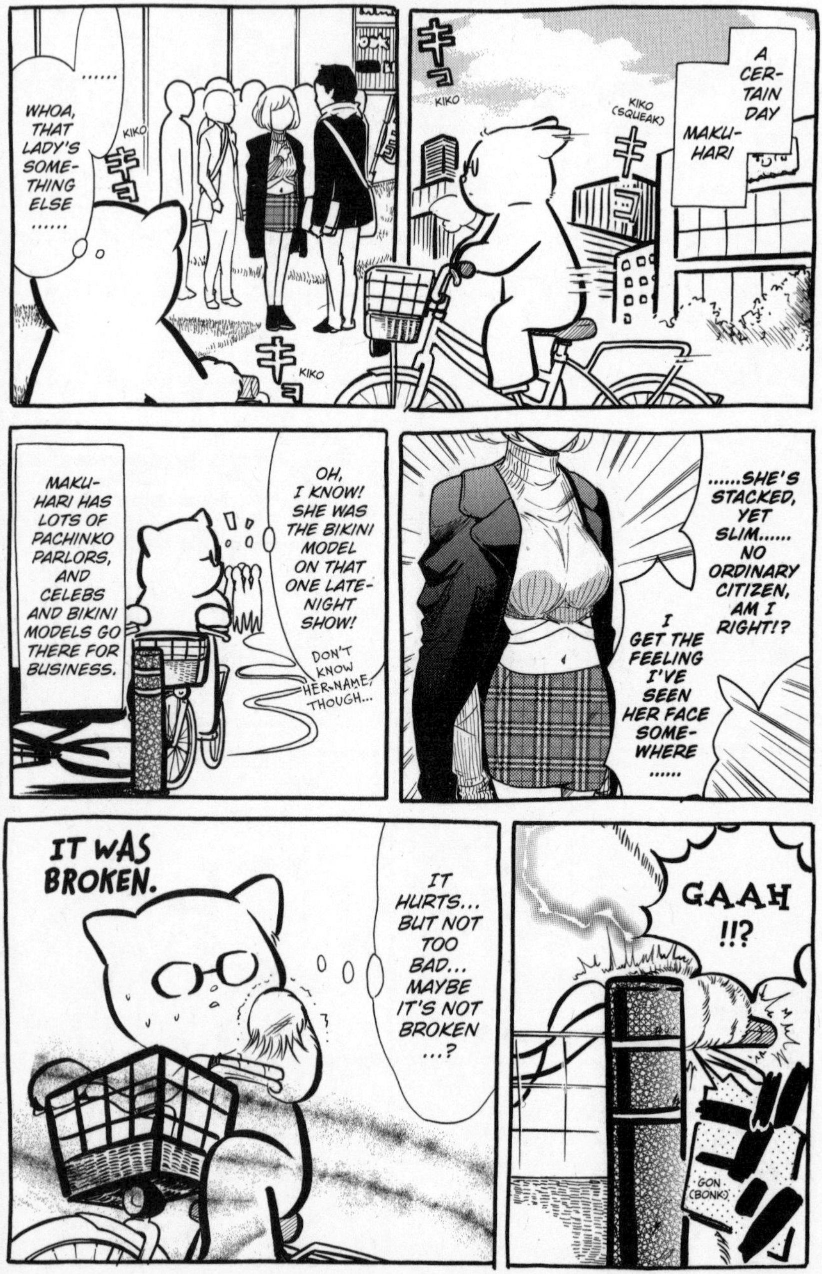
A CERTAIN DAY
MAKUHARI
KIKO (SQUEAK)
KIKO
......
WHOA, THAT LADY'S SOMETHING ELSE ......
KIKO
KIKO
......SHE'S STACKED, YET SLIM...... NO ORDINARY CITIZEN, AM I RIGHT!?
I GET THE FEELING I'VE SEEN HER FACE SOMEWHERE ......
OH, I KNOW! SHE WAS THE BIKINI MODEL ON THAT ONE LATE-NIGHT SHOW!
DON'T KNOW HER NAME, THOUGH...
MAKUHARI HAS LOTS OF PACHINKO PARLORS, AND CELEBS AND BIKINI MODELS GO THERE FOR BUSINESS.
GAAH !!?
GON (BONK)
IT HURTS... BUT NOT TOO BAD... MAYBE IT'S NOT BROKEN ...?
IT WAS BROKEN.

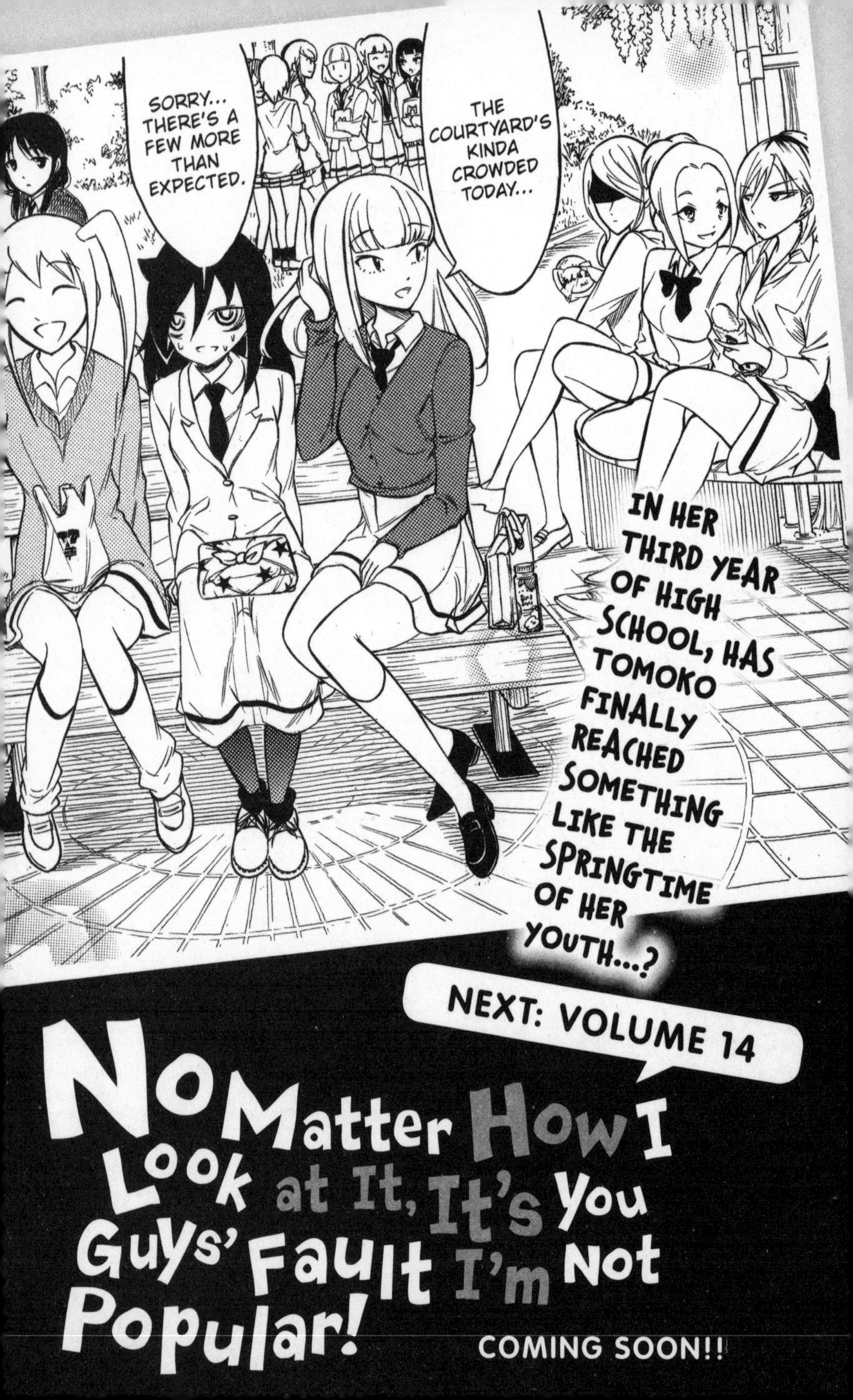
THE COURTYARD'S KINDA CROWDED TODAY...
SORRY... THERE'S A FEW MORE THAN EXPECTED.
IN HER THIRD YEAR OF HIGH SCHOOL, HAS TOMOKO FINALLY REACHED SOMETHING LIKE THE SPRINGTIME OF HER YOUTH...?

NEXT: VOLUME 14

No Matter How I Look at It, It's You Guys' Fault I'm Not Popular!

COMING SOON!!

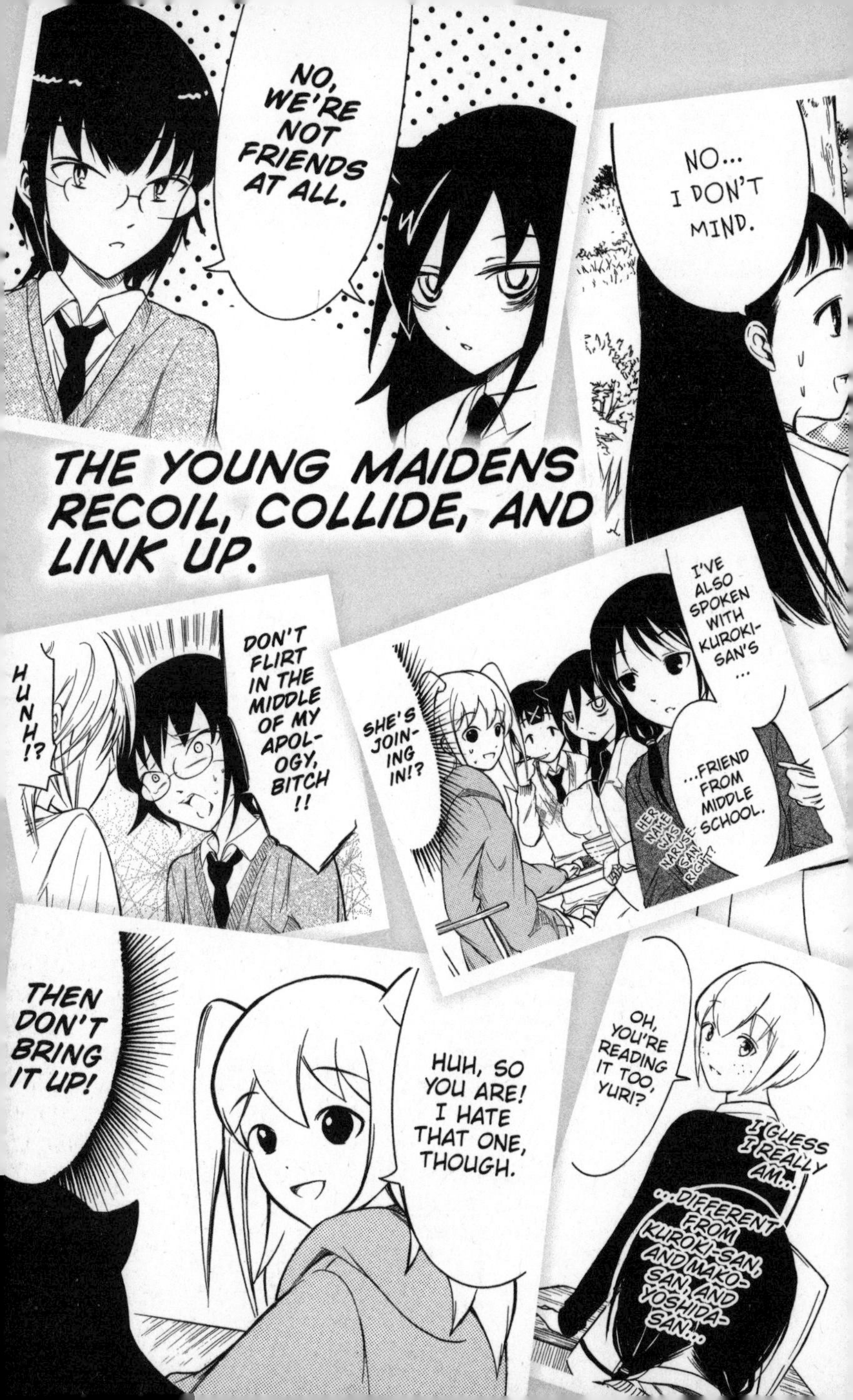
NO... I DON'T MIND.
NO, WE'RE NOT FRIENDS AT ALL.
THE YOUNG MAIDENS RECOIL, COLLIDE, AND LINK UP.
I'VE ALSO SPOKEN WITH KUROKI-SAN'S ...
...FRIEND FROM MIDDLE SCHOOL.
HER NAME WAS NARUSE-SAN, RIGHT?
SHE'S JOIN-ING IN!?
DON'T FLIRT IN THE MIDDLE OF MY APOL-OGY, BITCH!!
HUNH!?
OH, YOU'RE READING IT TOO, YURI?
I GUESS I REALLY AM...
...DIFFERENT FROM KUROKI-SAN AND MAKO-SAN, AND YOSHIDA-SAN...
HUH, SO YOU ARE! I HATE THAT ONE, THOUGH.
THEN DON'T BRING IT UP!

TRANSLATION NOTES

PAGE 4
It may seem weird for **"getting giddy over Mousey"** to be a **delinquent trait**, but much of that can be chalked up to emulating American culture, and Disney is very American. This is also why delinquents who dye their hair lighter are called Yankees.

PAGE 17
Tabelog is a Japanese crowd-sourced restaurant-review site, similar to Yelp, but specifically for restaurants.

PAGE 38
Using rock-paper-scissors to decide ride pairs also occurs in the manga and anime series *Kiss Him, Not Me* (*Watashi ga Motete Dousunda*; aka., the other *WataMote*), where main character, Kae Serinuma, suggests it for her group of six riding swan boats.

PAGE 47
Paddy Panda Choir, or *Inaka Panda Gasshoudan*, is a parody of Country Bear Jamboree (called "Country Bear Theater" at Tokyo Disneyland), but here it's very much rural Japan-style.

PAGE 48
The singing sound effect the first panda makes, **"Boeee,"** is well known in Japan as the sound of bully character Gian from children's manga *Doraemon* singing loudly and off-key.

PAGE 50
Meeting Kowarith is a parody of the **Stitch Encounter** attraction at Tokyo Disneyland. As of publication, there hasn't been a Stitch attraction exactly like this one at any of the North-American Disney parks, but it can be visited under the name Stitch Live! at Disneyland Paris, and a similar audience-interaction format is used at Turtle Talk with Crush. Also, the name "Kowarith" is a mashup of "koala," the original name "Stitch," and *kowai*, the Japanese word for "scary." The catchphrase "Waihaa!" is "Hawaii" with the syllables flipped, which they're using in place of the actual Hawaiian greeting Aloha.

PAGE 51
U●J is Universal Studios Japan (USJ), which is located in Osaka, a city with a very influential comedy scene.

PAGE 57
Tomoko calls Yuri **"Buster"** here, but in the original, it's *omae*, an abrupt word for "you" used most commonly by men. The plural version, *omaera*, is what gets translated as "you guys" in the title of this series (and in Yoshida's line on the next page).

PAGE 64
Hina and Tomoko are holding their arms up together to form a **heart shape**. This pose is called the MiyoMana Pose, after the two *Seventeen* (Japan) magazine models who popularized it: Ayaka Miyoshi and Manami Enosawa.

PAGE 65
Komi and Tomoko are right that **zeroing**, known more commonly in Japan as "zero in" thanks to a manga series by that title, is an actual term for a practice used by snipers.

PAGE 81
The original serialized version of this chapter pointed more strongly to Tomoko talking about the family from *Crayon Shin-chan* as **"that one famous anime."** The voice in the clip she plays on the next page would then be the baby sister.

PAGE 91
Sea is referring to Tokyo DisneySea, the aquatic-themed sister park of Disneyland Tokyo. Though located right by Disneyland, it's a separate park requiring a separate admission, so Yoshida's friend spent an awful lot of money to be able to buy that plush rabbit in addition to the cost of the plush itself.

PAGE 99
In Japanese, Tomoko's thought of **"It's okay to bite this instead of blowing it, right!?"** is actually a pun on *soshaku* ("chewing") and *sokushaku* ("fellatio performed immediately without washing the penis first").

PAGE 129
Kouhai is the antonym for the common term of respect *senpai* and means someone junior to a specific person.

NO MATTER HOW I LOOK AT IT, IT'S YOU GUYS' FAULT I'M NOT POPULAR! ⑬

Nico Tanigawa

Translation/Adaptation: Krista Shipley, Karie Shipley
Lettering: Bianca Pistillo

WATASHI GA MOTENAI NOWA DOU KANGAETEMO OMAERA GA WARUI! Volume 13 © 2018 Nico Tanigawa / SQUARE ENIX CO., LTD. First published in Japan in 2018 by SQUARE ENIX CO., LTD. English translation rights arranged with SQUARE ENIX CO., LTD. and Yen Press, LLC through Tuttle-Mori Agency, Inc., Tokyo.

English translation ©2019 by SQUARE ENIX CO., LTD.

Yen Press
1290 Avenue of the Americas
New York, NY 10104

Visit us!
↗ yenpress.com
↗ facebook.com/yenpress
↗ twitter.com/yenpress
↗ yenpress.tumblr.com
↗ instagram.com/yenpress

First Yen Press Edition: March 2019

Yen Press is an imprint of Yen Press, LLC.
The Yen Press name and logo are trademarks of Yen Press, LLC.

Library of Congress Control Number: 2013498929

ISBNs: 978-1-9753-0344-0 (paperback)
       978-1-9753-0345-7 (ebook)

10 9 8 7 6 5 4 3 2 1

WOR

Printed in the United States of America